Also by David Lamb

THE AFRICANS

THE ARABS

Stolen Season

STOLEN SEASON

A Journey Through
America and Baseball's
Minor Leagues

David Lamb

Random House New York

Grateful acknowledgment is made to the following for permission to reprint previously
published material:
Cherio Corporation: Excerpts from "Little Darlin'," words and music by Maurice Williams.
Copyright © 1957 by Excellorec Music Co. Copyright renewed 1985 by Cherio Corpora-
tion. International Copyright Secured. All Rights Reserved. Reprinted by permission.
Hal Leonard Publishing Corporation and Peer Music London: Excerpts from "(You've Got) the
Magic Touch," words and music by Buck Ram. Copyright © 1956, renewed 1984 by All
Nations Music and AMC, Inc. All rights reserved. Rights throughout the world excluding
the United States and Canada are administered by Peer Music London. Reprinted by
permission of Hal Leonard Publishing Corporation and Peer Music London.
Londontown Music, Inc.: Excerpts from "(Get Your Kicks on) Route 66" by Bobby Troup.
Copyright © Londontown Music. All rights reserved.

Library of Congress Cataloging-in-Publication Data

Lamb, David.
Stolen Season: a journey through America and baseball's minor leagues
by David S. Lamb.
p. cm.
ISBN 0-394-57608-X
1. Minor league baseball—United States. I. Title.
GV875.A1L36 1991
796.357'64'0973—dc20   90-45719

Manufactured in the United States of America
24689753
First Edition

BOOK DESIGN BY LILLY LANGOTSKY

FOR ERNIE, WHO HAD MANY FINE SEASONS,

THOUGH NOT ENOUGH,

AND BONNY; WALTER AND ERIN; HARRIET AND CHIP

Preface

This baseball journey was born in the rubble of Beirut while some maniacs were blowing away my hotel with tanks, chunk by chunk. I can't remember whose militia had taken over the city that day, but I can still hear the thundering artillery of the attacking Lebanese army. Behind the artillery came the rumble of tanks, advancing down Hamra Street, their high-explosive rounds pounding buildings a block away, on the corner, next door. Each round struck with a dull thud, accompanied a millisecond later by the sounds of shattering glass and falling brick.

I was living in Cairo then, in the early eighties, and had gone up to Beirut for the *Los Angeles Times* to cover Lebanon's orgy of national suicide. Together with a dozen other journalists, I had taken shelter in an abandoned nightclub in the Commodore Hotel's basement. The hotel shook as though a mighty storm had struck, and amid the deafening explosions we knew the Commodore's upper-floor rooms were now taking direct hits.

Jim Pringle, a Scotsman with whom I had covered the Vietnam war, the overthrow of both Idi Amin and Haile Selassie, a war in Somalia and another in Zaire, was sitting next to me on a couch with no legs. He held a notebook open to a blank page in one hand, a glass of whiskey in the other. An Olivetti typewriter rested on my knees, but I had no control over my shaky fingers and they slipped off the keys and struck at unwanted letters.

"We're getting too old for this shit," Pringle said.

"I'll tell you what," I said. "If we get out of here, I'm going to find something to write about that's a million miles from Beirut. Like baseball. Maybe I'll find some little ballpark in Montana and just sit there in the sunshine for a summer."

Two years later I came home to Los Angeles, the conversation with Pringle long forgotten. I revived a romance with baseball, spending many evenings at Dodger Stadium, which lay just over the hill from my home, and I cast about for some idea that would put me back in touch with a country I had left nearly a decade earlier for a life in Africa and the Middle East. I had covered so many miles as a foreign correspondent, propelled at a breakneck clip from story to story, that there were moments I wasn't quite sure where I had been, or where I was going. I yearned to move at a leisurely pace, free and unencumbered, and rediscover some old roads I had traveled as a youth. I wanted to find out if it was true that the past is but a prologue.

The opportunity came unexpectedly one night when, over dinner, my wife, Sandy, and I met a man named Geoff Cowan. What interested me was not that he was a film producer, writer or university professor in constitutional law. It was that he owned a professional baseball team, a minor league club in Northern California called the Stockton Ports. Having spent most of my time in the United States in major league cities, I had never even been to a minor league game, but I knew the marriage was perfect: America and the minor leagues, each a metaphor for the other. It was a road that led through what for me would be virgin territory, and back into the mist of my fondest childhood memory: a love affair with a team that no longer existed, the Milwaukee Braves.

Though the start of the minor league season was still four months away, I started laying plans almost immediately. I took an unpaid leave from the *Times* and, after securing a loan from the credit union, bought a secondhand mobile home that I named Forty-niner, honoring both my own age and the Gold Rush adventurers of my adopted state. I spent hours with *Baseball America's Directory* a vest-pocket guide listing all the minor league teams and their schedules. I plotted elaborate routings, then discarded them all, deciding that what I most wanted was to wander without an itinerary, following any road that interested me, whether it led to a ballpark or a back-road saloon. Baseball would be my reentry ticket to a country I had been gone from too long.

Robert Louis Stevenson was the one, I believe, who said the thrill of traveling was getting there, not being there. I agree. The wailing whistle of a train still conjures up images for me of distant prairies and unknown lands. Give me a road map or an official airline guide and I can lose myself for hours. My brother Ernie told me years ago of a friend at his boarding school who would sneak out of the dormitory late at night and sit on a rock overlooking the nearby highway, mesmerized by the parade of trailer trucks flashing by. He knew the silent language of their signals and the difference between a Peterbilt and a Mack. Ernie said everyone considered his friend odd. I thought him to be an admirable dreamer of the first order.

Here I should take a moment to avoid possible confusion, because many friends weren't quite sure what I meant when I mentioned my pending minor league journey. "Oh, that sounds interesting," one said. "Our son is in Little League, too." Others tried to steer me toward their favorite American Legion or softball team. I usually didn't bother to tell them what I had recently learned: The minors consist of fifteen leagues in North America (excluding two instructional circuits) and 150 teams, scattered from the timber towns of the Pacific Northwest to the steamy flatlands of Florida. (Eight teams are in Canada.) Four thousand players are employed there, full-time professionals, whose contracts, with a few exceptions, are owned by a major league club. If their careers go as planned, they ascend through the four levels of minor league baseball—Rookie League, Single-A, Double-A and Triple-A—and in a few years have reached The Show, an industry that has room for only 624 men. The career expectancy of a player who gets to the majors is five to six years.

Figuring in the players who fail to complete this journey, the cost of "developing" a major leaguer in the farm system is upwards of $2 million per man. Most teams, like Cowan's Stockton Ports in the California League, are privately owned and subsidized by the major league club with which they are affiliated. And most are worth a ton of money these days. Minor league attendance once again has climbed past 25 million a season—a popularity not seen since the advent of television—and the value of franchises has soared so high that one owner turned down a $10 million offer. Unlike the majors, the performers get no cut of the bonanza. They are but apprentices, the guardians of tomorrow's promises.

In the bottom rungs of the minors, players work for less than the minimum wage, feast on Big Macs and chocolate shakes, endure seventeen-hour bus trips from, say, Medicine Hat (in Alberta, Canada) to Salt Lake City and share more fun and more camaraderie than millionaire major leaguers could ever know. Their heritage in baseball's low-rent district is one of unpredictable happenings and of being constantly reminded of their expendability.

Infielder Buzzy Wares, for instance, had a good spring training in Montgomery with the St. Louis Browns in 1913 but didn't make the trip north. He was left behind to play in Montgomery, as rent for the Browns' use of the ballpark. The Brooklyn Dodgers bought the Reading team in the Eastern League in 1941 for three thousand dollars. It wasn't any of the players the Dodgers wanted; it was the team bus. In 1989, the Reno Silver Sox peddled one of their pitchers, Tim Fortugno, to the Milwaukee Brewers' organization for twenty-five hundred dollars—and twelve dozen baseballs. "I'm part of baseball trivia," said Fortugno with a note of triumph.

And it wasn't too many years ago that mysterious flashes of light were reported late at night in the clubhouse of the Lodi (California) Dodgers. This went on for more than a week. Finally a cop staked out the place and burst in the door. He found a man stretched out in his underpants on the trainer's table.

"Who the hell are you and what are you doing here?" the cop demanded.

"I'm the manager and I *live* here," came the sleepy reply.

I didn't know if life in the bush leagues was still lived like that or not, on a shoestring and a dream, but the more I learned about the minors, the surer I was that something old-fashioned and wonderful awaited me in the towns ahead. By the time the summer was over, Forty-niner and I would wander from California to Tucson, El Paso and Chattanooga, into Florida and up the Eastern seaboard to Elmira, New York, across the Midwest, through Montana and the Northwest and back into California. What I would find was baseball as I remembered it, played on real grass and in a time when the teams we cherished were ours for life.

Stolen Season

Prologue

Time consecrates and what is gray with age becomes religion.

—FRIEDRICH VON SCHILLER

Nostalgia is a dangerous obsession. It turns stumblebums into princes and dunghills into shining mountain peaks. It makes yesterday sweeter than tomorrow can ever be. But nostalgia is an expression of faith, because inherent in our embrace of the past is the belief that rediscovering the lost values of our youth will return us to simpler, more innocent days. Isn't that, after all, what got Ronald Reagan elected president?

For men of my generation, men in their forties and early fifties, who grew up with thirty-game winners and .400 hitters, there were few aspects of life more full of mythology and wistful dreams than baseball. To be a fan was to be bonded to your contemporaries. Almost all of us had a favorite team we treasured as much as the memory of a first love. We all had a moment in a pennant drive or World Series—Bobby Thomson's home run at Coogan's Bluff or Willie Mays's over-the-shoulder catch of the thundering drive off the bat of Vic Wertz or Lew Burdette single-handedly whipping the Yankees for Milwaukee's only championship—that even now, we can tell you exactly where we were when it happened, just as surely as we know precisely what we were doing the day JFK was shot.

I remember John McPhee, who has written a good deal about sports, once saying that most of the topics of his books and articles are rooted in interests he had as a youth. Thus I am not abashed to share a story from a golden season long ago. It explains why, at an age when I should have known better, I was about to head off on a back-roads journey to distant ballparks seemingly stolen from one of Norman Rockwell's *Saturday Evening Post* covers.

In the spring of 1955, when I was fourteen, I had mastered most of life's mysteries and understood that baseball, more than politics, religion or any other national institution, was what the rhythms of our days were all about. I was in love with a girl named Tootsie Weisenbach that year and wore my hair in a DA—which stood for duck's ass—though I certainly wasn't a hood, as toughs with slicked-down, swept-back hair were known in the fifties. I played second base on the school baseball team and wasn't very good at it. I loved *Gunsmoke* on TV and mourned the loss of *The Lone Ranger* on radio. I thought Davy Crockett coonskin caps were cool, grieved when James Dean died in the crash of his Porsche Spider on California Route 46, considered Evan Hunter's *The Blackboard Jungle* the steamiest book ever written and would have mortgaged my baseball mitt just to ride in a V-8 Chevy coupe.

Eisenhower was president then and the country, prosperous and secure, was feeling good about itself. I didn't realize it at the time, of course, but America that year was as much in transition as I was. The first McDonald's opened, outside Chicago, and in the empty citrus lands of Southern California, the first visitors poured into Disneyland. Television was becoming our prime source of entertainment; only one radio show—*Dragnet*—remained on the list of Top Fourteen most-popular evening programs. Elvis Presley appeared, as did the *Village Voice* and beatniks and rock 'n' roll, with Bill Haley's "Rock around the Clock" and Chuck Berry's "Maybelline" shooting up the *Billboard* charts. In Montgomery a black seamstress named Rosa Parks boarded a city bus after work, was told to move to the rear, refused and was arrested. She later said she wasn't trying to start a revolution. She was just tired.

But more pressing matters occupied my thoughts as the New England snows melted that spring. My beloved Boston Braves had deserted me two seasons earlier—the first franchise to leave a city in fifty years—and my suffering was severe. I had stopped collecting the Wheaties box tops, which, along with a quarter, used to get me a bleacher seat in Braves Field, and I took to hanging around Warren Spahn's Diner on Commonwealth Avenue, across from the abandoned ballpark, talking baseball with whoever had memories.

The only moments of intimacy with my heroes came now when the *Milwaukee* Braves played the Brooklyn Dodgers; I would lug the family's large Zenith radio up to my bedroom (we had no TV) and, if the night skies were clear, by fine-tuning the dial, I could find the voice of Brooklyn's announcer, Vin Scully, stirring my imagination through the static with a picture more real than any television screen could ever offer.

Sometimes, on Scully-less nights, I would lie in bed and narrate an entire Braves game. Warren Spahn almost always pitched, though occasionally I gave Chet Nichols a start, and whenever the game was on the line, mysteriously it would be Eddie Mathews at the plate, even, I suspect, if he had to bat out of turn from time to time.

All right, here's the situation. Spahn's pitched a gem tonight—a two-hitter and he didn't walk a man—and now Mathews can win it for him. We've got another capacity crowd on hand at County Stadium and they're on the edge of their seats. Mathews is two for three as he steps into the box with the Johnny Logan, the winning run, on second. Here's the pitch from Haddix. Mathews swings. There's a long drive heading back toward deep right field. . . .

"What's going on up there, Dave?" my father would shout from downstairs. "Cut out that noise. You've got school tomorrow. You're meant to be asleep."

"Sorry. I'm going, Dad," I'd lie, for under my breath the game was still in progress: "*. . .It's way, way back there. This ball is gone!*

Number forty-two for Mathews! Listen to that crowd!" I'd cup my hands to my mouth and breathe out with a soft *whhhaaaaaaa* and the roar of thirty thousand fans would fill the room, for only me to hear.

I don't recall now how the idea to close the distance between Boston and Milwaukee came to me, but one evening after dinner, I went up to my room and, using my father's pen and a piece of my mother's stationery, wrote a letter to *The Milwaukee Journal* that would rearrange the heavens.

The letter was addressed to the *Journal*'s sports editor, whose name I did not know, and began: "Dear Sir: I have what at first might seem like a stupid idea. I want to write for the *Journal* a story about the Braves, daily, weekly, monthly, or as often as you like. This I would be more than glad to do free." I went on to present a strong case: I would write "through teen-age eyes" what it was like to lose your team, and I pledged my allegiance to Milwaukee, whose fans had gone daffy over the Braves, showering the players with free cars, food, clothes and the largest season's attendance in baseball history. On or off the field, the Braves could do no wrong. When pitcher Bob Ruhl was pulled over for speeding and the cop saw whom he had stopped, he put away his citation book and said, "Just an autograph will do."

Looking back, I doubt I even expected a reply. Certainly I didn't realize that I had just taken the first step toward a newspaper career that one day would lead me to all seven continents as a foreign correspondent. But a week or so later my mother called me in from the yard: "Western Union's on the phone. There's a telegram for you." It was from the *Journal*'s sports editor, a man named Russell G. Lynch, and he was, I learned later, one of the people responsible for convincing Lou Perini to move his team from Boston to Milwaukee. His wire was my first lesson in the succinctness of journalistic style. It said, "Send special delivery airmail by Thursday three hundred words whether Dittmer or O'Connell should start at second. Lynch."

Within minutes, heart pounding and hands shaking, I was at the small oak desk in my bedroom, struggling over the first newspaper lead of my life. The article, which is still pasted in my scrapbook, took three days to write and began: "When Charlie Grimm hands his starting line-up to the umpire-in-chief on opening day, 1955, Danny O'Connell, the chisel-chinned Irishman, will be playing second base." Not bad for a fourteen-year-old. Concise, direct, a little color, an air of authority. I probably couldn't do much better today. (And I was right to boot: O'Connell did start at second.)

Lynch wrote back: "First contribution received. Not bad. Now, be prepared to have Dittmer fans jump on you, and we have a lot of them here. Sportswriters who make comments must develop thick skin." I was terrorized thinking I might have said anything to offend a single Braves fan, let alone, God forbid, a Braves player. Lynch also added a postscript: "Get a typewriter if you plan to be a writer."

My brothers and I did not receive presents from our parents except on birthdays and at Christmas, but in this case Dad agreed that a typewriter was an educational expense. Together we went to a dingy stationery shop in Brookline Village and rented a Royal upright for nine dollars a month. I was in business. Each Wednesday during the 1955 season—a rookie year for both Chuck Tanner and me—I wrote my column, banging away with two fingers. I sent it off on Thursday with a twenty-six-cent special-delivery airmail stamp and saw it printed, spelling errors and all, in the *Journal*'s Sunday sports section.

The year was one of my happiest, a time of simple hero worship. I was generous in my comments, lauding the Braves' accomplishments with flowery adulation. Lynch urged me to be tougher, but I resisted. My heroes were cast in the image of God, and in the conflict between being a sportswriter and a fan, I stood firmly on the side of the latter.

Throughout May and June I collected All-Star ballots on behalf of Johnny Logan—alas, Ernie Banks would start at short for the National League that summer—and received a note, thanking me for my efforts, that was signed, "Your pal, Johnny Logan." A kiss from Tootsie couldn't have set my heart more aflutter. I also saved my allowance to place calls to various Braves players in far-flung cities. I tracked down Bobby Thomson before a game in the Milwaukee clubhouse and found Del Crandall in the lobby of Philadelphia's Warwick Hotel. When he actually answered my page, I was so overwhelmed the only question I could think to ask was: "How come ballplayers say 'ain't' if they went to school?" I don't remember his response.

Fan mail started to arrive regularly—as, one day, did a large box from Milwaukee. In it was a Rawlings infielder's glove, autographed by every member of the Braves. My feet didn't touch ground for a week. On the little finger alone were the signatures of Hank Aaron, Andy Pafko, Gene Conley and Jim Pendleton. The glove has traveled with me all these years to homes in a dozen cities on four continents and rests today, shellacked and unused, on an office shelf, between my collection of Africa books and those on the Middle East.

I had always believed that the Braves had paid for the glove and mailed it to me. Now, after an afternoon spent with my scrapbooks, I find that isn't quite true. Lynch had been responsible. But he reassured me, in a letter I apparently had chosen not to pay careful attention to: "If the idea had been suggested to the players, they might have provided the glove, although if you ever have contact with players, you'll find that few like to part with money."

Lynch went on to say in that letter: "If you are to be a writer, there is one thing you must know. A gift or a favor must not influence your writing. When you find it necessary to be critical or feel like second-guessing, go right ahead. The right kind of people, ballplayers and others, understand that a writer must be honest in what he tells the public and in his opinions."

Those were weighty words for a young writer-fan to digest, but I thought about them and tried to respond. Charlie Grimm, I wrote, blew a game against the Dodgers by not pinch-hitting for Conley in the eleventh inning; Aaron ought to get a shot at the leadoff slot and Pafko should start regularly in left; the Braves, falling farther behind Brooklyn by the day, needed to "put their noses to the grindstone and hustle out of their doldrums."

My tone had changed. A line had been crossed.

"That's how I hoped you would write in the first place," Lynch said, finally offering faint praise. "Keep right on kibitzing."

About that time, in July or August, I received a letter from a Milwaukee businessman, Charles Meyer, whose family-run company made organ pipes for churches. He wrote that he and his wife, Florence, would like to invite me, at their expense, to Milwaukee in September for a seven-game home stand. He would arrange, through Lynch, to have me meet the players and get passes for the clubhouse and press box. Could I come?

Sweet Jesus, yes!

I had turned fifteen by then and had begun smoking an occasional Lucky Strike. As Dad drove me to Logan Airport on Labor Day, he had some words of advice: "Be yourself, son; remember to say 'thank you'; and don't smoke in public. In fact, I don't approve of you smoking, period." He handed me the ticket Mr. Meyer had forwarded. The fare, first class, round trip, was $112. Thunderheads hung on the horizon and I prayed the pilot did not intend to fly through them. My United prop was bound for Cleveland, where I would make a connection to Milwaukee, and I had visions of never seeing home again. Had I been given the chance, I probably would have forsaken my journey on the spot and stayed right there in Boston, to be forever the dreamer of a mystical land and its men of summer.

The Meyers lived in a dark wood-frame house full of family portraits and antique furniture in an old part of Milwaukee. They were fine people, elderly, quiet and almost timid, who expected no compensation for their generosity other than the opportunity to share my excitement. "I am sure I will be amply repaid by your appreciation," Mr. Meyer had written me earlier, and for many years afterward, until death ended the Meyers' half-century marriage, we regularly exchanged lengthy letters and a Christmas phone call.

My first night in Milwaukee—when the visitors were Stan Hack's Chicago Cubs—the Meyers turned me over to Bob Wolf, a *Journal* sportswriter, who had a wooden hand (the result, I think, of a Korean War wound) and had written a word in that day's paper I had to look up in the dictionary, *tantamount*. Wolf led me, trembling, into the Braves' clubhouse before the game. The scene remains frozen in my mind's eye: Bob Buhl is eating a piece of cheese by the trainer's table; Chuck Tanner, sitting next to the Braves ball boy, Chad Blossfield, who is about my age, is at his locker going through a stack of mail; Lew Burdette is putting on his uniform with the red tomahawk over the chest. I am introduced to Eddie Mathews, standing naked in front of a row of sinks, and he says, "You're the kid from Boston, aren't you?" My God, I just spoke to *Eddie Mathews*! I extend my hand, but he doesn't take it and turns back to the mirror to continue shaving.

Something had gone wrong. As I met the players one by one, I knew I was an intruder. A winter wind was blowing, and I didn't understand why. Only Tanner, the rookie who had hit a home run in his first major league at bat after laboring nine years in the minors, took the time to talk and make me feel that I had not invaded a fraternal sanctuary.

I was hurt and confused. After several days, I sought out the dean of the Braves, Warren Spahn, for consultation. Spahn was walking down the tunnel between the clubhouse and dugout when I caught up with him to ask why I had received an icy reception. He seemed to tower over me. He had a large nose and a face that was oddly handsome. His hands were not as big as I thought they would be. He was already in his mid-thirties and his talents as the winningest left-hander in history were Olympian.

"I'll tell you, Dave," he said. "You remember that article you wrote saying we weren't hustling? I think you said something about needing to put our noses to the grindstone."

I nodded solemnly. He went on: "Well, we're professionals and some of the players didn't think you ought to be making those judgments. It's not for you to tell pros they're not hustling."

"But, Mr. Spahn," I blurted out, "why did you *care*? I'm only *fifteen*."

Spahn laughed. "Someday you'll understand," he said. "In the meantime, relax. I don't think you'll have any more trouble with the boys. I'll tell them you're OK."

That may have been the most joyous moment of my young life. Not only had I been forgiven, I had been accepted. I felt a swell of confidence. Buhl shared some cheese with me after I assured him my ambition was to be a major league second baseman, not a sportswriter, and Logan said he and his wife, Dottie, would like me to drop by for lunch. Mathews chatted amiably about his chances of breaking Ruth's home-run record. Aaron gave me a hitting tip: Always keep your eye on the ball.

I summoned up the courage to ask the Braves general manager, John Quinn, if he might have some information I could use to write an exclusive for the *Journal* during my visit. Quinn was an astute baseball man with the red cheeks of a hard drinker. He wore blue suits and always seemed to have his hand in a pants pocket, shaking a fistful of change.

"Well," he said. "I heard Bobby Thomson's going to sell his house because he can't afford the property taxes in Milwaukee. That might be something."

Thomson approached me later that day in the stadium's parking lot. "Dave," he said, "I heard you might write something about my selling my house. You shouldn't do that, you know. That's a private matter."

"Oh, don't worry, Bobby," I replied, forgetting all that Russ Lynch had taught me. "If you don't want me to, I won't say anything."

The rest of the week flew by. I moved, with apparent purpose, from the playing field to the press box just like a real sportswriter, blushed when fans at County Stadium asked for my autograph and Braves announcer Earl Gillespie put me on his pregame interview show, and talked with Lynch during a barbecue at his house about pursuing a life in baseball.

"You've got to grow up and forget about the baseball business," he said. "Just forget that bunk. Find something worthwhile to do with your life."

Finally it came time to enter the *Journal*'s newsroom—a huge, energized place that was alive with clacking typewriters and harried men—to write my final article before returning to Boston. I noticed an interesting line in that column as I thumbed through my scrapbook recently: "Everything I wrote this past year was strictly an opinion and I can honestly say that I don't regret a single word I have ever written." The prose needs some work but I like the mildly defiant ring. Perhaps I was learning the difference between being accepted and being respected and had come to understand that even our heroes are not always heroic.

The *Journal*'s editors talked of bringing me back to Milwaukee in 1956 for a second season, but Lynch said no. "I can't tell you what publicity does to people," he wrote. "I've seen it many times in my nearly forty years in this business. You're a fine boy, and I would hate to see you change and feel that I was responsible for it because I let you write for the *Journal*. If you come here again, do it casually and quietly. I'll keep you out of this paper and you keep yourself out of any other. That's best."

Lynch and I corresponded for more than twenty-five years. He was a stern taskmaster and a valued mentor, and it was many years before I realized who the real hero of my golden summer had been. Lynch prodded me to take my college education more seriously— "The world's too full of deadwood as it is," he lamented—and urged me to find a profession that was honorable and satisfying, regardless of the salary. He challenged me to respect the nuances in the English language—"Tell me the difference between 'oral' and 'verbal,'" he once demanded—and critiqued the clippings I sent him after I got my first newspaper job in 1965. ("This one's OK, but you can do better.") By that time he had resigned as sports editor and was traveling the country for the *Journal* as the nation's first newspaper writer assigned full time to resource uses and conservation.

"Since you are a sports fan," he wrote during that period, "perhaps you will not understand when I say that the sports editor's work seemed sort of futile to me. I was in the entertainment field, and I am essentially a reporter. . . . And the Braves? Honestly, I have hardly given a thought to sports since I broke away. My attitude amazes me."

In a way, I did understand. The Braves consumed my life not much longer and eventually I wandered on to write about places where I found no heroes—Vietnam, Iran, Beirut, Ethiopia and the killing fields of Idi Amin's Uganda. But my affair with baseball lingered, for the older I became, the more the game whispered to me of being young and knowing no mountain too big to climb—of being all the things that could be no more—and I think I always knew that one day I would go back to try and recapture that magic of so many summers ago.

Chapter One

The golden moments in the stream of life rush past us,
and we see nothing but sand; the angels come to visit us,
and we only know them when they are gone.

—GEORGE ELIOT

Forty minutes out of Phoenix,
past the shopping centers and subdivisions that are pushing westward through orange groves and fields of sweet potatoes, I found
Johnny Neun standing in the March sunshine of yet another
spring. The old man carried a megaphone and wore number fifty-
eight on his uniform. His checks were ruddy and his white hair
thinning. "Now listen up, men," he said, and the young men
spread out on the grass at his feet did. They were silent and their
eyes followed him as he paced in a small circle, near the pitcher's
mound. His message was the sermon of a priest, and they listened
because "Mr. Johnny" had been to the fabled land of which all
young men dream.

"Today," he said, "I think it's important to remember how
careful you have to be about the way you live your life. It's to your
advantage not to do too many things off the field that interfere with
your life on the field. You turn on TV and you hear that some

committee or other is investigating things out of someone's past and lives get ruined. When you play this game, you're in the public eye. I once heard a great poet say that if you're going to go public in life, your life also belongs to the public. Be careful with your life. In the long run the thing that's going to be most precious to you, the thing you're going to treasure all your life, is your peace of mind."

Here he paused and rapped on the megaphone to make sure it was working, then went on: "Dig in and make sure you get the full benefit of your natural ability. Only a few of you are going to make it to the Big Club. But for the others, you ought to be able to leave, saying, 'I gave it my best.' Live your life today, be all you can be, and don't worry about the competition, don't worry about tomorrow. Don't worry about things you have no control over. Do it this way and someone may walk up and tap you on the shoulder and say, 'You're the one.' "

Johnny Neun—who played for Ty Cobb in the 1920s when Cobb managed the Detroit Tigers, who spent nearly four decades with the Yankees as manager, coach and scout, who managed the Cincinnati Reds and scouted and instructed for other organizations, including now the Milwaukee Brewers—was eighty-eight when I met him at the Brewers' minor league camp in Arizona. It was his sixty-ninth consecutive spring training. Neun was as timeless as baseball itself, his mind alert, his step spry, and when the morning workouts ended and the heat became withering, he would retire to a chair in the shadow of the clubhouse. There, on the slight rise above the three adjoining baseball diamonds, he would watch men young enough to be his great-grandchildren pursue the major league dream he had already fulfilled. He would make notes and see nuances in a pitcher's delivery or a first baseman's footwork that escaped me entirely and all the while his face would be creased by the slightest of smiles.

Like many men whose lives had been spent in the secure, innocent confines of professional baseball, Neun was blessed with the most wonderful of afflictions—terminal adolescence. He'd walk half naked, dragging a fungo bat, through the coaches' locker room, regaling the Brewers' minor league instructors and managers with stories of how he helped make a first baseman out of a third baseman named Moose Skowron and how Ty Cobb used to tell rookies, "You, kid. You better invest in Coca-Cola. That stock's better than land."

Neun made me think of my father, not because they were similar but because they were so different. Dad had lived to almost Neun's age before the cancer triumphed. He was a sober, stern man, decent and honest beyond measure. He had no hobbies and few interests other than business and the welfare of his family, and in his final years I don't remember much levity around our home. At heart Dad was always the Englishman of his birth, reserved, controlled, private, and the thought of him as an old man, bare-assed, dragging a game stick used by children around a room of laughing men, sharing yarns out of a past he seldom spoke of, was preposterous.

"Mr. Johnny," I said one day, trying to be tactful, "I was wondering if you think it's, well, unusual, that here you are almost ninety and you're hanging out in a clubhouse with a bunch of men in their underwear and you're hitting grounders to kids who have hardly heard of Ty Cobb."

"Oh no, not at all," he said. "Sure, I appreciate the fact that I'm getting older every year, but I don't *feel* old. I think this keeps me young. Working with the prospects in spring training, big-league scouting in the summer, that's good mental therapy. I see so many good men that lose that. As my doctor said, 'Johnny, you're a remarkable man.' I said, 'Doc, what do you want me to do next year to keep fit?' and he said, 'Just do what you did last year.' "

The Milwaukee Brewers' minor league spring-training camp was in Peoria, Arizona, and I had flown there for a week in mid-March, hoping to get an idea of what the minors were about and to meet some people I would encounter on the road once the season got under way. Forty-niner remained in Los Angeles, getting outfitted for the trip: new tires, a CB radio, a tune-up and a set of cooking utensils. Although I know few more perfect sights than the symmetry and colors of a baseball field caught in the soft spotlight glow of early evening, I had started worrying by then how far removed from baseball I had become during my years abroad. I couldn't even name a single major league starting lineup anymore, except perhaps that of my hometown Dodgers, and when in the box scores I saw names such as Bell, Griffey, Francona, I'd be amazed these old-timers had held on so long. Then I'd find out they weren't the players I remembered at all; they were their sons.

What I found in spring training was not merely a revival of the seasons and spirits. What I found was a dream that was desperate and young men who were hostage to that dream, to the longing of reaching what they called The Bigs, The Show or simply Up There. They played, in these first early days of their professional lives, not for future fame and fortune but for confirmation—confirmation that they were as good as they had been told all their lives they were. They never publicly acknowledged the fear of failure—only one of fourteen minor leaguers ever makes it to the majors—yet apprehension lurked in the promise of spring and in the long season of bus trips ahead. As one player told me: "A guy's not making it, he sees the end coming, and his sweat starts having a different smell."

The first cuts in spring training usually come about the third week of March. One team, the Atlanta Braves, carries out these career executions in the most humiliating fashion, sending a golf cart onto the field during pregame warm-ups. You can hear the gasps of nervous breathing as the cart makes its way through the rows of stretching, bending athletes. When it stops in front of an unsuspecting player, the young man gets in under the watchful eyes of what are soon to be his ex-teammates and heads to the club-house, where, he knows, Hank Aaron, the Braves minor league director, is waiting for him with a plane ticket home.

"Get in. Hank wants to see you," a trainer driving the cart said one day, stopping in front of a tall outfielder. The player, who was doing stretching exercises, remained immobilized, his fingertips touching his toes, his head between his legs. "Hank wants to see you," the trainer repeated.

Still the player did not move. "Fuck Hank!" he finally said. "I'm not getting in that cart!"

The Milwaukee Brewers were stocked deep with talent at the spring camp I visited, having, as usual, more minor league applicants than available positions. So on a warm Arizona evening in late March, while Milwaukee was buried under a foot of snow,

Johnny Neun and two dozen men wearing polo shirts and slacks gathered in Room 1026 at the Roadway Inn for the one ritual of spring that none enjoyed.

"What we need to think about," said Bruce Manno, the Brewers farm director, "is who we've seen the last four or five days and determine if we feel we can make a judgment on them for possible cuts tomorrow. If anyone feels he'd like to see a little more of the player before deciding, that's fine. We'll take another look. I want to make sure we have no doubts."

Manno was thirty-five, intense, ambitious, a workaholic whose endless hours at the ballpark—even on Sundays in the off-season—had cost him his marriage. He was a company man with compassionate instincts, and players who asked him where they stood with the Milwaukee organization got straight answers. To his left, also facing the assembled scouts, instructors and managers, sat Bob Humphreys, second in command, a former marine and a journeyman big-league pitcher in the sixties. The riches of today's game had escaped men of Humphreys' age—his top salary had been twenty-five thousand after nine years in the majors—and to him, any player who treated lightly the development of his skills was guilty of nothing less than a felony. The current generation of athletes, Humphreys thought, was bigger, stronger and faster than his had been, and mentally neither as tough nor as hungry.

"First the pitchers," Manno said. "I want to talk about Kevin Price."

Roland LeBlanc and Walter Youse, two of Milwaukee's scouting supervisors, spoke up from the back row almost at once. They were elderly men who would not have looked out of place at the bar of an Elks lodge in Des Moines or Cedar Rapids. At the exhibition games I hadn't initially even been aware of their presence. Yet once I intentionally looked for them, they were always there, somewhere just out of the line of vision, watching play wordlessly and, as each had been doing for more than half a century, handicapping a young man's potential for advancement. If their baseball lingo had been replaced with the parlance of the racetrack, I could have been at Santa Anita, among bettors analyzing the performance of thoroughbreds from the *Racing Form*.

"I saw the pitcher the other day," LeBlanc said. "Top fastball

70 [mph]. Mostly 68. Slider, 71 to 76 and that's his best pitch. Doesn't throw too good if you ask me."

"I saw him first time out," Youse said. "He was about the same. No, I didn't like what I saw."

"Do you have any reservations at all about letting him go?" Manno asked.

"How old's this guy?" someone asked before LeBlanc or Youse could answer.

"Twenty-six. Twenty-seven in July," Manno said.

"Old, then, isn't he."

"He had a lot of success in Double-A," Manno said, as though hoping someone would talk him out of the inevitable. "And he had fifty saves in Triple-A. But he's pitched for nine years. That's quite a while, and I'm not sure how much opportunity we can give him with our list of pitchers. Anyone want to see him in another outing? Anyone not in favor of letting him go tomorrow?"

There was silence. Manno's assistant, Judd Schemmel, walked up to the blackboard at Manno's back and wrote in big block letters: "1. KEVIN PRICE."

An outfielder and infielder went next—"An 80 mph fastball, knee-high, went right by him," a talent scout said of the in-fielder—and then I was surprised to hear Manno ask about Finney Rajchel. He was a lanky, blond catcher from Ohio, with a degree in psychology and a .300 batting average in the winter instructional league the Brewers run for rookie prospects. For eighteen years, from Little League through college, he had been the team star. Now, suddenly, he was surrounded by a hundred peers whose talents matched, and often exceeded, his own.

"The younger players get nervous when the cuts start," Rajchel had told me a couple of days earlier. "They get quieter. Some don't eat. But I'm older. I had a good winter. Catchers are in demand. I know I'm safe. Even if things don't work out, though, I'm in a little different situation than most of these guys. I've got a degree to fall back on."

Roland LeBlanc was the first to respond to Manno: "He doesn't look like a prospect to me. But he's a tough dude. He got hit today everywhere but under the foot and he hung in there."

"His arm's real scattered," said Walter Youse. "He's throwing standing up instead of in a crouch. He didn't show me much."

"He's a great kid, but I just don't think he can help us in the organization and he's twenty-four already," said Dave Huppert, manager of the Stockton Ports. Huppert had been a distinguished minor league catcher whose major league totals showed twenty-one at bats over two seasons, one hit and seven strikeouts.

The communal breakfast room at the Brewers' motel was solemn the next morning. "I heard the staff met last night and the first cuts are today," someone whispered to a friend. Plates with half-eaten stacks of pancakes and scrambled eggs were pushed aside, and players boarded the buses for the practice fields well before the 7:15 A.M. deadline. No one spoke of the morning's headlines, which seemed trivial in comparison to the personal struggle for survival of a dream: An Exxon tanker had gone aground in Alaska's Prince William Sound, spilling twelve million gallons of crude; the University of Utah announced that two scientists had produced fusion at room temperature; the Bush administration and the Democratic Congress had agreed to a new policy for promoting democracy in Nicaragua.

Finney Rajchel was taking off his shirt by his locker when the Denver trainer, Peter Kolb, approached. "Finney, don't dress yet," he said. "Bruce Manno wants to see you."

Rajchel stood up, his face suddenly gone pale. He took a deep breath, straightened his shoulders and, with eyes focused on the far wall, walked down the corridor, past the coaches. A sign taped over a row of lockers said: IF YOU CAN NOT PRAISE, IT IS DISHONEST TO CRITICIZE. The coaches did not look at him, nor did he look at them.

By the time Rajchel left Manno's office the other players had changed into their uniforms and were on the diamonds. The clubhouse was empty. Rajchel sat alone for a long time in front of his locker. His former manager in the instructional league, Alex Taveras, came over, put his hand on the catcher's arm and said, "You gave it your best shot, Finney. No one can ask more." After a while, Rajchel fished a quarter from his jeans and went looking for a pay phone to call his wife. The clubhouse attendant tore off the taped name marker over Rajchel's locker and tossed it in a waste-basket. Nearby a radio tuned to KJOY 1012 blared: "More sunshine today with temperatures in the nineties. It's another magic day in the valley."

Rajchel and the other casualties of spring would soon be forgotten. And in ten days, Greg Vaughn, Bill Spiers, Gary Sheffield—tomorrow's stars who would be in The Show before the year was out—and a hundred others would board planes and buses for the journey north. When the angels came to visit, they would be ready. Each was sure of one thing, that one day the announcer in Milwaukee's County Stadium would say, "Now batting for the Brewers . . ." and the name would be his.

County Stadium had been a special place to me, ever since my romance with Milwaukee, and I envied them going there. Long ago, though, my Braves had fled Milwaukee, as they had Boston, to take up residency in Atlanta, and tenancy of County Stadium now belonged to the Milwaukee Brewers, who were once the Seattle Pilots. But from the summers of my youth I can still call into focus every player on the 1955 Braves—Eddie Mathews, Warren Spahn, Del Crandall, Johnny Logan, Chuck Tanner—for those are the men who lived and worked in a time when giants walked the earth.

Baseball was much in the news when I got back to Los Angeles from spring training, and most of it seemed better suited to the *National Enquirer* or *Forbes* magazine than the sports pages. Pete Rose, having caught Ty Cobb as the most prolific hitter in history and gone on to become a manager, was facing a lifetime ban for betting on baseball games. The Red Sox were trying to trade baseball's best hitter, Wade Boggs, who had a wife at home and a well-publicized mistress on the road. No one wanted him. Mr. Clean, Steve Garvey, had impregnated two women and married a third. Two players had missed spring training because they were in drug rehabilitation. Rickey Henderson said the Yankees had lost last year's pennant partly because they drank too much. A players' strike or an owners' lockout loomed over the 1990 season. Frank Viola turned down a three-year contract worth nearly $8 million and accused the Minnesota Twins of not negotiating in good faith.

No sooner had the American League's twenty-four-year-old MVP, Jose Canseco, signed a new contract, calling for a *raise* of $1.2 million a year, than he started getting more speeding tickets than base hits. After Canseco was arrested carrying a 9-mm semiautomatic handgun, his general manager, Sandy Adlerson, sounded a lament for all the fast-lane victims of sudden megadollar stardom: "My evaluation of Jose is that he is a very naïve young man who doesn't grasp the magnitude of the interest in him as an individual or the consequences of not abiding by the same rules that apply to you and me."

The night before the start of the minor league season, Sandy prepared a Last Supper for me: cold lobster tails, a hot artichoke and endive salad, each dish a favorite. We talked about finding a town for a weekend rendezvous a month or so down the road, and I felt a tug of loneliness that made me swallow. If it had been raining, I might have declared the season canceled. My feet were restless but my heart was not.

"Promise me one thing," Sandy said.

"Anything."

"That you won't come home chewing tobacco."

I left Los Angeles the next morning in the worst April heat wave in California history. I had no plan other than to start the season with the Stockton Ports, descendants of Mighty Casey's Mudville Nine, and to be home by September when minor league pennants had been decided and new champions crowned. In the interim, my twenty-foot-long RV (recreational vehicle) would be my home and office, my meeting hall and traveling saloon.

Forty-niner and I moved down Benton Way and crossed Sunset Boulevard near Dodger Stadium. I had told friends that I intended to travel not a single interstate on this rural journey, but after briefly consulting a map, it became apparent there was no logical way to get out of L.A. on surface streets. I swung onto the freeway and headed north, my first covenant with the open road already broken.

From California's
San Joaquin Valley
to the Southwest Deserts
April 7 – May 29

Chapter Two

We got sunshine. We got fresh air. Let's play two.

—ERNIE BANKS

Spring training was over and now the real business was at hand. Carl Dunn's bus with three million miles under the hood was making its way north, its passengers twisted into odd shapes that each hoped would induce sleep. Soft banter came from the rear of the coach, where Steve Monson and Dan Fitzpatrick had started a blackjack game on an upside-down trash can. From somewhere in the darkness there was an occasional *spttttt* as a stream of tobacco juice struck a drinking cup stuffed with paper napkins. The miles had become an eternity, as though there had never been a moment without the hum of tires and the steady clicking of Dunn's directional signals when he pulled out to pass. In the glint of headlights, the drivers Dunn rolled by had a glimpse of the sign on the bus's side. It said, STOCKTON PORTS. THE ONLY PROFESSIONAL BASEBALL TEAM IN THE SAN JOAQUIN VALLEY.

The Ports worked for the Milwaukee Brewers, at the Single-A

poverty level, where players shine their own baseball shoes, get eleven dollars a day meal-money on the road and grouch about their misfortune hardly at all. Milwaukee sent its best young talent to Stockton—twenty-one former Ports were in the majors at the start of the '89 season—and year after year the team put together one of the best winning records in baseball. It was a team blessed with an indefinable ingredient known as chemistry—a magical meshing of personalities and talents that made a man strive for a group as well as for himself. Good chemistry was like Mulligan stew: "You dump everything into a pot, heat and stir," a manager told me. "You never know how it's going to come out, but when it's right, the tastes complement each other beautifully." If a player's warm-up jacket fell onto the aisle of Dunn's bus, two dozen teammates would walk over it just to be mulish. And if the player needed twenty bucks until payday or encouragement to battle a slump, those same two dozen men stood ready to help.

The bus was an excellent place to figure out the hierarchy of a team. The manager always sat in the front seat on the passenger side, his pitching coach across the aisle or just behind him. The veterans staked out the rear seat, which offered a smoother ride (and better snoozing) and was out of earshot of the manager. The divisions within a club were not based on race or talent, but rather on position and longevity. Pitchers tended to hang around with pitchers, rookies with rookies, and those groups sat more or less clustered together in the coach. Players whose reading habits included anything more serious than USA Today formed another group, the smallest.

Carl Dunn, or "busie," as the players called him, had never liked baseball until he began driving the Ports on their fifteen-thousand-mile annual journey through the California League three years ago. Now he couldn't get enough of it. He was fifty-eight, a retired Greyhound driver living on a small pension and the $950 a month he made from the Ports. The players viewed him as their father confessor, and he in turn worried about the ones who were so intent in their pursuit that they recognized no world other than baseball.

"Sometimes I tell the boys they're not going to have this job forever, and I don't think they hear a word I say," Dunn said to me at one point. "But I guess everyone's got a right to dream."

I asked him what his own dreams were.

"Mine? It's too late for me to have any special dreams. I've had my chances. I don't fantasize or want anything elite. I just want to be happy, have a little financial security. That's all."

In something like forty thousand hours behind the wheel, Dunn had never had an accident or even gotten a citation. "I'm not a bragger," he said, "but I'm damn good at what I do, and I know it." His service awards from Greyhound included a gold watch and a handsome mantel clock. Greyhound had taken good care of its people in those days, but then the company went sour, torn by a bitter labor dispute, industry deregulation and new management. When Dunn pulled into the Sacramento terminal on the last run of a thirty-year career, he looked around the loading dock, hoping some executive would be there to extend a word of thanks. No one was. The only person who bothered to say farewell was his pal, the dispatcher.

The tip of Dunn's cigarette glowed in the darkened coach. It was 3:15 A.M. He pulled off Highway 99 and drove through the deserted streets of Stockton, turning down Alpine Avenue toward Billy Hebert Field, where the team would play its home opener the next night against the Palm Springs Angels. The players stumbled off the bus, kicking aside beer cans from the aisle. Jim Poulin, the young trainer from Connecticut, headed for the deserted clubhouse, where he would stay until dawn, washing uniforms. Only a couple of the players had cars. The others dumped their blue equipment bags on the pavement and stood about, as though waiting for something to happen.

"Hey, busie, aren't you taking us home?" one asked.

"This is home," said Dunn, who had the flu and felt cranky. "My job's to get you to the ballpark, not shuttle you around town at all hours of the night."

The players lived six miles away, in the Willow Glen apartment complex, where, for the 142-game season, they would bunk four to a unit, often furnishing their rooms with nothing more than a beanbag chair, a mattress on the floor and a TV set. With paychecks that didn't total much more than six hundred dollars a month, after taxes, their necessities were Big Macs and six-packs, not sofas and end tables.

"How many you guys got taxi fare or transportation?" Dunn finally asked, standing in the bus's open door. Only half a dozen hands went up.

"OK, you got thirty seconds to get back on board if you want a ride down to the Willow Glen."

The California League dates back to 1891. For a long time its teams were in towns clustered along Highway 99, the inland route stretching through the state's agricultural heartland, from Stockton to Bakersfield. Then as California's population swung southward, so did some of the franchises, into desert towns that hold the overflow from Los Angeles: San Bernardino, Riverside and Palm Springs. The climate, the quality of the parks and the caliber of talent—one quarter of all major leaguers have labored in the Cal League—make the circuit a favorite hunting ground for scouts and an important development arena for farm directors.

It was into these towns of the San Joaquin Valley that the Dust Bowl migrants came in the thirties, attracted by the promise of sunshine, orange groves and well-paying jobs. John Steinbeck settled the Joad family in Bakersfield, and Merle Haggard, another child of the Dust Bowl, landed there, too. The valley was the home of the underdog, and in a state that places a premium on glamour, in many ways it still is. The people who walk the streets of Bakersfield and Stockton have the shuffling presence of second-generation Okies dealt a tough hand in life.

By the early eighties Stockton had begun attracting a new breed of migrants that Steinbeck would not have recognized—yuppies fleeing over the hills from the San Francisco Bay Area, in search of cleaner air and more affordable housing. But in spirit Stockton remained minor league, unpretentious and a bit weary, a town whose place in history started and ended when its inland port supplied the goods needed to sustain the California Gold Rush of 1849.

In a poll of the three hundred best places to live in the United States, *Money* magazine rated Stockton No. 292, just behind Yuba

City, California, best known for a mass murder committed by migrant worker Juan Corona twenty years earlier. I rather liked Stockton and thought the poll unfair. Besides, if I had been running the survey, no town with a professional baseball team would have been allowed to rank so low, because the presence of a minor league club makes, I think, a significant contribution to a community's civic pride and quality of life.

"It's the same old bullshit," George Sangster of the Chamber of Commerce told the *Stockton Record* when asked to comment on the poll. "We don't have a ballet of metropolitan quality. We don't have 'Roller Derby' or 'Wrestle Mania' or all these high-class cultural events. But who cares?"

Stockton was controlled politically by wealthy land developers, and it rattled them that, except for the success of the Ports, the news Stockton generated was almost always bad. The town got unwelcome headlines when Patrick Purdy, a deranged drifter, turned his rifle on a crowded school yard a few blocks from Billy Hebert Field, killing or wounding thirty-four children. (When the mayor advocated banning semiautomatic weapons, conservatives in town launched a petition to have her recalled.) Stockton got into the news again when Mark Stebbins, a dark-complected white man with curly hair, ran for City Council, posing as a black, and won. His opponent was Ralph Lee White, a black bail bondsman. White's campaign to have Stebbins recalled succeeded, and White took the contested seat. But it turned out White had coerced people into signing the recall petition, so he, too, was ousted. When I got to Stockton he had just announced his candidacy for state controller, advocating the legalization of drugs and promising friends and enemies alike, "We will not go away."

"I've got one ambition this season—to say, 'So long, Stockton' and know I'm on the move," said Steve Monson, a failed catcher in the Philadelphia organization who was making an impressive comeback as a pitcher in the Milwaukee chain. His sentiment was shared by every minor leaguer from Oregon to Georgia. Each one wanted to prove he was too good to be where he was. The next classification up is where he thought he deserved to play, and for Monson, that meant the El Paso Diablos in the Double-A Texas League. The El Paso team even *flew* between cities.

Monson was built like a cement block on which someone had painted a blond flattop. He cultivated the image of a tough guy, glowering and mumbling wisecracks through clenched teeth, all of which did little to conceal the fact that his heart was as soft as a teddy bear's. If he had an attribute, besides a strong right arm, it was the intensity of his confidence and competitive fire, for he pursued his baseball dream with missionary zeal. He had quit football his senior year in high school so injuries would not interfere with baseball. In the off-season he worked the graveyard shift at a convenience store so he could lift weights during the day. He ran before each game until sweat poured off him and his legs wobbled. Never far from his mind were the words of his father, a sheet-metal worker in Maryland, who had pushed him toward baseball as the ticket to a better life.

"No one's going to give you anything," the father had said many times. "You've got to earn it all yourself."

This was to be Monson's fifth season in pro ball and his second at Stockton. Talking to him in the dugout, what struck me was that the pressure of the minor leagues—the pressure to succeed and advance or be gone—had taken part of his youth from him. He spoke of "turning my life around for baseball," of the need for a pension plan in the minors, of the fear of debilitating injuries, and of a book he'd like to write titled *Highs and Lows: My Life in Baseball.* Somehow those were things one might expect to hear from a much older man. Monson was twenty-two.

"You watch me pitch, and you'll see," Monson said. "I'm aggressive. I like to intimidate, like I'm coming after you, so what are you going to do? You won't see me smile. I do that for atmosphere. I want batters to think, This guy doesn't fool around. He doesn't take shit from anyone."

In spring training, after a fine first season in Stockton, Monson had been scheduled for promotion to El Paso. He had told his girlfriend he would quit baseball rather than return to Stockton. Then one day after throwing a few innings in Arizona, his arm "knotted up." The soreness continued, affecting his velocity, and Milwaukee put him back on Carl Dunn's bus for another ride through the California League.

He called his girlfriend when he learned he was going back to

Stockton and she reminded him of his promise to quit. "I know
I said that," Monson told her, "but I can't just walk out on this
opportunity. Baseball's all I have. It's all I can do."

The Ports had opened the season on the road, in San Bernardino, a week before their predawn arrival in Stockton. Forty-niner
had performed well on the drive from Los Angeles, though I
frequently had to ease off the accelerator and remind myself, "Slow
down. There's no hurry." This new tempo felt strange, for I had
been rushing all my life, a hostage of deadlines and schedules and
itineraries. Now I had none.

I pulled into La Quinta Inn and staked out a "room" in the
parking lot. For the next five months I would shower and sleep and
dine in my small aluminum world on wheels. Home each night
would be spent wherever I chose to set the brake, and accommodations would not cost a dime. The Ports had just gotten in from
Stockton. I parked in the shadow of Dunn's bus, hoping the shade
would provide some relief from the heat. It was noontime, and I
didn't have the vaguest idea how I would spend the afternoon, let
alone the summer. The players were in the motel, dozing or watching television, so I did what I always do in a new town: I went
looking for a local newspaper.

San Bernardino was a city with a population of one hundred
thousand plus and no identity, other than its proximity to Los
Angeles. Then in 1986 actor Mark Harmon and some associates
bought the Ventura Gulls for $235,000, moved the franchise to
San Bernardino and called it the Spirit. San Bernardinians finally
had something that was *theirs,* and they responded by filling Fiscalino Field with the largest crowds the California League had ever
known. Everyone had told Harmon a team was doomed to fail in
a town so close to a major league market. He hadn't listened, and
now he owned a club that would have fetched a million dollars or
more and was the most successful sports operation in the history
of California's Inland Empire.

I learned most of this from *The Sun,* which I found in a vending
machine outside one of San Bernardino's ubiquitous coffee shops.
The paper that day ran a sixteen-page insert on the start of the Cal
League season—something I had never seen even in a major league

city—and also printed a critique of the city's newest restaurant, the International House of Pancakes. The reviewer rated the cuisine two stars but found the tomato sauce that smothered a chicken-spaghetti combination "unexciting."

The Ports played miserably in the opening series against the Spirit. Fiscalino Field's three thousand seats were full for each game, and as Port pitchers were battered from the mound the PA man in the press box would play "Till We Meet Again" and fans would stand in unison, slowly waving good-bye. Stockton nearly gave away the first game, letting San Bernardino score four runs in the ninth, then the second night, couldn't hold a 6–2 lead and did lose in the ninth. The Ports slipped onto the bus without a word for the ride back to their motel.

Dave Huppert, the Stockton manager I had met in spring training, let them get settled, then rose from his front-row seat. He had been the California League Manager of the Year the previous season and he knew one thing for sure: His job was to develop players' skills, but if he didn't win, too, he wasn't going anywhere, and Stockton was not where he intended to spend his career.

He yanked the door shut and said, "Close the windows." Now there were two worlds: outside, the fans, walking toward their cars, having had an evening's entertainment at a game that would soon be forgotten; and inside, a business meeting of deadly serious young men whose jobs depended on performance and who would sometimes carry the memory of a ghastly misplay with them for years.

"OK, we fucking lost, but that's not what pisses me off," Huppert said, struggling to keep control of his voice. "We came out of spring training with a policy—a fucking policy that we were going to fucking protect our players. We gave up fourteen fucking hits tonight. These guys aren't that fucking good. We put seven runs on the board and that ought to be good enough to fucking win. We had a couple of guys drilled, and do I see you knocking down any of their fucking guys in return? Next time I tell you to knock down a hitter and you don't, it'll cost you a hundred bucks. One hundred fucking bucks. You got to start earning your share of the plate. So we lost. Big deal. We're going to lose a lot fucking more this season, but if you want to stay on this team, you gotta start playing like professionals. . . .

"The bus leaves the motel for the park at eleven-fifteen tomorrow morning." Then he sat down. I wanted to scribble some notes, but felt uncomfortable, like an interloper suddenly privy to a family's most intimate secrets, so I looked out the window, pretending I wasn't paying attention. Carl Dunn started the engine. There wasn't a sound from the players, not even a *spttttt*, on the ten-minute ride back to La Quinta.

A few days later the Ports escaped San Bernardino with their lives intact, though not their pride. Their youngest player, a nineteen-year-old catcher from Australia, Dave Nilsson, wasn't hitting, and their oldest, twenty-five-year-old Dan Fitzpatrick, wasn't pitching, having reinjured his arm. Fitz knew his career prospects were fading. "But I keep thinking of those guys you hear about who've been around seven, eight years," he said, "then something falls into place and bang! They're in The Bigs. I'm not ready to give it up yet."

The organist at Sam Lynn Ballpark in Bakersfield, the Ports' second stop on their way back to Stockton, was a kindred soul. Bob Kapler had grown up in Iowa in the fifties, loving the Milwaukee Braves, and he still grumbled that Clem Labine was a felon for beaning Joe Adcock after Adcock had hit four home runs against the Dodgers in a game in 1954. "Don't forget, Adcock also got a double that day," I said, and Kapler grinned, knowing he had found a friend who remembered the world as he did. Kapler sat on the field level, directly behind home plate, the transistor radio in his breast pocket bringing him the voice of Vin Scully at Dodger Stadium, a hundred miles south. He had been born blind, and I thought his nightly presence at the park was testimony to the power of baseball as a game of the imagination.

"What do you 'see' on the field?" I asked. "Is it the same game I see?"

"What do I see? I see the same thing you see when your palm touches your forehead. Absolutely nothing. I don't know what colors look like. I don't know what darkness is. I don't think in terms of seeing, only in terms of other senses—touching, hearing, smelling. For instance, I don't normally think of ballparks in terms of smell, but this year we have cotton candy here for the first time, and I'm aware of that.

"I would say it's wrong to say I can visualize what's happening on the field, but I understand a batter running to first. I understand which is left field and which is right field. From a tactile point of view, I understand a batter hitting the ball and someone running after it. I think I appreciate baseball more than other sports because it's a game my mind can grasp. It's not just a rush of people playing against a clock. It's got pacing and orderliness, a sort of structure."

Kapler read a Braille edition of *The New York Times* between innings and after each game would call in the night's results to neighboring newspapers, dictating an entire box score from memory. His game "eyes" were provided by a mentally slow teenage neighbor, Daron, who sat next to the organ, maintaining a running commentary in a monotone voice. As Daron announced each new batter, Kapler would play several chords from an appropriate song. For the player from Indiana, it was "Back Home in Indiana," and for catcher Lance Rice it was, "Slow Boat to China," though that selection was so esoteric only one or two fans behind Kapler ever clapped.

"That's a single, Bob. Man on first," Daron would say.

Kapler would keep talking as though Daron's voice were coming from a radio. "I play here during the season and I play Friday lunches at the Kiwanis but what I'd really like—"

"Ball one, Bob. Outside and high."

"—is to find someplace where I could play dinner music. Not just because I need the money—"

"That's a strike. Fastball. Still a man on first."

"—but because I like to play. I played in a piano lounge back in the sixties and people told me I did very well, that they liked my voice—"

"He's going to steal, Bob." Kapler's fingers were poised on the keys. "No, wait, he's back on first."

"—The thing is that I play older music, and there's not much demand for that anymore. . . ."

There was a mighty crack. "That ball's out of here, Bob. It's going to be a home run!"

Kapler struck a couple of triumphant notes but no cheering voices rose from the stands.

Daron waited a moment, then said, "Sorry, Bob. He caught it."

I awoke the morning after meeting Kapler in another motel parking lot. There was a rattling outside, like the sound of raccoons foraging through a trash can. I lit a burner on the stove to make coffee and parted the yellow curtain over the sink. On top of a nearby dumpster was a man on all fours, pawing for aluminum cans, which he would toss onto the pavement below. After a while he scampered out of the container, crunched the cans, collected his pile and walked off, bent under the weight of the two green plastic bags slung over his shoulder.

The season was hardly a week old and already my life seemed unalterably changed. Almost all the minor league games are at night, even on Sunday, and with most teams playing every night, the days of the week became indistinguishable. Every day felt like Saturday. If I asked a pitcher when he was scheduled to start, he wouldn't reply with a specific day. Rather he'd say something like "I'm pitching the third game of the series." For him, too, there were no more Tuesdays or Thursdays.

I stopped reading the Los Angeles Times and The New York Times and started buying the local papers, which often boiled international news down to a few capsule paragraphs. My universe grew smaller. When I asked a player what he had heard about the explosion on the battleship USS Iowa that had killed dozens of sailors, he thought I was talking about the state and said, "I didn't hear anything. How'd it happen—a hurricane?"

Slowly I was learning what the players already knew: that any establishment without a drive-through window was not really a restaurant and that you filled up at dinner by loading extra relish and onions onto your ballpark hot dogs. The players' criterion for a good motel was one that had cable TV and the ESPN sports network; mine was one that had a large, well-lit parking lot, where Forty-niner and I could safely spend the night.

I also was discovering something in the bush leagues that I thought had disappeared from professional baseball. It was intimacy. General managers often knew every season ticket holder by face and maybe by name. Players, not yet haunted by the constant glare of stardom, signed autographs and chatted with kids as if it were a pleasure instead of a chore. Even the ballparks were homey. They were small, with the box seats usually starting on field level, and from almost anywhere, you could hear the umpire's voice and see the expression on the pitcher's face.

The Ports continued to struggle in Bakersfield but were jelling as a team. Charlie Montoyo and Pat Listach started making the double play, scooping up everything hit near second like vacuum cleaners. John Jaha, the grandson of a Lebanese immigrant, dropped his hands at Huppert's insistence, eliminating a hitch in his swing, and began slashing hits all over the place. Right fielder Bobby Jones, as swift as an elk, stopped dwelling on his discontent over being in Stockton for a third year and decided to just go out every day and play hard and have fun. His batting average climbed.

"Hey, Bobby," Carl Dunn called out from the grandstands before the start of a game. "Hit one out tonight and I owe you a steak dinner."

Jones homered on his first at bat and pointed to his stomach when, trotting back to the dugout, he caught Dunn's eye. Then he homered again the seventh and Dunn yelled, "Wait a minute. I didn't say anything about buying you the whole cow."

The Ports still managed to lose and Huppert traipsed back to the bus and shut the door. Here it comes again, Jones thought. But this time Huppert was playing a different psychological game. Before he had wanted to shock the players; now he wanted to settle them and strengthen their confidences.

"We'll straighten this out," he said. "You guys are busting your butts, and Derk [Rob Derksen, the pitching coach] and I appreciate that. This is the best fucking team in the league. No one's got the pitching we've got, no one's got the hitting. What I don't want to hear is any bad-attitude shit, like we're snake-bitten or something 'cause we've lost some close ones. This is a fucking good team. Remember that."

"And, Mo," he said to Monson, who along with Fitzpatrick

owned the rear seat of the bus as the team's veterans, "you're pitching tomorrow, so you don't have time tonight to screw another fat fucking broad, right?"

"Can I get a little skull?" Monson shot back.

Huppert laughed and someone behind me said, "That Mo, he'll say anything. Oh my, what a team we've got." I could almost hear the ice melting and the next day the Ports started winning.

Monson, working with the emotion of a bricklayer, set down the Bakersfield Dodgers inning after inning, plodding off the mound stiff-legged, his eyes on the ground as though it were just another day at the office. The following night Mike Ignasiak pitched five scoreless innings, and by the time the Ports got back to Billy Hebert Field for their home opener, they were only half a game out of first place.

Chapter Three

In baseball, you don't know nuthin'.

—YOGI BERRA

Billy Hebert, a Stockton resident and California League player fatally wounded at Guadalcanal in 1942, was professional baseball's first casualty in World War II. I couldn't find a Ports player who had ever asked why the park carried the name it did; nor did I find any who were curious about Stockton's past, when this delta town situated on reclaimed bogland endured frequent floods and was known as Mudville. A professional team nicknamed the Mudville Nine played here then, in the forerunner of today's California League. Ernest Lawrence Thayer immortalized the team—and Casey's famous strikeout—with a poem published on the editorial page of the *San Francisco Examiner* in 1888. Thayer long contended the poem had no basis in fact. But players with names similiar to those in his verse—Conney, Barrows, Flynn—did play in that old league, and many people in Stockton insist the game that left no joy in Mudville really did take place, with the local Nine playing a team of touring major leaguers.

And so, one hundred and one years after Casey left Blake on second and Flynn a-hugging third, Stockton prepared for another opener. The night was cold, a welcome change from the desert heat I had left behind, and the Ports stayed in their clubhouse an unusually long time. There was a small black-and-white TV with a coat hanger jerry-rigged as an antenna next to a row of lockers, and a sign outside the trainer's room that said, CONSERVE WATER. SHORT SHOWER PLEASE. On a wall near the shower, the history of the season would be written under two pieces of tape. On one was the word EX-PORTS, on the other, IM-PORTS. When one of the Ports was released or promoted, the taped name label over his locker would be peeled off and placed under the former; and when a player joined the team, having been demoted from El Paso or sent up from Beloit or signed from another organization, his name would go under the latter.

The Ports general manager had hired a band for the opening-game festivities—"Mudville's Finest, Available for Intimate Bashes, Wakes and Fancy Balls." Three female skydivers circled in a plane overhead. (They would make a perfect landing on the infield just before the first pitch). The crowd was large, more than two thousand, and had arrived early. Season ticket holders, city councilmen and local VIPs drifted down to a new redwood deck in left field where there was free beer and pizza from Domino's. Los Angeles's district attorney Ira Reiner, who owned a minority inter-est in the Ports, had flown in from Southern California and was among the group on the deck. His eyes were focused on something past the soft new-mown grass and the outfield shadows of early evening. In his mind's eye, another game from another era was being played out:

The stands were full of women in long, flowered dresses and men wore brown hats and suspenders. The war was finally over and in Los Angeles's Wrigley Field, the Pacific Coast League title hung on the outcome of a sudden-death play-off game. The Los Angeles Angels and San Francisco Seals, both scoreless, had battled into the eighth inning, with Cal McLish

pitching for Los Angeles. Then L.A.'s clean-up hitter Clarence Maddern
smacked a fastball with the bases loaded that soared over the left-field fence.
The Angels were the champions!

"Whenever I'm in a minor league park," Reiner said, "that game comes back to me like it was yesterday. Suddenly it's 1947 again and I'm eleven years old."

The Ports handled Palm Springs with ease to move into first place. Mark Ambrose, who had married a local girl in a previous tour of duty in Stockton, was cheered on by twenty-five in-laws as he turned back the Angels in the opener. Two nights later Monson and Carl Moraw teamed up on a 7–0 shutout, with each earning a hundred-dollar check from Snyder Lithograph, a local company that rewarded stellar Port performances. Bobby Jones took over the Cal League home-run lead with six.

From the press box of each game, Buddy Meacham, who earned forty dollars a game as the public address announcer, official scorer and unaccompanied singer of the national anthem and "Take Me Out to the Ball Game," kept up the constant patter that is a hallmark of the minor leagues:

". . . Fans, if you've got lucky number five-one-three in your program, you just won a gift certificate from Parks. . . . Remember, you can watch the action tonight, then relive it tomorrow morning in the sports pages of the *Stockton Record*. . . . With the prom just around the corner, why not stop by and see the great selection of tuxedos at California Formal Wear. . . . Here are three more lucky bingo numbers from the insert in your scorecard: B-67, B-3, N-38. . . . We'd like to remind you that the Stockton Ports Little League Clinic next Saturday is sponsored by David and Sons Sunflower Seeds. . . ."

Each announcement brought in a few dollars. For a team like the Ports, which earned a modest profit of about thirty thousand dollars a season, that added up to significant revenue, and Meacham took his job seriously. The son of a Baptist preacher, he could have passed for a Hell's Angel with his wild black beard and generous girth that tore at his T-shirt and sagged over his belt. But Meacham was an amiable and gentle man whose only enemy was the long winter months that denied him his fix of baseball.

Meacham would show up at Ports' road games, two hundred miles from home, traveling on his own nickel, the backseat of his VW piled high with Burger King wrappers and milk shake containers. He'd have a pizza, catch seven or eight innings and make the long drive back home alone. When his previous employer, the Salinas Spurs, folded and took off for Southern California, he had a simple solution. He quit his job as a cabinetmaker and moved closer to Stockton so he could join the Ports.

The man who had cost Meacham his job with the Spurs was Jay Goldinger, a multimillionaire Beverly Hills investment counselor, who, by his own admission, was probably the dumbest owner in the history of minor league baseball. "Talk about klutzes, you're looking at Number One," he said one day over lunch. "If they ever give an award for the worst owner, I've got to be the winner, hands down."

Goldinger moved on the fast track with Southern California's high-stakes players. He flew his own jet, chewed his fingernails to the quick and had hurried back to Beverly Hills immediately after his wedding so he could be in his office for the opening of the Tokyo markets. He was thirty-three years old, and if he set aside an hour for lunch, at precisely fifty-nine minutes into the meal he would push aside his apple pie and announce, "Gotta run."

Owning a baseball team is an exhilarating ego trip—rather like running a popular restaurant where guests consider your fleeting presence a form of flattery—and Goldinger intended to fulfill his dream of being a major league owner by first learning the ropes in the minors. Without fanfare he had already become a baseball philanthropist, buying thousands of tickets to big-league games that were distributed free to underprivileged kids throughout the country and sponsoring a summer baseball camp for terminally ill children.

A few months before the 1987 season, flying blind on emotion and enthusiasm, he bought the inept, financially troubled Salinas Spurs. All he knew about the town was that Steinbeck used to write there. The park was in bad shape—for starters, it had so few toilets that fans often scaled the fence during games to use those in a nearby McDonald's—and more important, Salinas wasn't much of a baseball town. For most of the season it was so cold that the concession stands didn't sell ice cream, and even in June fans showed up at the gate with plastic trash bags stuffed with blankets. If a warm spell struck, people wanted to take advantage of their backyard or the nearby Pacific Ocean.

"I had no knowledge, no experience, no brains. I just walked in," Goldinger said. "I give a lot of speeches on investing, and I talk about emotional discipline. Well, emotion belongs in the bedroom and discipline in the boardroom and in Salinas I kept getting the two mixed up. I got my enthusiasm confused with my perception of how that enthusiasm could be transferred to running a business called a baseball team."

Goldinger started with what seemed a logical premise, but wasn't: He would model the Spurs after the most successful organization in major league baseball, the Los Angeles Dodgers. He transformed Municipal Field into a showcase park with a quarter million dollars of his own money. He tore out the cubbyhole press box and replaced it with a carpeted twelve-man computer-equipped skybox good enough for Red Smith. He commissioned the writing of a computer program to provide fans with detailed daily statistics. He remodeled the clubhouse and hired a major-league-sized staff of forty. He leased a luxury bus, replete with VCR and video monitors, for the players to travel in, and paid their rent, in return for a few hours' community work each month. He flew the manager and trainer into town before the season to speak at businessmen's luncheons, just as the Dodgers did. When he was able to sell only a few of the thirty-one advertising spaces on the outfield fence—a major source of revenue for all minor league clubs—he gave the rest to charities, letting them display their messages for free. He bought the radio rights to broadcast the Spurs games.

Ignoring all the rules that had made him rich, Goldinger had stopped being the businessman and had become the dreamer. He dreamed of being the man who saved baseball for Salinas, a hero to an entire community. And sometimes, just for a second in the crevices of the imagination, he saw himself sitting alone at the end of the dugout, the pennant a base hit away, and heard the manager saying, "Goldinger, it's up to you. Grab a bat."

Salinas Municipal Field had thirty-five hundred seats, and as a result of heavy advertising six thousand fans showed up on opening night. Goldinger stood at the gate, wearing his Spurs cap, taking tickets. Fans asked for autographs and a group in left field chanted, "Goldinger! Goldinger! Goldinger!" for the man who had rescued the franchise and kept it from moving elsewhere. *Good Morning, America* came and did a story and there was playful talk of Goldinger running for mayor. See, thought Goldinger, if you love baseball enough, this is a snap.

Then the fans went back to listening to the San Francisco Giants games or whatever they did on weekday nights. The Spurs started losing. Some nights no reporters showed up in the new press box. The general manager fell sick with mononucleosis and had to take leave, and the concessions manager was fired. The players kept getting lost and showing up late, if at all, for the community events they were to attend in return for their rent. The team gave away free tickets to boys' clubs but the kids didn't come because they couldn't find adults to bring them. Not one sponsor bought a single advertising spot on the Spurs broadcasts, and when the station lost its transmission from the park during a game, no one called to complain. The station offered cash prizes for the answers to easy quiz questions—"Who was the first player to hit sixty home runs?"—but no one called then, either. The reason, Goldinger later surmised, was that no one was listening. *No one*.

Goldinger's losses were rocketing but he reasoned that he might still be able to salvage the season if he could hire a capable general manager and stage a successful fireworks display on July Fourth. Two months into the season he found Maryann Hudson, who had worked in the Dodgers publicity office for three years and, wanting to be a baseball writer, had gone back to college to get a journalism degree. Her job as general manager turned out to be mostly damage control.

"I remember waking up in mid-June one night and saying to myself, 'Holy shit, I'll bet they haven't even ordered the fireworks for the Fourth,' " Hudson recalled. "They hadn't. Well, we finally found a company that promised to deliver them on the night of the game. That's the quickest they could fill the order. We've got a capacity crowd on hand that night, and the fireworks don't come by the sixth inning, the seventh inning. I'm getting comatose. Then we get a call that the driver bringing them down from San Francisco had an accident and wasn't going to make it."

"Ladies and gentlemen," said Buddy Meacham, who was sitting next to Hudson in the press box, "we regret to inform you . . ." The fans started pelting them with everything within reach even before he had finished his announcement, and Meacham quickly added, "The Spurs would like to invite you back Sunday for a free chicken barbecue."

Goldinger got depressed. He came to Salinas less and less and started to feel relief when the Spurs were traveling because the team lost less money on the road than it did at home. He called a friend in La Jolla seeking advice, and the friend suggested that Goldinger give the Spurs to charity. He tried but no charity wanted them. Finally at season's end he got his chance to jump ship. He sold the team and the new owners—major leaguer Ken Brett and his brothers—moved it to Riverside.

"At least I was man enough to admit failure and get out," said Goldinger, who still makes sure thousands of kids get to see major league games every summer but who no longer dreams of being part of baseball, at any level.

Goldinger had missed a basic truth: not every town wants to be big league. When the luster wore off, Salinas considered Goldinger just an outsider who had bought himself an adult toy. They resented his wealth, joking that he had so much money he could even afford to buy another vowel for the Reno pitching coach, Eli Grba. Besides Hudson, who remained a friend, only one person from Salinas—a Spurs player—ever dropped Goldinger a note after he and the team had left to say thanks for giving it a major league shot.

For Salinas, though perhaps not for Goldinger, the story had a happy ending and the town was without baseball for only a year. What happened was that the stands at John Euless Park in Fresno were declared unsafe because of termite damage and torn down, leaving the Fresno Suns homeless, and seventy-year-old Joe Buzas bought the franchise. If Buzas had been born in the Old West, he would have been a horse trader. He had owned more than a dozen minor league teams over the past thirty years, including the Reading (Pennsylvania) club, which he bought for $1 in 1976 and sold for $1 million in 1987, and he heard no voices calling him to the plate in the last of the ninth.

His search for a new home took him no farther than Salinas, where Goldinger had left behind one of the finest facilities in the Cal League. The Salinas Spurs were reborn. Buzas sold all the outfield advertising space that Goldinger had given away, peddled thirty-three thousand dollars' worth of season tickets, pared the staff to skeletal dimensions and forgot about broadcasting any games. He was on his way to turning around another franchise.

"The secret's in making a team a hands-on operation," Buzas said. "You can't stretch beyond your means and you have to know your limits. I've got one ticket seller. If it gets busy, I jump in. If I need more help, I go into stands to get some fans. I've even grabbed umpires coming into the park and said, 'Get to work,' and they've collected tickets. In the Eastern League once, I had the league president taking tickets."

Salinas was one of six teams in the minors without a major league affiliation. To be an "independent" is usually a kiss of death, so Buzas took on a Japanese partner and got Japan to send him— and pay for—seven players. He talked the San Francisco Giants into supplying him with another fifteen, who weren't quite good enough to make the Giants' California League team in San Jose. For a manager, the Giants found a baseball itinerant who had been out of the game for two years and was making a six-figure salary in Los Angeles as a door-to-door salesman, having decided reluctantly that it was time to settle down and make some money.

Tim Ireland was thirty-six and had never owned a house or a stick of furniture or been married. His major league career stats showed one hit in seven at bats. He had played for minor league teams all over the country and been released ten times. He had played in Japan and Italy. Once he had hopped a plane for Australia on a moment's notice to apply for a coaching job, only to be edged out by someone else. When the Giants called offering the Salinas job, it took him not a second to decide to take a pay cut, which I imagined to be in the range of eighty thousand dollars a year.

I watched him hitting pop-ups to his infielders one night in Stockton, before a game with the Ports. He was trim and tanned and relaxed. He had a thin mustache and a toothpick stuck in the corner of his mouth. "Thataway to play last night; that's what I want you to do every night," he'd shout to a player. Then he'd toss the ball up again and hit another pop-up, and I thought how miserable he must have been in a coat and tie, knocking on doors, his feet on pavement instead of grass. Ireland was like a lot of people I met on my journey. He had found the level of his own contentment.

The young Japanese players on Ireland's team came from two major league clubs, the Daiei Hawks and the Yakult Sallows. Unlike American players, who go to Japan as neither teachers nor students but merely to display diminishing skills, they had come to polish their talents and to learn. They traveled with their own translator, Kota Ishijima, who sat behind the group during team meetings in the clubhouse, repeating in Japanese Ireland's comments on the night's play.

"Of course," Ishijima said, "I don't directly translate the *motherfuckers* and the *fuck this* and *fuck that*. I sort of work around that. But they get the idea when their manager is displeased."

Actually, the verbal attacks didn't bother the Japanese at all, because in Japan, where cleanup hitters often bunt and team performance is more important than that of the individual, they were accustomed to being beaten. The Hawks's farm director used to pummel his players bloody for unsatisfactory play in 1988 (he was later fired), and if a player broke curfew, he could expect to be physically assaulted by his manager and coaches. Ireland had an ambidextrous pitcher on his staff, Yuki Kaseda, and during a particularly bad outing in Japan, his manager had walked out to the mound in the third inning and knocked him cold with a right to the chin. A national TV audience watched.

Ishijima, who had worked for an advertising agency in New York for ten years, gave his players two messages for minor league survival in America, one of which was Stay away from junk food; it's too greasy. But they had ignored him and were devouring it in vast quantities, particularly Big Macs and French fries. And he also told them not to mention their salaries; such talk would only cause friction. Each earned more than forty thousand dollars a season— about fifteen times what their American teammates made—and, as ballplayers on every level are in Japan, were national heroes. Each had a fan club and a lucrative contract with a sporting goods firm. They did not crash into walls in pursuit of outfield flies and they seemed to take victory as stoically as defeat.

"You could say our players are spoiled early," Ishijima said. "They have great talent but they don't have the aggressiveness or the competitiveness of your players. They lack this"—he tapped his heart. "That's why your minor leagues will be good for them. They will learn hunger."

Chapter Four

Sports and gam[bl]ing, whether pursued from a desire of
gain or the love of pleasure, are as ruinous to the temper
and disposition of the one addicted to them, as they are
to his fame and fortune.

—RICHARD E. BURTON

Joe DiMaggio was born an
hour or so up the road from Stockton, in Martinez, which, according to some, also gave birth to the first martini. DiMaggio, a high
school dropout, used to read comics in the Yankees' clubhouse and
was confounded when a reporter once asked him for a quote. "I
didn't know what a quote was," he later recalled. "I thought it was
some kind of soft drink." But when a friend asked me if I could
invite one living American to an evening at my dinner table, who
would it be? I unhesitatingly answered, "Joe DiMaggio." Though
I'm not sure what we would have talked about, DiMaggio has
always been the protagonist of my baseball mythology. It is not just
his remembered skills that appeal. It is the vulnerability, the hint
of buried pain, in his quiet gray-haired bearing. The presence
makes him at once appear serene and sad. He is interesting because
we do not know him, and Joe D. could have grown old only as he
has, with grace and in privacy.

The Ports had swept the four-game series from Tim Ireland's reborn Salinas Spurs and, leaving Stockton, I wanted to swing through Martinez and spend a morning with the DiMaggio legend. I called the Martinez Chamber of Commerce to inquire how the town had commemorated its most famous son and what I should see.

"There's not a thing, I hate to say," a woman told me. "We used to have a restaurant that had a lot of DiMaggio memorabilia, but it closed last December. Save yourself a trip. There's nothing."

So I headed east, toward the Sierra Nevada. Fifty miles out of Stockton a sign warned me that Sonora Pass was still closed by snow at Cow Creek, just beyond Strawberry. Looking for a lower, northern pass, I turned up into the Mother Lode country where Mark Twain and Bret Harte once lived and wrote, passing through old gold-rush towns that weren't on my map and counties I had never heard of. The road climbed and the mountain snows deepened. I topped the tree line, skirting a ridge along the roof of the world. Clustered pines appeared in the dusk as blotches of green paint on distant peaks. The empty road was mine alone.

Forty-niner never quivered, handling each rise at a steady speed. Unlike the sleek RVs that had swept by me in the valleys, Forty-niner's lines were those of a draft horse, not a thoroughbred. Its frame was boxlike and its sturdy, powerful appearance had said to me at first meeting, "I like the high, tough roads." I counted dearly on that promise being kept.

About two weeks before Forty-niner and I had set off from Los Angeles, the excitement of the pending trip gave way to a feeling of uneasiness. Five months seemed too long to be alone. The miles seemed too many on unfamiliar roads. In one dream I bartered with a motel owner, trying to make an even swap—my RV for eight free nights at his motel. In another, I walked into an unfamiliar clubhouse. The players parted in ghostly silence as I entered and my steps carried me through a wall of mist and back into the night. I awoke in a sweat, and I knew my life had grown too comfortable, too secure.

The stars were out when I neared Bishop, the California town where Route 6 ends its back roads' journey from Provincetown, Massachusetts. I pulled off the highway and parked near a river.

Forty-niner was only twenty feet from stem to stern, hardly longer than a car, and every space had been utilized. There were little cupboards and drawers, a dinette table in the rear, a double bed over the driver's unit and a bathroom the size of a broom closet. I turned on the interior lights, opened a bottle of California Burgundy the Ports' team doctor, Joe Serra, had given me and put a can of Campbell's vegetable soup on the stove.

Forty-niner rocked to and fro in the wind that whistled through the pines. I tried to remember the last time I had spent a night this far from another person. Even in the isolation of Vietnam's hilltop firebases, one had not been really alone. I went to sleep hearing the rushing waters of the river and did not stir until the sun had dried the morning's dew.

Beyond Bishop and Death Valley lay Las Vegas, home of the Las Vegas Stars of the Triple-A Pacific Coast League. Twenty-five years earlier, after earning my freedom from the U.S. Army, I had piled all my belongings into a battered Mercury and driven West, looking for a newspaper job and a new life far from traditional Boston. It had never occurred to me to head in any direction other than west. I had no leads and found no encouragement as in town after town I appeared unannounced at the desk of city editors. The Mercury died in Reno and I bought a bus ticket for Las Vegas with my last twenty-dollar bill. The paper there, the *Review-Journal*, needed someone to cover the police beat, and I went to work the next morning for ninety dollars a week. Having been kicked out of an Eastern prep school my senior year for taking sports bets, Las Vegas seemed an appropriate place to begin my newspaper career.

In the Las Vegas Stars clubhouse, as in the clubhouse of every minor league team, there hangs a large sign, printed in English and Spanish, that contains Professional Baseball Rule 21 dealing with misconduct. It says in part:

> (d) BETTING ON BALL GAMES. Any player, umpire or club or League official or employee, who shall bet any sum whatsoever upon any baseball game in connection with which the bettor has no duty to perform shall be declared ineligible for one year.
>
> Any player, umpire or club or League official or employee, who

shall bet any sum whatsoever upon any baseball game in connection
with which the bettor has a duty to perform shall be declared permanently ineligible . . . DO NOT ASSAULT UMPIRES. . . . KEEP YOUR HEAD.

Had Pete Rose read these signs? Rose, who twice a month drew
a check from the Cincinnati Reds for $41,667.67, had been a
frequent topic of conversation in the California League because of
the gambling allegations against him. It was common knowledge in
baseball that he had quietly moved thousands of dollars in
memorabilia, wearing as many as thirty or forty uniforms a year so
he could sign the discards and put them out to bid. A recent Rose
uniform brought about a thousand dollars retail, an early flannel
four times that much. He understood nothing of the world except
the art of hitting and the pleasure of money, and when his daughter complained publicly that he hadn't been much of a father, Rose
replied, "How could she say that? I just bought her a Mercedes."
Charlie Hustle, Inc., was someone to feel sorry about, not for, but
at least he had given me an excuse to stop off in Vegas and learn
how to bet a ball game.

According to the magazine *Gaming & Wagering Business*, Americans bet (legally and illegally) more than $22 billion annually on
sports events, an amount greater than Bulgaria's national budget.
If gambling were a single corporation, it would be the nation's
fifteenth most prosperous company, ranking just behind Chrysler
and ahead of Philip Morris. As Pete Rose once said of the Super
Bowl, "If you can't bet on it, who the hell would watch it?"

Baseball is the toughest game to beat consistently and the one
that requires the most discipline in money management. The long
season, the frequency of streaks and the fact that even the finest
teams lose sixty or seventy times a year gives baseball such an
unpredictable balance that lopsided odds of three to one on a
particular game are seen only a few times in an entire season. On
top of that, baseball is difficult to handicap because no one player
dominates the game as does a high-scoring center in basketball or
a quarterback in football. Often the difference between victory and
defeat is a gimpy-legged utility infielder or a rookie just up from
Louisville or Pawtucket. Journeyman Bucky Dent changed the

world with one swing of his bat. So did weak-hitting Sandy Amoros, with one sparkling World Series catch.

Baseball also has a unique purity: gamblers bet into a line of odds and win only when the team they wagered on wins. In football and basketball, you bet into a point spread and can win even when your team loses, as long as it loses by a smaller margin than the book-makers had predicted. Because the house's "hold" (profit margin) is smaller in baseball than in other sports—less than 2 percent, or about the same as a grocery store—most Las Vegas casinos no longer make a serious effort to attract the baseball gambler, having found easier ways to empty a man's wallet. One relic remains, though—the Stardust, whose glitzy façade covers the soul of an old-fashioned bookie joint.

The Stardust was built in the fifties with mob money out of Chicago. Its casino runs for a quarter of a mile along the Strip. Tucked into one corner, past the crap tables where dealers are watched by pit bosses and pit bosses are watched by unseen men through one-way mirrors in the ceiling (Las Vegas wasn't built on trust), is Scott Schettler's office. From that small windowless room, at 8:00 A.M. each day, comes the most widely followed baseball line in the country, the one that influences what bookmakers from Los Angeles to Miami will offer their clients.

Schettler, who came out of a gambling background in western Pennsylvania, and I landed in Las Vegas at about the same time. Vegas was a small town in the sixties. The casinos were run by mobsters, whom the locals considered respectable because they gave money to charity and did their killing outside the city limits. High rollers put on tuxedos when Sinatra opened at the Sands. The tallest building on Las Vegas Boulevard was the Desert Inn, whose third-floor cocktail lounge was known as the Top of the Strip. Then Howard Hughes bought up the Strip, corporations took over the gaming saloons, and executives who didn't know the difference between a natural and a full house discovered that slot machines were more valuable than blackjack or crap tables (slots do not go on strike or need health insurance). Suddenly three-thousand-room hotels with slot-filled casinos larger than football fields sprang from the desert. Open-collar shirts and trendy jogging suits replaced tuxedos at showroom openings. Vegas was no longer intimate and slightly wicked; it was just big, a town where class had given way to mass.

"The school I went to is done, history," Schettler said. "Other guys in this business now are accountants, bottom-line guys in coats and ties. There's no operation like the Stardust's left. The school is closed."

When Schettler first started making baseball odds, he paid cleaning crews at Las Vegas's McCarran Airport to collect discarded sports pages from incoming flights, thus giving him access to home-town information that others in Nevada didn't have. Today, in an era of informational blitz, there are few meaningful insider secrets in baseball, and the Stardust runs a handicappers' library where three sports wires give gamblers the same data that Schettler uses to establish his line.

Much of it was arcane, but I suppose it was important. Damon Berryhill had tendinitis in his right shoulder, Eddie Murray was hitting .415 lifetime with the bases loaded, the wind in Cincinnati was blowing 7 to 14 mph from left to right field. The Stardust also made available copies of *Sports Form: America's Gaming Gazette*. The week's edition I saw carried a page-one photo of poker champion John "Austin Squatty" Jenkins. The caption said he had been fatally shot in the head while visiting a cemetery in Texas. It didn't say what he was doing in the cemetery or why he had been shot, but a columnist for the paper noted: "He was very versatile and played just about every game and played them well."

In the three-story-high sportsbook outside Schettler's office, a hundred or so men and a couple of women sat in front of thirty-four wall-mounted TV screens. Their sounds were not those of the ballpark. Instead of collective cheers and approving *ahhhhhs* for a stirring play, what I heard was intense and individual: a piercing moan as a rally failed or, when a sinking liner fell for a Phillies' hit with a man on second and the score tied, a gravelly voice bellowing, "Now run, you bastard, run!"

"Harry, ought'n we get outta here?" said a man whose pallor led me to believe he had never seen sunlight. "We been here all day. I gotta eat something or I'm gonna die right in this chair and they ain't gonna let you play next to no stiff."

"Nah," Harry said. "I'm getting crushed. I gotta stick it out for the Dodgers game."

Schettler was little moved by gambling emotions. He looked on himself as an agent, bringing together two players who wanted to back opposite teams in the same game. His goal was not to pick winners but to establish "true" odds, odds that attracted the same amount of money on each team. When that happened, the Stardust could pay off the winner with the loser's money and keep the vigorish, or commission, that is built into every posted price. It couldn't lose. Even "wise guys" (professional gamblers) like Lem Banker had trouble if there weren't any bargains to shop for.

Lem Banker was barefoot and sweaty from lifting weights when I knocked on his door. He lived in a Spanish-style home a few miles from the Stardust. A Mercedes 500SL convertible and a bronze Cadillac with the license plate LEM were parked out front, and in the back, near the swimming pool and a punching bag, were two satellite TV dishes. There was a television in every room, a short-wave radio in the sauna and a high-speed UPI sports wire on the kitchen counter, chattering with baseball news, scores, updates and injury reports. It was Banker's sixty-second birthday, and he had made so much money in his business—betting on ball games—that he figured he finally had turned the corner and could not go broke now even if he hit a prolonged losing streak. Banker was one of those people in Vegas no one ever said hello to. Instead they'd ask, "Whodaya like?"

"I'll tell you this," said the six-foot-three Banker, pacing around his kitchen, full of nervous energy. "There are more casualties in baseball than in any other sport. Unless you know what you're doing, betting baseball is like trying to cross the desert with no water and no map. It's a long season and in today's economy you got to bet at least a thousand a game to make money. You can't have emotional favorites. You got to bet a lot of underdogs. My wife used to ask who the best pitcher in baseball was, and I'd say, 'Sandy Koufax,' and she'd say, 'Then how come you're always betting against him?' "

The grandson of Russian Jews, Banker had lived a dangerous life. "The people I grew up with were so tough, when they commis-

sioned the battleship *New Jersey* and pulled up the anchor, there
was a bookmaker and a shylock tied to the chain," he said. Banker
had moved gambling money around New Jersey for some mob
characters, taken bets in his father's candy store in Union City and
spent more time at the racetrack than he did in the college class-
room. He was, he figured, too heavy for light work and too light
for heavy work, leading his father to make the observation:
"You're a bum and you'll always be a bum." But in 1958, tired of
dodging the law, Banker moved to Las Vegas, and Nevada gave
him what no other state could: legitimacy and an honest profession.

"You know what advice I give people who want to be gamblers?
I tell 'em, 'Forget it,' " he said. "It's too tough. Too much pressure.
I always had courage but I didn't have a lot of money to start. It
took a home run by some guy whose name I forget, in the eighth
off Koufax, to keep me going once. He doesn't get the home run
and I'm knocked right out of business, broke."

Banker bet only baseball, football and basketball, dismissing the
stock market, horse races and all casino games as too chancy. He
spent several hours each night making his own line—assigning
values to opposing pitchers, comparing clubs' on-base averages,
considering streaks, bull pens, injuries to regulars (but not substi-
tutes), and home-field advantage for teams such as the Red Sox
that played well in their own parks. When his odds differed from
those posted by Schettler or his competitors, it constituted a play.

"I'm like an engineer, a guy looking for gold," Banker said. "Like
if a guy throws a no-hitter, I can't wait to bet against him the next
time out because the price is going to be inflated." To find those
bargains, he employed two legmen with clipboards and beepers to
cruise the city's forty-five sportsbooks. He joked that one of them
had arrived in Vegas ten years ago with nothing but a ten-dollar
bill and the shirt on his back "and hasn't changed either one
since."

I asked Banker if he ever worried he would wake one morning
and find, like an aging athlete, that his skills had diminished.
Perhaps the concentration would ebb. Perhaps the instincts, the
desire, the luck would betray him. He evaded the question and
called up a story from his New Jersey past. I suspected that gamblers

must have no greater unspoken fear than the thought that they had made their last winning bet.

Banker had bet six ball games and was down eighty-five thousand dollars for the day when I met him later at Caesars Palace for dinner. One of his teams, Montreal, had blown a 4–0 lead and three others had lost in extra innings. He had a fifteen-thousand-dollar bet still working on the Yankees, who were ahead by a run in the sixth, but he gave the appearance of being more concerned with instructing the waiter on how to prepare his veal.

"I wish you'd at least get a little nervous about that Yankee bet," I said.

"Forget it; I had good figures today," he said, brushing away a waiter with a hand weighted down by gold jewelry. "I'll grind out small winning bets and get back on track. I figure I'm smarter than the bookmakers."

Banker was finishing his veal when a man appeared and said quietly in his ear, "Yankees, seven to five, a final." That cut his losses to seventy thousand. Banker nodded, took out some dental floss and said in a loud voice, "Hey, Antonio, you're going to bring over that dessert cart, right?"

I tried the Lem Banker school of gambling the next day. The Dodgers, with Fernando Valenzuela pitching, were posted at the Stardust as "-135," meaning Los Angeles was favored and a bettor had to put up $135 to win $100. I laid down forty dollars on Los Angeles and stayed around to see Valenzuela get clobbered and the Dodgers lose by a wide margin.

Damn, I thought, that was gas money to Tucson.

It was a funny reaction. I'd been traveling on an expense account for years, ever since I finished my minor league apprenticeship on the *Review-Journal* and a couple of other small papers. I'd check into the Brown Palace in Denver or the Olympic in Seattle without a second thought. I'd spend a hundred dollars of my publisher's money taking a source to dinner in Chicago or rent a car and drive halfway across Montana. But knowing that no one was going to reimburse me for what I spent had made me considerably more thrifty. I no longer took my comforts for granted, and the occasional luxuries I now allowed myself on the road—a good dinner with a bottle of wine, a trip to the dry cleaner rather than ironing my shirts on Forty-niner's dinette table—became events to be planned for and appreciated. So the thought of dropping forty bucks on Valenzuela bugged me until I crossed the state line and had been swallowed up by the vastness of the Arizona desert.

Chapter Five

You want to know why players can't let go of the game?
I'll tell you why. I've had sex, beer, good times, and
there's no ecstasy like winning. Nothing feels that good.

—DAN SNOVER, *rookie second baseman,*
Pulaski Braves

I had forgotten what a good
companion radio is. Television (like interstates) deadens our imagination while radio (like country roads) puts our minds back into
gear. I had brought some of my favorite tapes with me—Sinatra,
the We Five, Sarah Vaughan—as well as a small TV set that
plugged into the cigarette lighter. But before long Sarah stopped
singing, "Broken Hearted Melody" and television became only a
habit that was easily broken. I gave the set away.

The airwaves were full of talk shows as I drove on to Arizona—
"This is Jack in Dallas. I'm a first-time caller, so I'm a little bit
nervous. The problem I want to talk about is with my boy-
friend. . . ."—and what seemed to be on people's minds in the
summer of '89 was crime and drugs, the nation's failing education
system, AIDS and abortion. In Arizona, the radio brought me a
couple who were shopping together for condoms. "There are so
many," the thoughtful male voice said. "There's even one here in

your favorite color." The woman was reassured and said, "I'm so glad we're doing this together." Near Kingman, Arizona, where Clark Gable and Carole Lombard spent the first night of their honeymoon in 1939, the signal faded into static, then the static gave way to the clear voice of a friend come to visit.

"Here's Chris Speier, the veteran. Pena out of the stretch, a look at Riles on first and a throw over there." It was Vin Scully, the Dodgers' announcer and baseball's supersalesman. "This has been a big series between the Giants and Dodgers and a big payoff at the box office: over one hundred forty-four thousand dropped by. Hope you're making your plans to be with us when we come off the road next week. Pittsburgh, St. Louis and Chicago. It should be a great home stand at Dodger Stadium. See you there."

But even Scully could not beckon my spirit back to Los Angeles. To be lost in the expanses of the West was to appreciate America again. To move *through* the country, instead of over it at thirty thousand feet, to listen for the sounds of desert silence and find empty roads that slipped through empty towns was to be reminded of the extraordinary beauty of all we take for granted.

My destination in Arizona was Tucson's Hi Corbett Field, home of the Houston Astros' Triple-A farm team. I didn't know much about Tucson except that mob boss Joe Bonanno had retired there and the oldest player in the minor leagues, Ron Washington, still worked there, waiting for redemption and a return to The Show. The Toros were home all week, so rather than hurrying down the interstate, I got directions in Kingman and went looking for Route 66, the road that had carried a nation's dreams—and often its feet—west, toward sweeter water, greener fields, gentler breezes.

Route 66 had once stretched from the corner of Jackson Boulevard and Michigan Avenue in Chicago to the Pacific Ocean in Santa Monica, California, a journey of twenty-two hundred miles through three time zones, eight states and fifty-five towns. It was the way of westward wagon paths, the first national telegraph line, Okie refugees fleeing the Dust Bowl. *If you ever plan to motor West, travel my way, take the highway that's the best. . . .* No one ever thought of the road going East.

"It was the year after the war and my wife and I were driving

from Pennsylvania to California, in a 1941 Buick I'd bought with
the royalties from my first song, 'Daddy,' " said composer Bobby
Troup, who now lives outside Los Angeles. "The family had music
stores in Lancaster and Harrisburg that I could have gone into, but
I told my mother I had to find out if I had any talent and there
were only two places for a songwriter to go then—New York or Los
Angeles."

Somewhere, back in the early miles of the trip, his wife, Cynthia,
suggested he write a song about Highway 40 and Troup shrugged.
"Then later, out of Chicago, when we realized we'd be following
the same highway all the way to California," he recalled, "she
whispered, kind of hesitantly because of the put-down on her first
suggestion, 'Get your kicks on Route 66.' " He had two stanzas and
the melody written on a road map by the time they got to Los
Angeles, where Nat King Cole recorded the song, making it part
of America's musical lexicon:

> Won't you get hip to this timely tip
> When you make that California trip.
> Get your kicks on Route 66. . . .

I, like Troup, had discovered John Steinbeck's "mother road"
more or less by accident, as a teenager in the Burma-Shave days
when 66 was America's main street. Flashing neon signs on cafés
then said, EAT, the painted sides of red barns advised, CHEW MAIL
POUCH TOBACCO, and a billboard outside Albuquerque displayed a
sweating skull with the words: 700 MILES DESERT . . . WATER BAGS,
THERMOS JUGS, ICE. It was 1959 and Route 66 was still, as Jack
Kerouac had written, the symbol of existential wandering and
back-roads culture: "A fast car, a coast to reach and a woman at
the end of the road."

My best buddy, John Sherman, and I had left Boston early that
summer, hitchhiking for California, which seemed as distant and
full of wonderment to me as Milwaukee had four years earlier. We
had fifty dollars between us and I never felt richer or freer. The
unknown was our ally (instead of the threat it would occasionally
become as I grew older). We made it to New York the first night.
There, in a place on Fifty-sixth Street called the Las Vegas Club,

we were befriended at the bar by Errol Flynn, who, as I recall, had a seventeen-year-old date. Flynn paid for our evening of drink (New York was the only state where you could drink legally as a teenager), and flushed with our good fortune, John and I left, convinced that an El Dorado awaited us at the road's end.

A truck driver in Indiana told us Route 66 was the best way West and I was surprised that one highway reached so far. We slept in roadside ditches along the way when we couldn't get rides, peeled potatoes and scrubbed floors in exchange for free restaurant meals and survived a summer of California poverty by working at a string of busboy jobs, from which John would invariably get fired for incompetence. We were a team and John's dismissal would lead to my quitting in protest. (John remembers it the other way round, believing it was I who kept getting us fired.) At any rate, his loyalty was never in question, and when I was arrested in Tijuana, just across the border from San Diego, and driven away to jail for urinating in a filthy alley that had been urinated in many times, I can still see John pounding on the window of my departing police car, yelling, "Hey! Hey! Take me, too, God dammit! I want to go, too!"

That summer was like a stint in the minor leagues. It taught us the techniques of survival. I don't remember much about the little towns on Route 66 John and I hitchhiked through, but I doubt I attached as much romance to the highway then as I do now that the great road West is dead.

U.S. Route 66 disappeared from the maps of America at 2:30 one September afternoon in 1984, when the last stretch of Interstate 40 was completed outside Williams, Arizona. At that precise moment the way-station towns that had straddled 66 emptied of traffic that would never come again. "We been bypassed," said the barber in Seligman, looking out the window of his shop. In the distance he could hear the hum of vehicles on the new superhighway, rushing through the franchised soul of America.

The day I got to Seligman, on my Tucson detour, an eighteen-wheeler followed me into town. It hissed to a stop in front of the barbershop, and Jim Scott climbed out of the cab. Finding the one-chair shop open but deserted, he walked into the grocery store next door, where the barber's brother, Joe, was passing time playing his guitar, accompanied by his friend Bob Lee on the fiddle. Scott sat on a crate, tapping his boot in time with the music, and waited for the barber to return.

The 137 miles of Route 66, now designated a state highway, that run from Seligman west to Topock on the California border represent the longest drivable stretch of the original road left in the country. The old road attracts some curious wanderers but nary a long-haul trucker, and I asked Scott why he had come off the interstate. He said the barber, Angel Delgadillo, had been cutting his hair for years, and besides, what was the challenge of highballing it from Chicago to L.A. if the road had not an unexpected turn, not a traffic light or a single town to slow the pace?

"Every once in a while I still come over 66 just to get the feel of it," Scott said. "I saw every mile of that interstate being built and what it's done is make things impersonal. Anyone can herd a truck up and down the freeway, but I remember when you had real respect as a trucker.

"We took care of each other. We sat together in the cafés. You never pulled back into a lane without blinking a thank-you on your lights. And if someone was broke down along the road—man or woman, it didn't matter—you offered help. Now we don't even stop. Things have gotten so uncourteous, it's unreal. People'll throw you the bird today and honk to make sure you see it. Far's I'm concerned, the whole damn world's changed."

The barber came back after a while and, seeing Scott's rig parked in front of his shop, went into the grocery store to get his only customer of the afternoon. Angel Delgadillo talked as he clipped. He had been born in Seligman sixty-one years ago, and he devoted most of his energies now to an association the neighboring towns had formed to promote the surviving miles of Route 66 as a historical landmark that would attract tourists. It would not be easy, they knew. The towns were dying and the young had left. What was there to offer except memories?

U.S. 66 used to turn off Main Street onto Railroad Avenue just before Delgadillo's shop. I stood alone in the middle of that empty road for a few minutes, hearing the *whoooosh* of traffic on Interstate 40 a mile or two away, and couldn't imagine that it had ever been clogged with trucks and buses and restless people.

The café Delgadillo's grandfather, Camilo, built and ran on Railroad Avenue was gone. Bud Brown's pool hall had collapsed. Frank Smith's convenience store was a pile of boards. The drugstore that held the high school graduation each June had been abandoned. All that stood in good repair was the Harvey House hotel next to the train station, where the town's children used to gather to hear stories of far-off towns recited by engineers and brakemen who carried the latest copies of *Life* and the *Saturday Evening Post.* But the Harvey House had been boarded up since 1954, its grassy courtyard now weed-dead, and when Amtrak's Southwest Chief passenger train out of Chicago hurried through Seligman each night just before midnight, it was only a silvery blur, hurtling toward Los Angeles, acknowledging the town with nothing more than a wailing salute of its whistle.

"Angel," I said, "you're spending all this time trying to get people back on 66 just to see what the past looked like. Why does it matter? Why hang on to what's done and gone?"

"I don't know," he said slowly. Then he thought for a moment and added: "No, darnit, I do know. It's because years ago we had family, more togetherness. Mothers didn't have to work. Fathers didn't have to moonlight just to afford the things we think we should have. We're so materialistic now and family life's gone because of it. This association we've started has caught people's imagination. It's not done with the state or with the county. We the people are doing it. That's how it used to be years ago. We meet every month, someplace along the route, and I notice this togetherness I'm talking about comes out at the meetings. We're all fighting together to save something important.

"The American people are finally starting to realize we're plowing under our orchards, our schools, our heritage, and we don't have much to begin with compared to Europe. We're destroying too much of ourselves. Why not slow down? The fastest, straightest road doesn't always head you in the best direction."

I left Seligman at dusk and raced a Sante Fe freight across the high desert. Forty-niner fell steadily behind. By the time I got to Truxton, in the foothills of the Laughing Mountains, Ray and Mildred Barker were getting ready to close the Frontier Cafe and Motel. Across the street, by a shuttered Mobilgas station, a metal sign bearing the likeness of a red flying horse rattled in the wind. The Barkers' only customer, a local rancher, finished his coffee and drifted out. Barker put a hamburger on the grill for me—I had fallen into the habit of ordering hamburgers as a reflex reaction without even looking at menus—and pulled down the shades. With no rooms rented and no traffic on state Route 66, he didn't bother to turn on the neon VACANCY sign.

Barker was a thin, quiet man of retirement age who worked seven days a week. He and his wife had last taken a vacation eleven years ago, driving over to Reno in their new Dodge, but for some reason or other there had been a riot in Reno that weekend and they had come back the next day. He hated cities and didn't care much for straying far from home.

"I was raised on an Oklahoma farm," he said. "I knew how to drive a tractor, how to plow, not much else. I'd never even seen the ocean till World War II. Then they sent me plumb over to China. It was quite an experience."

"Would you ever like to go back to China as a tourist?" I asked.

"No, I don't think that'd really interest me. Tell you the truth, China didn't impress me that much. Too many people. The streets always crowded. It seemed to me China had a lot of problems. I don't know if the poverty's still there, but I suspect it is. No, Truxton's all we want. Besides, put me in a big city and I'd worry about who it'd be safe to talk to.

"When I-40 opened up, Mildred and I looked around, considered different areas. But at our age we didn't figure we could better ourselves much so we just decided to stick it out. We're getting up there in years, you know, and you gotta consider that. You may not make a lot of money here, but you still eat, you have a bed, you have warmth. All in all, I don't know that a man needs much more than that. I can always look around and find people a lot worse off."

I met a good many Ray Barkers and Angel Delgadillos in the small towns I passed through, and their directness always put me at ease. They reminded me how little those of us who live in major-league cities know about the rest of America, in part, I think, because television divorces us from—rather than introduces us to—our country. It tells us about city people and city dreams that are inherently dreams of discontentment, and it tempts us with images of a life that in reality are obtainable only by the rich.

"I'm learnin' one thing good. Learnin' it all the time, ever' day," Ma Joad said in *Grapes of Wrath* as the Joads moved over Route 66. "If you're in trouble or hurt or need—go to poor people. They're the only ones that'll help—the only ones."

The Pacific Coast League, of which the Tucson Toros are members, was formed in 1903, the year the Boston Red Sox defeated the Pittsburgh Pirates five games to three in the first World Series and nine years before Arizona became a state. By then baseball had evolved into the game we know today. Batters had lost the right to call for a high or low pitch, the number of balls needed for a walk had been reduced from nine to five to four and catchers had begun stationing themselves directly behind the plate, rather than taking the ball on a bounce off to one side. Although umpires still swept off the plate with long-handled brooms and a club employee walked through the stands with a megaphone to announce starting lineups and substitutions, what the fans saw in those early PCL games—the rules, the pacing, the positioning of players, the key statistics—was virtually identical with what I would see nearly a century later. Baseball had established its continuity between the generations; in the years ahead there would be wars, depressions and technological revolutions, yet baseball would remain the same. It was the one national institution we could rely on to be constant.

Until 1958, when major league baseball ventured west of the Mississippi and the Brooklyn Dodgers and New York Giants took up residency in California, many Pacific Coast League veterans didn't much care about getting jobs in the big leagues. They often earned better salaries in the PCL, with its 225-game schedule, had better working conditions, with its temperate climate and relatively short train trips, and they played in front of bigger crowds. "The best thing about a long season was that you had a short off-season; there were less days you had to carry a lunch bag to the factory," recalled sixty-three-year-old Dale Long.

The minors today exist for the sole purpose of developing talent for the major leagues, with each of the twenty-six Triple-A clubs being affiliated with one of the twenty-six big-league teams. But the minor leagues of a few decades ago were truly independent entities, free from the pressures and edicts of Major League Baseball. They were a place where a man could spend his entire career and a place where fading stars could make one last hurrah after their big-league days were over. Herman Pillette pitched in the PCL for twenty-three years, winning more games than Don Drysdale did in the National League; he didn't retire until he was forty-seven, in 1945. Arnold "Jigger" Statz played eighteen years for the Los Angeles Angels and collected more hits in the PCL than Willie Mays did in twenty-two years with the National League's Giants. When Vince DiMaggio's ten-year career ended in 1946, he didn't slip quietly back to his family in San Francisco; he returned to the California League (and led the league in home runs).

I arrived at Hi Corbett Field in Tucson fifty years to the day that Lou Gehrig, a victim of amyotrophic lateral sclerosis, had played the last of his 2,130 consecutive games for the New York Yankees. The first few days with a new team were always difficult because seldom did I know anyone—usually I didn't even know anyone's name—and clubhouses are not places where strangers are made to feel at home. They are the chapter room of a fraternity, private sanctuaries for public performers who are protective of the brotherhood. Casual conversations did not come easily until I had been around for three or four days, quietly in the background, listening instead of talking.

At first meeting the players viewed me with studied indifference. No one expressed even mild curiosity about my trip and no one ever asked, What's it like living in an RV? Where are the best parks? What league has the toughest travel schedule? Or, who are *you*? Occasionally I'd try to get those early encounters off dead center by dropping in a line or two that usually sparked a conversation in other settings. "What I remember about living in Africa . . ." I'd say, or, "The great thing about Australia . . ." It didn't work. Baseball was the only common denominator of discussion, and the older a player was, the more uncomfortable he became talking about topics other than himself.

There was a distinct change in the collective personalities of ballplayers as they progressed toward the major leagues. In the low classifications, still unsure of their own ability, they were approachable, unguarded, trusting. In Triple-A, having been exposed to adulation, the whiff of big money and a drumbeat of reporters' repetitive questions, they had taken on the trappings of celebrities: They spoke in clichés, echoing lines that seemed to come from a Standard Reference Guide to Acceptable Baseball Responses, and by the time they reached the majors, most were essentially self-centered.

After Gorman Thomas, for instance, signed a multimillion-dollar contract with Milwaukee—his skills began fading almost before the ink was dry—the Brewers decided to turn their talented young infielder, Paul Molitor, into an outfielder, thus forcing Thomas to move from center to right field. One of the Brewer coaches, Sam Suplizio, called Thomas aside and said, "Gorman, this kid can use a lot of help learning the outfield. He's going to look up to you. I hope you'll help him make the transition."

"Fuck him," Thomas said.

My detour onto Route 66 and my time in Las Vegas had sidetracked me. It had been a week since I had been in a ballpark and walking into Hi Corbett Field was like going home. I moved through the concourse to savor the moment I find the most exciting in any park, that moment at the top of the ramp when, as though curtains had parted, you see the field for the first time, spread out below you, a blanket of grass bounded by long white chalked lines and crowned with a cinder warning track in the outer reaches of the outfield. Surely a great battle is going to be settled here tonight, I always thought.

The Toros were a perennially weak team, having made the playoffs only twice in twenty-one years and never having won a PCL championship. But that did not concern me, and I was pleased to learn that their manager, Bob Skinner, was an old baseball foot soldier I remembered from my youth. Skinner had spent thirty-two of his fifty-seven years in the majors, as a manager, coach and player. Unlike the young managers I met whose desire to escape the minors took on desperate proportions, Skinner didn't mind being back where he had started. He had secured the maximum major league pension and had nothing left to prove. He was happy to still be part of the only professional life he had ever known.

It was five hours before game time when I walked into the Toros' clubhouse. Skinner and his pitching coach, Eddie Watt (who had won thirty-eight games in a ten-year big-league career) were the only ones there, except for infielder Ron Washington who was always the first player to arrive. A long porcelain trough stretched along one wall. There were two signs above it. One said, GONE BUT NOT FORGOTTEN, and listed the names of three players who had not survived their first month with Tucson. The one below said, PLEASE DO NOT THROW SUNFLOWER SEEDS OR BUTTS IN URINAL. Skinner was half dressed, his stocking feet extended on his desk. The "dip" cup for his periodic stream of tobacco juice was close at hand.

I asked him about his job. He was surprised at how inadequate minor league defense was, particularly in lateral movement, compared with the majors, and said he had never quite gotten used to sitting down with a player to discuss some future move and being told, "I'll check with my agent." His most important task, he said, was trying to teach the players how to concentrate. I thought it strange that men who had been professionals for four or five years had trouble concentrating.

Watt, who was putting on his uniform, said, "A lot of times bad concentration is just a catchall for a lack of success. When someone says a player doesn't concentrate, what he often means is that the player lacks motivation. If people aren't smart enough to see what the average salary is on the major league level today, if that doesn't motivate them, then I can't. Maybe you've got to pass out free blow jobs for base hits to motivate them. That's the big difference with the past. Sure, we had to make a living, but we played primarily for enjoyment. Today the motivating force is money and greed."

A small crowd showed up for the game that night—the Cleveland Indians use Hi Corbett Field for spring training and the entire Toros' season is always something of an anticlimax—and when the temperature was announced as a chilly 67 degrees, everyone booed. Gary Cooper, greeted with a bugled cavalry charge as he came to bat, led off with a single (though with a name like that, I think those of us in the stands had the right to expect a home run), and the Toros scored twice in the first against the Edmonton Trappers.

The man who caught my attention was No. 12, the Toros shortstop, Ron Washington. At thirty-seven, he was four years older than the oldest starting shortstop in the major leagues, Ozzie Smith, and was earning approximately $2.2 million per season less. He looked younger in uniform than he had when I saw him sitting in jeans and a T-shirt by the clubhouse bench press and noticed his receding hairline and worried face. Hardship Day—the name he used to describe the time when the body no longer did what the mind commanded and the last game drew near—was almost at hand.

Washington had a presence that said major league. I saw him range far to his left, spear a ball and, propelling himself off his right foot, throw to first to get his man by a seam. (Now *that*, Skinner would say, was lateral movement.) Washington referred to each plate appearance not as an at bat but as an opportunity, and when he missed an opportunity, he would clench his left fist and give his head a quick shake on the way back to the dugout. Baseball was still fun to him, and each game pushed so much adrenaline through his system that, after taking the bus back to his apartment on Broadway, it was three or four hours before his body calmed down and he could sleep.

Nine months earlier Washington had been the starting short-stop for the Cleveland Indians, capping an eleven-year major league career that had been reached via stops in Sarasota, Waterloo, San Jose, Jacksonville, Waterbury, San Antonio, Albuquerque, Tidewater, Toledo and Rochester. He was an anachronism in today's minor leagues of young athletes on the ascent, and I suspected that what had kept him around so long probably had as much to do with his mental toughness as with his physical prowess.

One of ten children, he was raised in the projects of New Orleans. Although his parents did not come to his high school games, they always set aside enough money to provide him with the essentials of life—balls, bats, gloves, baseball shoes. In 1970, Washington paid his way to the Kansas City Royals Baseball Academy. If he had negotiated the contract offered him there, he could have gotten five thousand dollars. But talk didn't interest him; he signed immediately and headed for Sarasota with his modest bonus—a new glove and a pair of spikes. "I was so happy just to sign, they could have kept the glove and shoes," he said. Later, in 1978, having made it to the Los Angeles Dodgers, doctors looked at his injured knee one day and said he would never play again. So here he was, eleven years after the operation, trim and fit, floating around the infield for the Toros and planning his return to The Bigs.

"If I get hit with the negative side of something," he said, "I turn it positive. I've never stuck my head behind my ass and run like a puppy in my life. Just so I go out onto the field every day a little more fired up than I was the day before, I'll be all right. I'll get back. The Astros know they got a major league shortstop down here."

The Edmonton Trappers, aided by Washington's two-base error, scored twice in the thirteenth inning to beat Tucson. Only eighty fans stayed to the end. I asked Washington if he wanted to have a drink and he said he knew a quiet place in the Park Mall called CPW. He would be there after he called his wife, who had remained in New Orleans because of uncertainty over whether he would stay in Tucson, get called up to Houston or be traded elsewhere. Washington called home after every game, and Gerri's first question always was "How'd you do tonight?"

CPW was the noisiest place I'd been in for years. There were crashing disco sounds and flashing lights and video monitors full of odd imagery. The women wore short skirts that ended far north of their knees and the young men favored faded jeans with tank tops that bore the labels of trendy sports gear. For the life of me I could not understand why anyone would wear a T-shirt advertising the name of a sneaker company. The bartender called me "sir" and brought me a drink (which cost exactly what Angel Delgadillo charged for a haircut on Route 66). I felt old, as out of place as an undertaker at a christening.

Judging from the applause he drew with each at bat, Washington was the most popular player on the Toros. But like most minor leaguers, his life in civilian clothes was an anonymous one, even in the town where he played, and he took his seat at the crowded bar, unrecognized. "Sorry," he said, apologizing for being late, "I had to explain the error to Gerri."

He was the first to admit that life in Triple-A—the holding tank for the major leagues—wasn't bad. Unlike the low classifications, players in the three Triple-A leagues—the PCL, American Association and International League—flew between cities and earned nearly as much as a union plumber. They had spacious clubhouses. Their games were broadcast on the radio, and there were three umpires instead of two on the field for each game. Some players, in fact, found their "comfort zones" in Triple-A. It was as though a spark within them died once they got this far, and they settled in to be Triple-A players with major league skills. As Watt had said, it was their mental discipline, not their bodies, that had betrayed them.

Washington believed, as did Satchel Paige, that age was a question of mind over matter. "If you don't mind, age don't matter." He was the only veteran player I would meet all summer who did not blame his minor league assignment on either some sinister plot or some callous front-office executive. "Still," he said, lighting a cigarette, "when you been to the top where everything's first class, you don't like coming back down. You have to worry about nourishing yourself on the meal money they pay you here. You can hear the hecklers real good with the small crowds. You get worn down with those 4:30 A.M. wake-up calls to catch another plane. Up There, everything's done for you. Down Here, you gotta do things for yourself.

"I'll tell you this. The sun shines bright every day in Tucson, but it doesn't shine as bright as it does in Houston. It shines bright in Houston even when it's raining."

It was 2:00 A.M. when I left the CPW and Forty-niner and I went looking for a quiet street to spend the night. Having had a few more drinks than intended, I stopped for coffee at a fast-food restaurant. The front door was locked for security reasons and only the drive-through window with its bulletproof glass was open. Forty-niner was eleven feet tall and would not fit under the low-hanging canopy over the drive-through area. So I parked and, feeling out of place for the second time that night, stood in line, between an '88 Oldsmobile and a Ford pickup, to place my order.

Chapter Six

The bottom line is people don't just come to minor
league games anymore. You have to go out and get them.
The days of handing out a one-dollar coupon and seeing
people show up are over.

—BILL SHANAHAN, *general manager,*
San Bernardino Spirit

Getting from Tucson (a city
that has lived under Spanish, Mexican, Confederate and American flags) to El Paso (which feels Mexican, not American) is a
straight shot down Interstate 10. But Angel Delgadillo's words
stayed with me: Avoid the fast, straight roads. I backtracked and
veered north through a moonscape strewn with boulders as big as
cars. "The region is altogether valueless," a government surveyor
said of Arizona in 1858. "After entering it, there is nothing to do
but leave." I passed Apache Tears Road and Dead Man Gulch and
wondered what dark secrets were buried in this open, empty land.

Everywhere in the desert there was mystery. In the rolling dunes
a scurrying world of insects and creatures lived, but I saw no life,
no movement. Colors blurred into a single hue, hiding dormant
gardens that would burst into bloom at the first touch of rain.
Cacti stood like semaphores on an ocean of sand, and in the
distance, down desert tracks, an occasional trailer home caught my

eye. It was not, I suspected, that the occupants had forsaken their dreams by stopping here; rather it was that they had no dreams, except perhaps to be left alone. Just surviving was enough. They lived uncluttered lives and if need be could move on, as man has always done in the desert.

The little towns along Highway 70 were not much more than frontier outposts. I stopped in one to read for a while on a park bench. The weathered wooden plaque nearby said in tribute to the town's fallen sons:

> Go spread the word,
> tell the passer-by,
> that in this little world,
> men knew how to die.

Farther down the road, just after dark, every teenager in Arizona seemed to have descended on Safford to drive bumper-to-bumper, car radios blaring, back and forth and back again, along a street with boarded-up shops. "Hey, granddad!" a girl yelled at me, pulling alongside Forty-niner. "You out cruisin' in that thing?" Her friends giggled. I shrugged and replayed what she had said. *Granddad,* indeed!

I left the Mountain Time Zone, crossed the Continental Divide in New Mexico and neared Texas, which has been home to more minor league teams (101) than any other state. The Texas League started play in 1888—five years before historian Frederick Jackson Turner declared the American frontier settled and seven years before gunslinger John Wesley Hardin was shot dead while rolling dice in El Paso. Hardin is buried in that old railroad and cattle town and that is where I was headed, to El Paso and the wacky Dudley Dome, the very symbol of minor league baseball's Second Golden Age.

In several towns between Stockton and El Paso I stopped in libraries to peruse local history and look (usually without success) for books on baseball history. This is what I learned: The sports editor of the *Spirit of the Times* in New York, William Trotter Porter, first called baseball "our national game" in the

1850s, but not until the Civil War when Union soldiers brought the game South did baseball become truly national. Confederate troops learned baseball from Northerners they had taken prisoner. Civilians learned it because wherever there were Union soldiers, even behind Confederate lines, there was a game. At Hilton Head, North Carolina, forty thousand Union soldiers gathered on Christmas Day, 1862, to see the 165th New York Volunteer Infantry take on a team from other regiments. By the time the war ended, baseball had become a symbol of national unity. It was the nation's first team sport, a game played the same everywhere, and the language of "rounders" had given way to labels that were uniquely American: Aces were now referred to as runs, hands had become innings, strikers were hitters and spectators were no longer cranks—they were fans.

Eleven years after Lee surrendered to Grant at the Appomattox Court House in Virginia, major league baseball was born with the formation of the National League. Within little more than a decade, independent minor leagues were flourishing throughout the country. Pennsylvania, Ohio, Kansas and Montana all had their own. Others stretched from New England to the Pacific Northwest. For most towns, particularly those in the still-isolated West, having a team was tantamount to being part of the nation's growth and progressive spirit.

"Salt Lake has for a number of years fostered the game of baseball," editorialized the *Salt Lake Tribune* in 1887. "In fact, our city would not be up in modern ideas did she not do so. In these times baseball clubs are almost an imperative necessity."

The minors remained a hodgepodge of unrelated leagues until 1901 when the threat of player raids by the National League and the just-established American League threatened extinction. In order to protect their interests and exert their independence, the presidents of seven minor leagues traveled to Chicago in early September that year and after a daylong session at the Leland Hotel declared the birth of the National Association of Professional Baseball Leagues. Maximum player salaries were set at eighteen hundred dollars a season.

"With it all," a reporter in *Sporting Life* wrote of the meeting, "there was a dignity of manner and fixity of purpose that impressed all with a feeling that the professional interests of the great game in its broadest field and its highest state was safe in the hands of this new organization."

The sovereignty of the minor leagues meant that team owners held absolute power over their players. Jack Dunn, for instance, president of the Baltimore Orioles in the International League, peddled his teenaged pitcher, Babe Ruth, and two other players to the Red Sox for thirty thousand dollars in 1914, but denied future Hall of Famer Lefty Grove a place in the major leagues for five years, until the Philadelphia Athletics met his asking price of one hundred thousand dollars.

While Grove was pitching in servitude for Dunn, the St. Louis Cardinals hired a man who would change the structure of minor league baseball. The Cards were deeply in debt and had never won a pennant when Branch Rickey took over the team in 1919. They were so poor they wore the same uniforms at home and on the road and held spring training in St. Louis instead of Florida. Rickey was known as a keen judge of talent, and if he approached a minor league team to express interest in a player, the price would immediately go up, and the club would wire other owners in the league to say Rickey was looking for a shortstop or whatever. If he sent one of his prospects to a minor league team for seasoning, he invariably got double-crossed, and the owner would sell the player.

"That kind of thing drove me mad," Rickey said. "I pondered long on it, and finally concluded that if we were too poor to buy, we would have to raise our own."

What Rickey did, surreptitiously at first, was start the farm system. He quietly bought into the Houston Buffaloes in the Texas League, then wangled command of the Fort Smith team in the Western Association. He got control of the entire player supply in the Nebraska State and Arkansas-Missouri leagues. By 1940 the Cardinals owned thirty-two minor league teams outright and had working agreements with eight others. "We'd have three hundred ballplayers at spring training," recalled Stan Musial. "Everyone was known by a number, not his name. You'd look on the board in the morning and if your number was up there, it meant you were going to play." The baseball establishment led by the commissioner, Kenesaw Mountain Landis, viewed the experiment as a challenge to the major leagues' authority, and the chunky Rickey was introduced at the annual baseball meetings one year as "Piggly-Wiggly." The last laugh, however, belonged to Rickey. By 1942 he had brought St. Louis its fifth pennant. "Luck," Rickey said, "is the residue of design."

Rickey's Chain Gang, as critics had called the farm system, was copied by the other National and American League teams, creating a huge minor league expansion. So many prospects were on hand at the Brooklyn Dodgers' Florida spring-training camp in 1948 that players wore uniforms with triple-digit numbers and the line outside the team cafeteria each evening stretched for blocks. The minors reached the pinnacle of their popularity the next year, when 464 teams in fifty-nine leagues drew forty-two million Americans.

From Bangor, Maine, to Oakland, California, great feats took place. Eighteen-year-old Joe DiMaggio hit safely in sixty-one straight games for the San Francisco Seals in the Pacific Coast League. Joe Bauman, who ran a gas station in the off-season, hit 72 home runs and drove in 224 runs for Rosewell (New Mexico) in the Longhorn League. Ray "Little Buffalo" Perry hit .411 and .404 in consecutive seasons for Reading (California) in the Far West League (which players called the Far Worst League) and after each game took up his other duties as team president, general manager, bus driver, trainer and league vice president. History quickly forgot men like Bauman and Perry, neither of whom ever saw an at bat in the majors, because the minors were but the stepchild of a grander place where the real records were set and cherished.

The minors' Golden Age was short-lived. By the 1950s leagues were dying as fast as afternoon newspapers were folding. Those wonderful names—the Anthracite League, the Sunset League, the Tobacco State League, the Iron and Oil Association, the Panhandle Pecos Valley League—were to be no more. Americans had found a new pastime and they kept their televisions turned on an average of seven hours and two minutes a day. Minor league attendance dipped below nine million.

·   ·   ·

El Paso seemed an unlikely place to stage the revival of minor league baseball and Jim Paul, a Vietnam vet who thought the infield fly rule had something to do with zipping up your pants, appeared an improbable candidate to be its guardian saint. But if I had to pick one franchise that placed a premium on fun, that made every game a rollicking adventure, the El Paso Diablos were the winners, hands down. No one else even came close.

Built like a horseshoe around the Franklin Mountains—which were named for a nineteenth-century confidence man—El Paso is a blue-collar, beer-and-nachos-for-breakfast town. It has the fifth lowest per capita income in the United States. With a population that is 65 percent Hispanic, most earning the minimum wage on assembly lines and in apparel factories, it reminded me more of the Third World than it did of boisterous, blustery Texas, where capitalism is considered the cure of all ills. "This isn't a murderin' town," a cop told me, "but it's a thievin' town. Your body's pretty safe walking down the street. As for your property, that ain't worth a nickel."

Like many cities, El Paso's personality had been split in two by the construction of a superhighway. To the north of Interstate 10 (which takes you from Los Angeles to Jacksonville without so much as a traffic light to interrupt the rush) were the white middle-class neighborhoods. The university, the best shopping centers, the finest homes stood there, in the Franklin foothills. To the south were the crime-infested projects, the gangs and graffiti, the impoverished Hispanics. That's where the Dudley Dome was, in the heart of south El Paso, just a long home run from Mexico and the waist-deep waters of the Rio Grande. "We've been lucky," Jim Paul, the Diablos owner, remarked. "We've never had anyone shot here."

Paul had bought the failing Diablos franchise in 1974 with a borrowed thousand dollars and later had sold his home on Rim Road to raise the cash to keep the team afloat. His first order of business was to work out a truce with the neighborhood gangs. At that time the Diablos drew in a season what most major league clubs did in a day. Fans used to fall asleep in the stands during the dreary games, and when Gene Autry was brought in one night as guest of honor, the PA man forgot to announce his presence. Paul needed every dime. He told the young toughs who hung around outside that balls hit into the parking lot during batting practice had to be returned. If they weren't, Paul and his assistant, Rick Parr, would tear out of the park in pursuit. They would return a few minutes later, often bloody but always with the ball. When Parr caught one young man testing him, straddling the fence and saying he was coming in for free, Parr walked over and knocked him back off the fence with a right to the chin. Territorial rights had been established. The gangs declared the Dudley Dome neutral turf. It was now an island of safety in the middle of Fort Apache.

Actually the Dudley Dome wasn't a dome at all. It was an uncovered park, but because it never seemed to rain on the field during a game—even when summer squalls were drenching everything within spitting distance, including the parking lot—almost no one referred to the stadium by its proper name, Dudley Field. Dudley was as grand a park as I had ever seen. It was sixty-five years old and full of odd angles, nooks and crannies. The grandstands were built with adobe brick, and there was a small hill in center field that covered an irrigation ditch, resulting in marvelous battles between man and ball. The outfield wall, made of plywood, was held up by two-by-fours and had once fallen down in a mild gale, and on the front of the stadium, in yellow letters twelve feet high, was the word BASEBALL. On every beam, every wall, every dark little crevice a sign had been painted—there were fifty-one on the outfield fence alone—to advertise products ranging from IBM to Gold's Gym. The word around Dudley was that if you stood still long enough, you'd find something like DOMINO'S DELIVERS written on your back and Paul would sell you for a few hundred bucks.

My first day in El Paso, I found Jim Paul in his second-floor office. He was wearing new cowboy boots, purchased with the proceeds of a winning hundred-dollar bet on Sunday Silence in the Kentucky Derby, and was looking out a book-sized window at the lines in front of the ticket booths. He took small crowds as a personal insult and didn't like what he saw, though game time was still an hour away. "The crowd doesn't look good tonight," he muttered. "I may have bombed on this one." Two umpires were with him, each in a state of panic. They had been stricken with severe diarrhea and doubted they could go nine innings without making dashes to the toilet. "Tell your radio guy and the PA man not to say anything if we disappear, please," one of them said. The umpires ran down the list of restaurants where they had eaten in El Paso, and as each name was mentioned Paul would say, "Nothing the matter with that place."

"I've been so sick I haven't even had a drink for two nights," the tall umpire said.

"That may be your problem right there," Paul replied.

Paul had transformed the Diablos into one of baseball's most successful franchises by understanding two axioms that many of his peers had been slow to grasp. First, minor league baseball may be the only business in the country in which the stockholders have no control over their product. The product—team performance—is controlled by The Big Club, whose prime concern is its own welfare, not building bush-league champions. If it needs to move a player in the heat of El Paso's or San Antonio's pennant drive, it will. In 1983, for instance, the Chicago White Sox depleted their Triple-A roster at Denver on the eve of Denver's championship series against Louisville, calling up the Bears' eleven top players, and, oddly enough, the manager, too. Louisville won in four straight games. So Paul and other operators can't promote their product around a player, who soon may be gone, or even around a team. They have to sell entertainment, not baseball.

Second, organized baseball has traditionally been the most conservative of businesses, resistant to change and—by the standards of corporations that do not enjoy a monopoly—backward. Open your gates, the reckoning went, and the faithful will come. No one dared try a new idea; they only worked at what had been perfected by others.

But turning the Dudley Dome into a nightly carnival that overshadowed the game itself had made the purists shudder and had brought such loud complaints from other Texas League owners that league president Bobby Bragan hurried into El Paso. He took one look at the shenanigans and the standing-room-only crowds and told the owners: "Why don't you try some of this shit, too. Maybe you'd fill up your parks the way Paul has."

Paul had comforted the umpires, helped his son Robbie, the

Diablos batboy, with his homework and was now sprawled on the stairs outside his office. He said, "In the sixties, baseball sat on its ass and said, 'We're the national pastime; come see us.' So what happens? Attendance dwindles and the seventies become a hotbed for NFL football. No one bothered to call attention to baseball. We still had the older generation. They'd come forever. But we'd lost the younger generation, who didn't remember this was the national pastime. They had a lot of other ways to spend their time.

"Ten years ago you didn't hear anything in the parks but organs, and organs are for funerals. We played rock 'n' roll. We danced in the aisles. We had a promotion every night and gave away trucks and pizzas and had ten-cent hotdog nights and brought in the Famous Chicken. We had jugglers and mimes. What we did was to make it fun to come to the park. And what do you see now if you go up to Milwaukee or Chicago today? They're playing rock 'n' roll and dancing in the aisles. Well, welcome to the modern world, major leagues."

The Diablos were playing the Arkansas Travelers my first night in El Paso. The skies had cleared and a good crowd had shown up after all. I left Paul's office and walked into the stands just as the PA announcer, Paul Strelzin, a junior high school principal who had grown up in Brooklyn and played football at the University of New Hampshire, was testing his mike. On the top of the visiting team's dugout was painted in red the word ENEMY. Strelzin's voice boomed through Dudley Field:

"Well, the umpires have arrived, fans. Finally. Behind the plate tonight is Jeff Henrichs, just back from helping clean up the oil spill in Alaska. At first is his illegitimate brother-in-law, Cris Jones. Fearless Dick Fossa is at third. He sells panty hose in the off-season. . . .

"Now here are your starting lineups for the El Paso Diii-aaaa-blos! Leading off, Rambo Sambo. Batting second and playing second, the professor of fieldology and batology, Frank Mattox . . . Andre the Giiiiiiant Killer David in left field . . . in right, Sandy Go Go Guerrrrrrrr-ero . . ."

By the second inning the Diablos' Diamond Girls were dancing on the roof of the dugout. Strelzin was playing "Charge!" on his kazoo and waving a green flag out the window of his booth. Shon

"The Avenger" Ashley responded with a three-run triple and moments later two thousand fans were on their feet, waving white tissues they had been given at the gate as the Travelers' starting pitcher plodded off the mound. "It's sayonara time," Strelzin yelled. "See ya later, baby." The pitcher shot Strelzin a threatening glance and disappeared into the dugout.

Strelzin was used to abuse. He had been tossed out of games by umpires and been smacked in the face with a pie thrown by the Wichita Wranglers. One player, "Cobra Joe" Frazier, who went on to manage the New York Mets, had once invited Strelzin to meet him under the stands and had waited for him with a baseball bat. Another, Jerry Bell, just demoted to El Paso from the major leagues, got so angered by Strelzin's chatter that he refused to pitch and stalked off the mound, flashing him the finger as he went. Bell stormed into the clubhouse and did seven hundred dollars in damage.

The fans were alive now with two outs, hollering the Diablos on. "You want more runs?" Strelzin thundered. "You want to pummel these guys? Do you want to pound them? Do you want to rub their noses in the dirt? Do you want to make them go home?"

"Yeah, yeah, yeah," came the chorus from the stands.

"And what team scores more runs with two outs than any team in baseball?"

"The Diablos!" roared the crowd.

Strelzin had asked that question so many times over the years that El Paso's come-from-behind heroics had become part of minor league lore. You could, in fact, ask almost anyone who had ever played in the Texas League, from Orel Hershiser to Brooks Robinson, what team in baseball scored the most runs with two outs, and the unhesitating answer always was "The El Paso Diablos." It was an intriguing statistic, and I asked Strelzin where he had learned it.

"Oh, I made it up," he said.

Section CC, just in front of Strelzin's booth, was the repository for the most serious Diablos fans. The group there came every night: Jim Parker, a cigar-smoking computer analyst who had a collection of ninety-six thousand baseball cards in his laundry room and recorded every play on his scorecard; Mitch Malott, nearly eighty, an exceedingly gentle fellow who from time to time would emit a terrible bellow—"Aw, come on, ump! That was a strike when I played"—then chuckle at his own mischievousness; Ralph Banner, his shiny bald head a trademark of Row 6 for nearly forty years, who still mourned the loss of the Cohen brothers, Syd and Andy. The seats they had occupied for so many seasons, two rows down, had been empty all season.

I asked if the Cohens had been elderly. "Not at first," Banner said, "but they sure got that way at the end."

Mitch Malott wore white suspenders, blue sneakers and one of his numerous minor league baseball caps, which he would replace only if El Paso lost. He sat with his feet draped over the seat in front, his hands folded between his knees like a young boy. Every year he took a road trip with the Diablos and last year, when he didn't have the money to go on with the team from San Antonio to Wichita, the players offered to chip in five dollars apiece to cover his expenses. He said no, he couldn't accept, because they had less money than he did.

"All winter long," he said, "I keep waiting for baseball to begin. The Dome's my summer home. I can remember when we just had wooden benches up here and down there was an organ. My wife used to come out here quite a bit with me then, before she passed away. She used to tell me I had just one fault; I never met a stranger I didn't like."

I had lost track of the game talking to Malott and hardly saw the ball Sandy Guerrero banged over the right field fence and into the El Paso Zoo. Suddenly Malott was out of his seat, hurrying down the aisle while reaching for his wallet. Guerrero circled the bases, then slowly made his way along the infield wall, where Malott and seventy or so fans waited, each holding out a dollar bill. Guerrero cheerfully piled the crumpled bills into his batting helmet, one by one, chatting, shaking hands, signing autographs. The ritual, dating back to barnstorming days when underpaid players counted on fan contributions to survive, is celebrated after every Diablos home run and struck me as symbolic of what makes minor league baseball unique among professional sports: there is an intimacy between player and fan.

Walkie-talkie in hand, ringmaster Jim Paul had stationed himself in his "skybox," a rickety cubicle above the concession stands that offered mesquite-grilled chicken and meatball kabobs and were staffed by some of the same youths who used to hassle him in the parking lot. He brought three kids onto the field between the third and fourth innings and at the bases had STRIKE-O signs placed that advertised Bob Goff's appliance store. Anyone who threw a ball through a hole in the signs won a television set. Balls whizzed wildly about the infield, forcing the Arkansas pitcher, who was trying to warm up on the mound, to flee for cover; the TV was safe for another night. After the fifth, Paul put an employee in a chicken costume on second base and stationed a little girl chosen from the stands midway between first and second. If the girl, running, could beat the chicken, walking, she would win ten dollars.

"Move the kid up," a fan shouted.

"Like hell," Paul shot back. "You ain't paying the ten bucks. She stays where she is."

The crowd cheered as the girl, her tiny legs churning like the blades of an eggbeater, rounded second, closed the gap at third and flew down the stretch. The Diablos catcher, Tim Torricelli, intercepted the chicken with a hip block inches from victory and the girl crossed home plate, a winner, to thunderous applause.

"Don't you love it?" Paul laughed, slapping his knee in delight. "Isn't this wonderful?"

The fans thought it was. While other owners weren't doing much more in the mid-seventies than setting off fireworks on the Fourth of July, Paul was putting on a different promotion every single night. One night there were free kazoos at the gate; another, beer cost only a dime. Attendance doubled his first year in El Paso and set a Texas League record the next. He still had a dreadful team, and therein lay an important lesson: Unlike the majors, winning or losing in the minors has only a minimal effect on a team's attendance. Word of the Diablos' success spread. Paul put on a minor league seminar in El Paso at season's end to exchange marketing ideas with other executives; eight people showed up. But before long, the annual seminar was drawing two hundred participants and even the stodgiest owners had become P. T. Barnums with nightly promotions, giveaways, discounted tickets and non–baseball food that ranged from smoked turkey drumsticks at Sec

Taylor Stadium in Des Moines to stuffed potatoes at Derks Field in Salt Lake City. By the late eighties, minor league attendance had more than doubled from the bleak days of early television, and one team, the Buffalo Bisons, was outdrawing three major league clubs.

Alas for the Diablos, they did not score with two outs in any inning, and the Arkansas Travelers rallied to win, 10–8. Mitch Malott gathered up his blue cushion and said to Jim Parker, "Tomorrow night I'm wearing a different cap." I drove out toward the airport, where the Hilton offered excellent complimentary accommodations—a level paved parking lot, good lighting for security and no street noise. Forty-niner picked out a new El Dorado to spend the night next to and I walked into the bar to drink some whiskey.

The woman down the way, nursing a vodka on the rocks, was a food rep from California. She had the blurry eyes and washed-out expression of someone who had spent many nights alone at the bar. She seemed desperate for conversation and turned to the three Arkansas players who had just walked in, fresh from their victory at Dudley. "What brings you to town?" she asked pitching coach Chris Maloney.

"I'm a Traveler," he said.

"I am, too," she said, "but what do you *do?*"

Chapter Seven

I never dreamt at night about playing major league ball
and from that standpoint, I always felt odd.

—FRANK MATTOX, *second baseman, El Paso Diablos*

The Diablos were struggling.
They had no fire and no core of veteran team leaders. They were
losing games they should have won, and the more they lost, the
tenser their clubhouse became. Players showered after a game and
couldn't get out of the park fast enough. In baseball parlance, "to
struggle" is a euphemism for "to fail." No cellar-dwelling manager
would say, "My team is so bad it doesn't even belong in this
league." Instead he says, "We're struggling." Nor would a .220
hitter ever say he couldn't hit a curveball. "I'm struggling," he says,
as though a good attitude and a few breaks will overcome inepti-
tude.

But El Paso's supporters were tolerant. Minor league fans are
kinder than those in the majors to players, accepting less than
perfection in exchange for an honest display of effort and a little
humility. The only Diablo that El Paso had cold-shouldered had
been infielder Gary Sheffield, who had signed for a bonus in excess

of one hundred thousand dollars. He was weighted down with jewelry when he showed up at the Dudley Dome, had the gold initials "G-S" inlaid in his front teeth and drove a red pin-striped Corvette, given him by his uncle, Dwight Gooden, the New York Met's pitching star. After hitting his first home run as a Diablo, Sheffield had returned to the dugout, ignoring Mitch Malott and the other fans who pressed against the infield wall with their dollar bills extended. "Gary, you gotta go out there," the trainer, Jim Rowe, said. "It's a tradition." Sheffield stayed put and the fans never forgave him.

The next season Sheffield had returned to El Paso for an exhibition game, as a member of the Milwaukee Brewers. A TV reporter asked him what his fondest memory of the Texas League was, and the weak-hitting shortstop, who would end up back in the minors before the year was out, said, "I have none." That's where he and I differed. Some pretty interesting things have happened in the Texas League during a hundred-year history interrupted only by the Second World War, and I set aside in my notebook a section headed "TexLeg History."

Galveston, for instance, gave baseball its first Ladies Day, in 1888, building a special grandstand for women and admitting them for free Wednesday afternoons. "Don't fear to compromise your sex by attending the baseball game," encouraged the *Austin Statesman.* The next year a chap named Art Sunday left Houston to join Toledo in the International League. He immediately collected a bunch of bloop singles and forever more those mousey hits would be known as Texas leaguers. The Texas League also gave us the most lopsided game in the history of organized baseball, with Corsicana beating Texarkana 51–3 in 1902. (Some telegraph operators thought the score was an error and transmitted it as 5–3.) Catcher Nig Clarke hit eight home runs that afternoon. And although I had never been to Beaumont, it seemed the town's history could be traced through the different names it had given its Texas League team: The Blues, Millionaires, Orphans, Oilers, Exporters, Navigators, Roughnecks, Golden Gators. Houston's team had been known at various times by a marvelous contradiction of names: The Lambs, Red Stockings, Babies, Buffaloes, Moore's Marvels and Bluffs. Then there was Shreveport's Ken

Guettler, a slugger with glasses as thick as his bat. He hit sixty-two home runs in 1956, but couldn't manage more than five in any of the next three seasons and retired at the age of thirty-two, having never seen the majors.

I had been in El Paso for several days when Bruce Manno and Bob Humphreys—the men who ran the Brewers' spring camp in Arizona—showed up from Milwaukee to examine the wobbly Diablos. They sat together talking quietly behind the first-base dugout, Manno nibbling intently on sunflower seeds, Humphreys, the ex–major leaguer who looked like Bob Newhart, trying hard to contain himself when a Diablo failed to execute a basic play.

"Jimminee Christmas!" he cried softly as outfielder Darryel "Woo Woo" Walters committed a late-inning error that would cost the Diablos the game. Humphreys bolted from his seat and strode into the empty left-field grandstands, where he stood alone, hands in his pockets, the collar of his windbreaker turned up against the cold wind, his back to the diamond, unable to watch. Walters retired to the dugout once the game had ended. The other players disappeared into their clubhouses, the lights atop Dudley Field flickered off. Still, Walters sat there, his chin in the palms of his hands, a silhouette at the end of the dugout, looking out over the dark, empty park.

Manno, who was the Brewers' farm director and assistant general manager, considered the jump from one of the seventy-eight Single-A teams to Double-A—a classification with twenty-six teams divided among three circuits (the Texas, Eastern and Southern Leagues)—the toughest step in the minors. It was the army's equivalent of being promoted from private to staff sergeant, the difference between being a recruit and a careerist. Pitchers in Double-A cannot survive with just a fastball, as they could in Single-A, and batters are more patient and selective. Finesse becomes as important as power. Manno decided that some Diablos players were over their heads in Double-A, others were over the hill, and in the next four days he rebuilt the team, making ten roster changes.

He signed a journeyman slugger from Mexico and traded an old outfielder (he was twenty-five) to the Phillies organization. He released Brad Wheeler, whose arm had gone dead from throwing too many pitches. Wheeler had turned down a college scholarship in order to play pro ball and now, suddenly, at age twenty-seven, he was an ex-athlete with no marketable skill. Wheeler did not go home to Michigan immediately, and the night after his release, he was back at Dudley Field, running with the other pitchers. Then Manno sent one of the Brewers' best pitching prospects, Narciso Elvira, back to Stockton. Elvira's desire had gotten sidetracked in spring training, after Milwaukee's million-dollar pitcher, Teddy Higuera, had taken his fellow Mexican under his wing. Higuera had paid Elvira's three-thousand-dollar dentist bill, bought his meals in Arizona and, the Brewers had heard, promised him fifty-thousand dollars to start a new life if his baseball career failed. Higuera had also given Elvira the use of his home and car in Ciudad de Juarez, just across the Rio Grande from El Paso, and Elvira, age twenty, arrived for the Diablos games every afternoon in a chauffeur-driven limousine.

With the demotion of Elvira, El Paso had a vacant pitcher's spot on the roster. One candidate to fill it was Steve Monson, the hard-nosed Stockton pitcher who had promised his girlfriend he would ride Carl Dunn's bus no more. Manno worried that Monson would get crushed in Double-A, relying too much on his high fastball. Besides that, El Paso's thin air made the spacious Dome a hitter's paradise that had psychologically destroyed more than a few pitchers. But Manno saw an intangible quality in Monson that he wanted to put to the test: "He's damn tough mentally. Sometimes you put a kid like that in this environment, let him sink or swim, and he'll rise to the occasion."

The night Manno decided to call up Monson, most of the Ports were celebrating another victory in a club called Basil's, back in Stockton. Monson ordered a third drink, or maybe it was a fourth, and a stranger next to him at the bar said, "I don't think you need another drink."

"Who the fuck are you to tell me how much I should drink!" Monson shot back. As far as anyone could remember, that's when the first punch was thrown and in a flash the Ports were back to back, taking on most of the bar. It was a fine exercise in charging team morale and the players returned to the Willow Glen apartment complex exhilarated.

Monson didn't fall asleep until 6:00 A.M. His phone rang two hours later and the Ports' pitching coach, Rob Derksen, told Monson to come over to his apartment, which was just down the street and around the corner.

"Management's complaining that there was too much noise last night," Derksen said, straight-faced. "What were you doing? Having a party?"

"No, we were just playing cards. It wasn't noisy."

"Well, they said it was. You've got to find a new place to live. You're going to have to live in El Paso."

Monson jabbed his right fist into the air in triumph. "Don't forget all you've learned here," said Derksen, who had been in Stockton for six years as a player and coach. Then Monson was on his way. Double-A at last. He landed in El Paso, dumped his four suitcases at the airport Hilton, and with his last ten-dollar bill caught a taxi straight to the Dudley Dome, where he changed into his new uniform. Seeing me in the clubhouse was confirmation that he really was on the march.

"Hey," he said, "when are you going to be in Denver? I may see you there, too." Denver was the Brewers' Triple-A club.

Monson was scheduled to pitch the night after his arrival. I got to the park early that afternoon and found one of the local fans outside, pleading with Rick Parr, the general manager, to let him into the game. Manny was on his knees, crying.

"You know the deal, Manny," Parr said. "You're sober, I let you in for free. You're drunk, you don't get in at all." Parr had once kept Manny sober for thirty straight days with the threat of denying him baseball, but on this day, his humanitarian ploy had clearly failed and Manny would not be on hand for the debut of Monson, whom Paul Strelzin, the announcer, would introduce as "Monsoon" Monson.

"I've won everywhere I've been and I'll win here, too. I can carry this club," Monson said before the game. He pitched six solid innings, striking out seven, and left with a 4–2 lead. He stretched out on the rubdown table in the trainer's room, wearing an I-told-you-so grin. "My fastball was ninety-one [mph] and my curve was clocked at eighty-seven," he said, speaking quietly because other players were around. "I threw seventeen change-ups. And they said

I didn't have a breaking ball. Ha! So when did you say you were going to be in Denver?"

Monson was blue-collar, and he was the type of player who made farm directors and old-time managers comfortable. Players who questioned and asked why, who had aspirations beyond baseball, were often thought to lack motivation. But those who came right off the minor-league assembly line, who didn't let intellect get in the way of the task at hand, who weren't too outrageous or too colorful or too outspoken, were the ones credited with having desire and a good attitude. They were to the corporate world of baseball what oranges were to a citrus farmer.

Frank Mattox, the Diablos switch-hitting second baseman, had thought a good deal about this and concluded that the structure of minor league baseball was built on conformity. If Mattox had a flaw as an athlete, it was that he did too much thinking. He had a degree from the University of California at Berkeley in the political economy of natural resources. His father was a pharmacist and his mother had recently gone back to school and gotten her business degree. "She has mega-knowledge and a library you wouldn't believe," he said. He perceived, correctly I think, that his education was a subtle career detriment.

When Mattox sat out a game with a sprained thumb on his throwing hand, I asked one of the Brewers' roving instructors—an older man who had toiled many years in baseball—how he regarded Mattox. "Good ballplayer," the man said, "but he has a lot of *nagging* injuries. He went to Berkeley, you know. That's an education for you." The implication was that a less educated athlete would have more limited options in life and thus a greater need to succeed and more intensity. That wasn't quite true, though. It was that Mattox's desire was on a different, less desperate level, and that unnerved traditionalists. They had a hard time accepting that 60 percent of today's minor leaguers had attended college, and that some had already figured out baseball was not the only world in the universe.

Mattox didn't devote the winter to menial jobs in order to spend hours working out, as the Big Club liked; he found opportunities that would benefit him in a postbaseball career. Once he had gone to Europe in the off-season. He had two books on his bedside table: one on building vocabulary, the other on learning how to speed-read. He talked about forming a pool of minor league players to speak out against drugs, do community work and be available for corporations looking for particular skills. His confidence seemed unrelated to his abilities on the field.

The first professional goal Mattox had set for himself was one of time: If he didn't make the majors within three years, he would quit baseball. This was his fifth year in the minors, and his third at El Paso. He read his Bible often—"It's a great backbone whenever you get down and it helps you keep perspective when you get too high"—and he equated the minors to a false retaining wall that players can lean against but which doesn't really offer support. There were moments when he thought he would feel a sense of great relief once this whole battle was settled, one way or another.

"Sometimes I look around and see the friends I went to college with climbing in their professions, doing well," Mattox said. "I feel a bit envious and I say, 'Wow, I'm missing out.' And they say, 'Boy, I wish I had the opportunity you've got. You might hit it big and get a shot at the majors.' Just to hear them say it makes me realize how lucky I am.

"Other players I know have baseball dreams. Two outs, last of the ninth. That kind of thing. They've told me about their dreams and it worried me for a long time that I didn't dream baseball. Maybe it's just that I don't remember my dreams, because I do have one: It's to play with the best, in the majors, just one day in my life. You take a physicist, an engineer, whatever, and he doesn't get that chance, but a baseball player does. I'd make sure all the relatives I hadn't seen for a long time got to the game. To have my relatives and friends see me out there, knowing that I had obtained what I had set out after, even if it was just for a minute in life, that would be lightning."

Well before meeting Mattox, I had decided I would have made a bad sportswriter and a worse general manager. I was glad Russ Lynch had steered me away from baseball. I never would have been tough enough to release someone I liked, and I'm sure my feelings would have gotten in the way of what I wrote about this player or that. Mattox didn't know it, but he ensured a place for himself in my summer memories over lunch one day, shifting the conversation so that I, instead of he, took center stage. It was something no other player had done. "I'm sure a lot of players have asked you this," he said, incorrectly, "but what's it like, traveling around alone to all these ballparks? What made you do it?"

I had intended to stay in El Paso for only three or four days. On my tenth day there dark clouds swept down Interstate 10 and the first rain I had seen since leaving Los Angeles engulfed Dudley Field, ignoring the legends of the dome. The ubiquitous Marlboro man, who towers over the fence of almost every minor league park, swayed on his horse near the left-field line, his yellow rain slicker aglow in the dark evening. Out in the parking lot, I made coffee and spread my maps over Forty-niner's dinette table, to decide where I would go next.

A whole new rhythm had taken over my life. I was among travelers now, people who asked not "Where have you been?" but "Where are you going?" I thought of my friends back at the *Times* in Los Angeles, bent over their computers, in a carpeted newsroom as sedate as an insurance office, friends who wore coats and ties to work, weren't allowed to smoke—a third offense was cause for dismissal—and seldom drank too much anymore at the Redwood Saloon across the street. I did not envy them. City newsrooms used to be alive with loud voices and a sense of urgency. The camaraderie of the loners and eccentrics and rebellious characters who inhabited them had a veritable fragrance. But like major league clubhouses, they were now more the home of individuals than teams, and when the day's work was finished, everyone hurried off in his separate way. I called Sandy and felt distant, as though I had fallen into a universe removed from all that had been shared and familiar.

My only responsibility these days was having a full tank of gas and finding a ballpark. It was the simplest of lives, gladsome in a lonely sort of way, free from all the nettlesome obligations of middle-class stability. I had been surprised when so many friends had expressed envy as I set forth. Several had asked if they could join me along the way. One, a wealthy businessman, had said I was doing what he had always dreamed of doing. Now I knew why.

I had run away.

Chapter Eight

Fame is the perfume of heroic deeds.

—SOCRATES

My map of the western states ended at El Paso, and a notation in the margin said, "For adjoining area, see central states map." My final link to home had been cut. I spread out the new section and realized that escaping Texas would be a daunting task. Oklahoma, Arkansas and Louisiana all lay a hard day's drive or more away, across a flat, hot wasteland of numbing sameness. The Bedouin of the Arabian Peninsula would have felt much at home here. I had no timetable or planned itinerary and I wasn't expected in any particular place, so I decided Oklahoma was as good a destination as any. I checked *Baseball America's Directory* and found two teams listed in Oklahoma: The Oklahoma City 89ers, run by one of the few female chief executives in baseball, Patty Cox-Hampton, and the Tulsa Drillers, whose manager, Tommy Thompson, had spent nearly twenty years in the minors and in that time had, like his peers, earned not a penny toward any sort of pension.

About a hundred miles out of El Paso all traffic had to stop at a U.S. border checkpoint. I must have some psychological flaw because I am one of those persons who always feel mildly uncomfortable cashing a check in a bank or passing through immigration control at an airport, as though I were hiding some criminal guilt. Checkpoints unsettle me, too, and have ever since Beirut when daily you had to navigate a dozen or more roadblocks manned by gunmen wearing black pillowcases over their heads. If you produced the wrong pass or raised suspicion by some innocent gesture, the consequences could be dire. My hands would shake as I negotiated my freedom, a few blocks at a time, and I always wondered what face went with the cold eyes that stared me down through those cloth slits.

The uniformed border man had blue eyes and a Texas drawl. Was I a U.S. citizen? he asked. Where was I going? Was I transporting anyone? "You wouldn't be minding if I took a look, would you?" he asked. He came on board through the side door, checked my bunk, opened the bathroom door, glanced at the empty rear sofa by the dinette table and wished me a good journey. In five months of traveling, his was the only presence of national authority I would encounter. I drove off toward Pecos—where Judge Roy Bean once represented the only law for hundreds of miles around—thinking how much of our freedom we take for granted. In many of the countries where I had spent a considerable amount of time, such as Ethiopia and Iraq, citizens could not even move from one neighborhood to the next without government approval. In others official permission was needed to board a domestic flight. Here at home there wasn't anyone who had the right to tell me I couldn't follow any damn road I chose.

I clung to the interstate in Texas. The towns were far apart and I was usually ready for a cup of coffee when a sign beckoned me off the highway. At Angies Cafe in Fort Hancock, two elderly ladies, Miss Herbie and Miss Lillian, sipped lemonade through straws and talked about tornadoes. A large picture of the late John Wayne hung on the wall, and on the jukebox the late Ricky Nelson sang "I'm a Travelin' Man." The faces I saw in this long, lonely stretch of Texas were so ordinary as to be beautiful. They were the faces of working people, weathered and creased by heat and cold and wind. Their dusty jeans were the color of the land; their dresses came from the Sears catalog. The women wore no makeup; the men never removed their Stetsons. They talked in low voices in the cafés, leaning across the table, and their hands bore what I have always considered, perhaps naïvely, to be a badge of trustworthiness: calluses.

It took me two days to get into north Texas, and look as I did, I never found a single bar in any of the little towns along the way. Fine sand hung in the air like talcum powder, clogging my nostrils, and I felt in need of company and a glass of whiskey. Finally, close to midnight, in Archer City, a speck of a town at the junction of routes 79 and 25, I noticed what appeared to be an oasis: a long, squat building near the police station with boarded-up windows and a neon sign that said COKE. It was American Legion Post 198. I was probably the only person on the entire *Los Angeles Times* staff who was a card-carrying member of both the Elks and the Legion, an affiliation my colleagues thought strange but one I found useful when traveling in rural America.

Post 198, it turned out, was the only place within rifle-shot range where you could get a drink. There was a dart game going on in the back room and half a dozen people at the bar. The barmaid, Carolyn Parish, was on the phone, as she would be until closing time, helping women track down their husbands. "Nope, haven't seen him," she was saying to a caller as I walked in. "Chris's here. George and Matt are here. Harry just left. But I haven't seen your man all night." On the wall behind her a sign reminded customers that Texas forbade carrying weapons in a place that served alcohol; the punishment for offenders was up to ten years in prison. Another said, WELCOME HOME, VIETNAM VETS, which was ironic, because the Legion had initially turned its back on Vietnam veterans, who, after all, hadn't fought in a *real* war, the old-timers said.

Mrs. Parish downed a straight shot of tequila. "I wasn't going to drink tonight," she said. "I promised myself that. But I need a little pick-me-up and I'll only do a few of these." Then she leaned over the bar and said confidentially, "You see that peach schnapps over there? I could down half a fifth of that stuff a night, but, you know, it's just too sweet." She said I was welcome to spend the night in the Legion's parking lot. That being the case, I allowed that another Canadian Club would be welcome. My sinuses were clearing quickly.

Archer City looked vaguely familiar, like a forgotten black-and-white photo in an old scrapbook. The next morning the abandoned and crumbling Royal Theater across from the courthouse jogged my memory, and I knew why. Archer City had been Anarene in *The Last Picture Show,* the film adaptation of Larry McMurtry's novel about the stultifying drabness of small-town Texas in the fifties. When the film opened in 1969, Archer City had gone en masse to Wichita Falls for the premiere, and its collective response of outrage was loud enough to muffle the prairie winds.

The Baptist preacher said the movie was sinful and urged his flock not to read the book or see the film. (He apparently had done neither.) Some residents accused McMurtry—who had graduated from the local high school—of being a Benedict Arnold, and reporters from around the country traipsed into town to see if Archer City truly was the end of the earth as Hollywood had portrayed it. McMurtry offered to debate his critics in a public forum at the American Legion. None accepted.

"Frankly, it was the Baptists that made all the noise," lifelong resident Jane Ceay told me. "I think it was mostly jealousy. Instead of being proud of Larry, they were resentful of his success. That's how small towns are."

Fickle as we are toward our heroes, McMurtry was not held in contempt long—only until the collapse in oil prices turned the north Texas economy sour. By the time I got to Archer City, McMurtry—who still did his writing on an old manual typewriter in the nearby family ranch house—had won a Pulitzer Prize, for *Lonesome Dove,* and with his sister had set up in his hometown the only bookstore between Abilene and Wichita Falls. The town had honored him with a testimonial dinner. It also needed jobs, and with McMurtry planning to film *Texasville,* a sequel to *The Last Picture Show,* in Archer City, locals were already inquiring where they could sign up as extras and asking what time the American Legion would hold the luncheon buffets for the crew.

·　·　·

Texas ends, mercifully, at the Red River, a little ways north of Archer City. I crossed into Oklahoma, and, after a few phone calls and a couple of wrong turns, found the country club in Broken Arrow. The man I was looking for was downstairs in the grill. He was bald, a little overweight and sixty-eight years old. But it was not difficult to picture him as I had always known him—his right leg pointed skyward, left arm bent behind the white Milwaukee uniform bearing No. 21, his face twisted in concentration, looking for all the world as if he were preparing to fly off the mound. I would have recognized Warren Spahn anywhere.

Spahn was sitting with his friend Marge Renard, whom he introduced as "my intelligent young lady." His eyes twinkled with mischief and darted about the room in search of a prank. "Hey, Scotty, come here," he called to a golfing buddy. He clasped Scotty's bald head to his own, and, bending forward, seemed to have produced two buttocks. "You ever seen a perfect asshole?" he asked. Spahn and Scotty broke into giggles and Marge looked away, smiling slightly as though to say, "Boys will be boys." Being with Spahn, as she had been for eight years, was to live in a time warp of laughter and innocence; it was to appreciate his joking reply when someone asked him if he enjoyed O. Henry. "Nah," Spahn had said, "the nuts get stuck in my teeth."

It is worth noting, I think, that I did not choose my boyhood idols idly. Like the Nelson family in *The Adventures of Ozzie and Harriet*, Warren Spahn had been part of my maturation. He had thrown his first big-league pitch when I was two years old and his last when I was twenty-five. In the interim he had achieved a consistency of excellence that may never be matched, collecting twenty victories in thirteen different seasons and winning more games than all but four pitchers in baseball history. He threw a no-hitter when he was forty, hit more home runs than any National League pitcher ever, and struck out at least a hundred batters for seventeen straight years. "What he had that made him great you can't teach, because it was in his heart," his former teammate Del Crandall said. Spahn was an intensely proud man who did not accept defeat as a natural consequence of anything but imperfection and who to this day could rattle off the bad pitches and the misplays that had cost him this game or that.

Once, in the early sixties, outfielder Mel Roach had misjudged Junior Gilliam's fly ball in the seventh inning, depriving Spahn of what would have been back-to-back no-hitters. When Roach saw Spahn at a golf tournament in Richmond nearly thirty years later, the first thing he did was apologize.

"Geez, Mel," Spahn said, "that was a lifetime ago. Forget it." But Roach hadn't forgotten, and neither had Spahn.

Catching up with a childhood hero and meeting, as adults and equals, was somehow confusing. What I saw across the table from me was really two Warren Spahns. One was a life-sized, amiable man full of baseball stories and shared memories, miserly to a fault, playful as a teenager, a man whose last twenty years probably had not been as adventurous or interesting as my own. The other was the baseball immortal, so much larger than life that just by association I felt a tingle of pride when others in the grill room would look at our table and whisper to one another, "Isn't that Warren Spahn over there by the window?"

Spahn remembered my Milwaukee visit as the young Boston writer-fan but had forgotten his role in mediating my acceptance into the Braves' fraternity. That had been thirty-four summers ago, and the structure of professional baseball had changed so much since then that Spahn—a member of the old guard who believed that competitive fire and hard work equated with success, or at least with decency—found the whining and drugs and Fortune 500 salaries of contemporary athletes to be simply incomprehensible. Spahn's top salary had been $87,500. Today, when the *average* major league salary is just short of $600,000 a year, Bret Saberhagen of the Kansas City Royals (who has had a losing year after each successful season) earns in eight innings what Spahn did in a season. For players in Spahn's era with longevity and proficiency, baseball offered entry into the middle class. For today's players, the reward for two or three good seasons is lifetime security as a member of the nouveaux riches.

"I used to sit there across the desk from John Quinn [the Braves general manager] every winter, after winning twenty-two, twenty-three games the year before, and he wouldn't even offer me more money. I'd say, 'John, what do I have to do to get a raise?' And he'd say, 'You're paid to win twenty.'

"He'd write down a figure on a piece of paper and push it across the desk to me without a word. I'd scratch it out, write in a new figure, and push it back. It would get so we didn't even have anything to argue about. John was always the gentleman. But was he ever stingy, and he usually had the last word. Of course, I later found out he was earning fifteen thousand a year, so I can understand why he didn't want to give it away.

"I was the senior citizen on the Braves ever since I was twenty-nine or thirty, and John was always training some left-hander like Juan Pizarro to take my place. We only had one-year contracts in those days, so I'd go to spring training, knowing I had to earn my job every year. I never felt that security they have today and I didn't want it. I think I became a better pitcher without it. It kept me hungry."

Spahn lived a couple of hours from Tulsa, on a ranch he and his late wife LoRene had bought in 1948, the year Spahn and Johnny Sain ("and pray for rain") had pitched the Boston Braves to the pennant. The Diamond Star had only fifty acres then. Today it sprawls over twenty-eight hundred acres, acquired parcel by parcel. During the off-season of many winters, Spahn built and patched fences, bulldozed the scrub to make hayfields and pasture-land, dug ponds to provide water for the cattle. By the time February arrived each year and he and LoRene packed the car for spring training in Florida, his spirit ached for the uncomplicated delights of a season in the sun.

The ranch house was really too big for one man to rumble around in alone, so Spahn no longer stayed home long enough to get bored or lonely. He was on the move constantly, capitalizing on the nostalgia industry that had made him a celebrity. His frequent-flyer account at Delta Air Lines alone was over a million miles (though he couldn't bring himself to cash in any miles and take a real vacation, as Marge wanted, because exchanging miles for tickets was like dipping into a savings account), and wherever he went, there was a blur of polite but badgering people, wanting to shake hands, wanting an autograph, wanting to talk. For those willing to sing for their supper, it was a tedious price to pay for fame, but it was not as painful as it would be if people had walked right by you and never even known who you were.

Spahn took me up to the Diamond Star for the night and we bounced over his property in a blue Jeep, following tracks that paralleled the Kiamichi Mountains. One of his heifers bellowed at our intrusion, and Spahn bellowed right back. I asked him if the character of baseball had changed since he left the game.

"I'll tell you one thing that's different," he said, shifting into first as the Jeep's wheels spun over hillside rock. "They talk about pressure today, but whatever happened to the word 'challenge' we used to use—the intensity to excel?

"It's that desire to be greater than the other guy that makes a person worth his salt, whether he's a petroleum engineer or a ballplayer or what, and I'm not sure the kids have it today the way we did. I'm not one of those guys who say everything was best in the old days. If there's a better way to do something, I want to learn it, but still, I'm just not sure the kids now have the same dedication we did. We've gotten too lazy as a nation, too spoiled.

"That saying—it's not whether you win or lose, but how you play the game—well, that's the dumbest thing I ever heard. You show me a good loser and I'll show you a loser, period, someone who didn't try hard enough. Lew [Burdette] and I roomed together for fourteen years and we were always challenging each other: Whatever you can do, I can do better, we'd say. It wasn't professional jealousy. It was just saying, 'Hey, pal, get off your butt. Try harder. Be better.'"

Spahn pitched until he was forty-four, splitting a final lackluster season between the New York Mets and San Francisco Giants after twenty years with the Braves. "The consensus of everyone in baseball," he said, "was that I played a year too long. Maybe I did. But I honestly thought I could still be a winner." The year after retiring, he went to work for the Mexico City Tigers as pitching coach and, for extra compensation, agreed to start a game. Word got around that Warren Spahn, future Hall of Famer, was trying a comeback in the bush leagues. Spahn insisted his stint was only a promotion to drew a crowd, though if he had performed well, I imagine he might have started planning his trip back to the majors.

There were two telephone answering machines in the den that

served as Spahn's office at the Diamond Star, but he never bothered to turn them on. He had no secretary, no agent, no staff. "I figure why hand it over to someone else if I can do it better myself," he said. Fan mail was stacked on his desk, much of it unopened, and on the office walls and shelves were trophies, plaques, pictures and mementos of a baseball life. Sometimes sitting there alone, Spahn—the son of a wallpaper salesman in Buffalo who made twenty-seven dollars a week, the holder of a battlefield commission earned for bravery in the battle for Remagen Bridge, the winningest left-hander of all time—would look up from his desk and say to himself, "Hey, did I really do all *that?*"

Spahn walked out to the bar in his living room, opened two beers and lit a cigarette. I asked him what he would be worth at today's prices. He smiled and rolled his eyes. "Look at it this way. Remember Thurman Munson, the Yankee catcher? He was killed piloting his own jet. Well, if he hadn't had all that money, he wouldn't have been able to buy a plane, would he? So maybe I was lucky. Hell, I'd just like to be twenty-one again and have all my hair."

We drank the beer on a deck by the bar, looking out at the shadow of mountains and a land that was all his. He loved the solitude of the Diamond Star and Oklahoma nights so clear each star seemed within reach. "You can hear the grasshoppers talking to you out here," he said. "It's only when I start talking back that I get worried." But before that happened, he would be gone, off to Seattle or Louisville or any one of a hundred places where his name was magic and a man was treated as though his greatest feats had happened only yesterday.

"I still see a lot of the people from the old Braves days as I travel around," he said, "but more and more I go back to Boston or Milwaukee and I ask people, 'Where's so-and-so?' and I find out they've died. Del Rice is dead, of course. Bob Trowbridge's gone. Sid's gone. You remember Bob Elliott? He's gone, too. I always thought those guys should have lived forever. Johnny Logan called from Milwaukee the other day. Dottie had died and he was really broken up. He said he was going to move back to his old hometown in upstate New York, and I said, 'John, don't do it if you're expecting to find your friends there. They'll be gone, too.' "

I asked Spahn the next day if he wanted to drive to Tulsa to see the Drillers play the El Paso Diablos. He had managed the Drillers for four years after returning from Mexico City, and I still remembered a wire-service photo of him standing in Tulsa's third-base box, recovering from knee surgery and supported by a crutch under each arm. He said he'd rather play golf. He hadn't sat through a full ball game in years. In fact, he didn't even like to watch baseball on TV because he'd holler at the manager to move his infield this way and that and cuss the pitcher's inability to perform fundamentals, and pretty soon he'd be so worked up he would have to turn the set off.

I left the Diamond Star Ranch, following the potholed road toward Hartshorne. Aspens lined the way and the blue sky was strewn with wisps of clouds. Spahn had ignored Dylan Thomas's edict and had gone gentle into that good night, without burning or raving to mark the close of day. "The secret, I guess," he had said the night before, "is making the most of wherever you're at in life. Some people look in the mirror and they're unhappy. What do I see? Well, I see someone with gray hair who's growing old, and you know what? It makes me feel good, sort of content. I like where I've been and where I'm at. Baseball and the military did that for me. They gave me everything."

Warren Spahn's batterymate on the Milwaukee championship teams of the fifties was Del Crandall. He and Spahn were together so long that on the field there was just one collective mind analyzing the positioning of players, playing to the weaknesses of batters, selecting pitches. Crandall had reached the majors as a teenager and hustled with such intensity that opposing players razzed him unmercifully. He had been arguably the best catcher in baseball in the prime of his sixteen-year big-league career, but did not have the big name to cash in on, as did Spahn, and was still at work, as a scout and roving instructor for the Milwaukee Brewers.

Crandall came into Tulsa with the El Paso Diablos the day I had been with Spahn. The Diablos had a talented young catcher, Tim McIntosh, a solid hitter with uncertain defensive skills and a pro-

pensity for hurling or kicking his batting helmet into the dugout
in moments of disgust, thus giving pitchers the impression that he
was more interested in his own successes and failures than he was
in controlling the game. The Brewers had dispatched Crandall to
teach McIntosh to play baseball the way he had.

"You've got this organization saying it believes you can be a
catcher," Crandall said to McIntosh in the clubhouse after the
Diablos had beaten the Drillers. "Maybe you haven't had that
commitment before, but you've got it now. You've got the talent.
You just can't let this"—Crandall tapped his forehead—"get in
the way."

"I appreciate that. That means a lot."

"Then what do you say we go back to El Paso Monday and get
to work?" asked the sixty-year-old Crandall.

"I can dig that," said the twenty-four-year-old McIntosh.

Crandall was different from other baseball people I met on the
road. Rather than wearing the summer civilian uniform of his
peers—a polo shirt, tan slacks and unshined shoes—he had on a
sports jacket, shirt with collar, matching gray trousers and buffed
loafers. He sat alone during the game, a few feet down the first-base
line where he had a good view of the catcher, rather than with the
gaggle of scouts behind home plate. In conversation, he used the
word "commitment" often, looked you straight in the eye, asked
questions and waited for your full reply. Crandall was as controlled
and reserved as Spahn was loose and extroverted. He didn't drink,
smoke, swear or tell dirty stories. "In a way, Del was too good for
baseball," his former teammate Bob Hazle once said. Baseball, I
thought, could have been a lonely life for someone who didn't find
nourishment sitting around a bar, swapping old stories like veterans of some remembered war.

The last of the Diablos had showered and left the clubhouse.
Their manager, Marc Bombard, called in his game report to the
dictaphone machine in Bruce Manno's office back in Milwaukee
and said, "Night, Del. See you tomorrow." Crandall turned to me.
"Are you in a hurry to get out of here?" "No," I said. "I've got all
summer." He did not recall the time I had had him paged at the
hotel in Philadelphia so many years earlier and had asked why

ballplayers said "ain't." But the fact that we had shared, in differ-ent ways, Milwaukee's rapt embrace of the old Boston Braves made us something less than strangers.

Crandall had flirted with the alien world outside baseball after his skills failed him in the mid-sixties. He had worked for an insurance company and hated it. He had opened a restaurant and found that the hours didn't equate with the compensation. He had become a sales rep and awakened every morning with knots in his stomach. Like so many others, it was only baseball that gave him the comfort he needed, and he had returned to a variety of assign-ments—manager, radio announcer, scout—in both the majors and the minors. He had, I think, been fired from all those jobs, which is no disgrace in baseball, though I suspect the sport's establish-ment is not at ease with those whose demeanor carries them out-side the mainstream of being "one of the boys."

"One thing that's surprised me is how few real friends from baseball you carry with you when your days as a player end," Crandall said. "I mean *real* friends, friends you'd turn to in a crisis. All that intensity and intimacy of being teammates for years, then suddenly it's gone. What's left is mostly acquaintances and stories of old times."

It was after midnight when we left Bombard's office. The lights in Tulsa County Stadium had been turned off, and only two vehi-cles remained in the parking lot, Crandall's rental car and Forty-niner. Crandall came on board to examine my home. He liked the layout and asked questions about my trip: Where did I sleep? How did I make contacts in a new town? Wasn't it lonely without my wife and friends? Before driving off, he said, "It takes an unusual person to do what you're doing." Coming from a man I had once lionized as being no less a giant than a dragon-slayer, I felt flattered.

Through the South
and into Appalachia
May 30–July 3

Chapter Nine

Next to religion, baseball has furnished a greater impact on American life than any other institution.

—PRESIDENT HERBERT HOOVER

In a little Tennessee town whose name now escapes me, I saw the glow of lights one evening. It came softly through the June darkness, from somewhere behind a grove of elms and past a village green, and I turned off the highway to find it. The road I followed meandered through a row of white clapboard homes whose porches were stacked with firewood and ended after a while in an open field. There was a baseball park in the field, very simple in construction, its outfield grass patchy and more brown than green. The lights I had seen from the highway shone from four tall wooden poles and cast a glare that danced unevenly over the diamond, leaving the young shortstop standing alone in a curtain of shadows.

I didn't know who was playing because there was no scoreboard and the players—who looked to be eleven or twelve years old—wore uniforms that bore not the names of teams but those of local establishments: a drugstore, a feed store, a gas station, a flower shop. The wooden bleachers along the first-base line held several dozen families, and they loudly cheered their boys on the field. "Come on, Jamie," a woman shouted to a little blond-haired batter. His cap was pulled down so firmly over his head that his ears stuck out. "You're the hitter up there. Wait for the one you want. Be ready up there, Jamie."

Jamie backed out of the box, scooped up a handful of dirt, and glared at the pitcher, just as Eddie Mathews would have done. The pitcher pawed at the mound. The third baseman pounded his glove and shouted, "No hitter up there, Billy. Burn one by him." The first baseman smoothed the earth in front of him with the toe of his sneaker and tossed away an imaginary pebble. "Attaway, Billy," he yelled. "Make 'im hit it."

These were the same rituals, the same language, I had known when I was Jamie's age. They were the same ones you saw and heard today if you watched a game on TV. From California to Tennessee they didn't vary, because baseball is so entwined with society's fiber that its mannerisms and vocabulary are inherited more than they are learned. They are like the Pledge of Allegiance, which one recites without ever being taught the words.

A good deal has been written about baseball being a metaphor for life. It moves with the seasons; it is a daily game, often slow and tedious, instead of the weekly spectacular that football stages; its participants are men of ordinary physical bearing, not steroid monsters padded with armor or seven-foot giants in short pants; its outcome, unlike that of other sports, is uncertain until the last moment—a three-run lead with two outs in the ninth can disappear with a single pitch, but two touchdowns in football or five baskets in basketball is an invincible margin with seconds left; there are no clocks, no time-outs, no rush of players commanded by an official's whistle (baseball, in fact, is the only game in which the defensive team has the ball), and at day's end the battle is never indecisive—there is one winner and one loser.

Americans love traditions and rituals and statistics that are meaningful and easily grasped, and baseball is full of them all. "Whoever wants to know the heart and mind of America had better learn baseball—the rules and realities of the game—and do it by watching some high school or small-town teams," the French-born author Jacques Barzun wrote in 1954. Babe Ruth's sixty home runs are part of our culture. So are the perennial failures of the Cubs and Red Sox, the onetime superiority of the Yankees. But I doubt that many kids know how many points Kareem Abdul-Jabbar scored in his career (or was it Wilt Chamberlain who scored the most?), how many touchdown passes Fran Tarkenton threw in his best season, whether the NBA Timberwolves play in Minneapolis or Seattle, or when the Packers last won a Superbowl.

Still, I don't think baseball is a metaphor for anything, let alone for life. It is simply the best game. The game where teamwork and individual performance are independent and interdependent. The game in which every player (except the foolish designated hitter) is expected to execute all offensive and defensive assignments. The game of perfect distances: Who was the genius, anyway, who figured out that a ball thrown from short and a runner dashing ninety feet from home would reach first at almost precisely the same moment, whereas eighty feet would have been too short and a hundred too long?

Baseball also endures because its myths and statistics endure. Winning twenty games or hitting .300 is still the same measure of excellence that it was in the 1920s. Hack Wilson's 190 RBIs in a single season is no lesser feat today than it was in 1930. And every schoolboy knows that Abner Doubleday invented baseball at Cooperstown, New York, in 1839; no matter that Doubleday was a plebe at West Point that year and had nothing to do with baseball—though as an artillery captain he did fire the first Union shot of the Civil War, from Fort Sumter in Charleston Harbor in 1861. For most Americans at the turn of the century, the idea that the young republic had borrowed its national pastime from England was repugnant; they wanted an American name attached to their American game, just as they had one associated with the invention of the electric light, the radio, the automobile, the airplane. In 1907 a commission of eminent baseball men (but no historians) settled the issue, albeit wrongly: Abner Doubleday, its report said, was the father of baseball.

If historical trivia delight you as much as they do me, I offer these other tidbits that are nice to know but not worth a trip to the library to find out:

—On a cold spring day in 1901, ice cream wasn't selling at the Polo Grounds, so the Giants concession's manager, Harry M. Stevens, sent out for some sausages. He boiled them, laid them lengthwise in rolls and dispatched his hawkers into the stands, shouting, "Get 'em while they're hot!" Thus was born one of the staples of the American diet, the hot dog.

—"Take Me Out to the Ball Game" was published in 1908. Neither the composer, Albert von Tilzer, nor the lyricist, Jack Norworth, had ever been to a ball game. But that didn't detract from the song's realism. Baseball was part of everything, and if you were an American, the atmosphere of a ballpark was understood intuitively.

—During an exhibition game in 1882, according to one account, Jasper Brennan, the coach of Manhattan College in New York, saw that fan were getting restless and suggested in the seventh inning that they stand up and stretch. Seven years later, in a World Series game between the New York Giants of the National League and the Brooklyn Bridegrooms of the American Association, the fans copied what had become part of Manhattan's game ritual, bequeathing us the seventh-inning stretch that for decades now has been synonymous with standing and singing "Take Me Out to the Ball Game."

—One baseball custom—dragging the infield after the fifth inning—doesn't have much to do with keeping the diamond in playable condition. Fred Haney came up with the idea in the fifties when he was managing the Hollywood Stars in the Pacific Coast League as an entrepreneurial ruse to give fans more time at the concession stands.

In 1885, when cattle prices crashed because of drought and overstocking and the open range of the West gave way to the introduction of fenced pastureland, the Chattanooga Lookouts played their first game. The team was named for Chattanooga's dominant physical feature, fog-shrouded Lookout Mountain, where in the Civil War's Battle Above the Clouds the Mississippi Valley was assured to the Union. Chattanooga has been a fine baseball town ever since those early days—Ruth and Gehrig played in exhibition games there; Satchel Paige began his forty-year career there—and I thought the Lookouts was an excellent name for a team because it reflected something of Chattanooga's history and tradition. I always felt disappointed when I found a team that had taken the name of its major league parent. What, after all, does the Helena Brewers say about Montana? (Wouldn't the Helena Gold Panners have been better?) The Auburn Astros, Gastonia Rangers and San Jose Giants are no better. The minor league names I liked spoke of local character and there were some terrific ones to choose from: the Nashville Sounds, Durham Bulls, Toledo Mud Hens, Butte Cooper Kings, Erie Sailors, Charleston Rainbows.

I arrived in Chattanooga on a Friday evening, and, never having been there before, headed directly for the Greyhound Terminal, which I found on the corner of Seventh and Chestnut streets. This is a custom that dates to my teenage days, when I used to hitchhike around the country and would seek out the terminal for two reasons. First, I like long-haul buses. I like to look at them, I like to ride in them, I like seeing them flash by in the night, their destination markers bearing the name of some city a thousand miles away. Second and more important, the Greyhound station gives me a sense of place, not only by putting me in the midst of downtown but also by fixing me within a region. It lets me know my routes of escape.

In Chattanooga, for instance, I learned that there were two daily departures to Birmingham and ten to Atlanta, although both cities were roughly the same distance away. That told me that the flow of money and goods out of southern Tennessee was linked to Georgia, not Alabama. On the long-distance runs, Chattanooga was listed as a twenty-minute snack stop, not a forty-five-minute meal stop, and that told me Chattanooga was neither a major metropolis nor a stopover on any great transcontinental route. Only two westbound buses passed through Chattanooga, one from Miami to Denver, the other from Orlando to Portland; the folder marked Schedule No. 76 indicated that the heaviest traffic through

Chattanooga was on north–south routes, not east–west, which I assumed had historical roots in the migration of blacks to the industrial North.

I might add that most friends consider my penchant for Greyhounds an aberration. When I lived in San Francisco I used to bring a lady of whom I was fond to the musty old bus terminal on Mission Street before dinner dates. I tried to explain to her the romance of buses headed for Chicago and Dallas and Las Vegas. She would stand in line with me, fidgeting with annoyance, as I inquired about connections in Atlanta for Augusta or what time the Boston departure arrived in Presque Isle, Maine. I suppose I was just testing her tolerance level, and before long she reached it, saying good-bye to both the Greyhounds and me.

Chattanooga is a pleasant city that moves at a poky pace. Largely destroyed in the Civil War, Sherman used it for a depot in his march from Atlanta to the sea. After the war, carpetbagger money flowed in as Northerners tried to turn the town into the Pittsburgh of the South. It remains the home of heavy industry. Many people told me if the city had been more aggressive thirty years ago, Chattanooga instead of Atlanta would today be the South's most important city. But the denizens—cautious, conservative Southerners to the core—liked things as they were. Even the Sunbelt expansion of the seventies slipped right by Chattanooga.

The Lookouts' marriage with Chattanooga was a good one, and the team was one of the few I had encountered that had a true local identity. While many other clubs had often changed names, switched cities and major league affiliations and never been part of local history, the Lookouts were arguably Chattanooga's most important institutional resource. They played in a fifty-nine-year-old stadium (only El Paso's Dudley Field and Rochester's Silver Stadium were older); they had shared in Chattanooga's cycles of prosperity and economic suffering; and they had, for more than thirty years, an owner whose popularity rivaled that of Tennessee's favorite son, Davy Crockett.

Joe Engel, who took over the Lookouts in 1929, was the grandest promoter the minor leagues had ever known. During the depression he opened his stadium on Christmas Day and served twenty-seven thousand free dinners to the needy. At one game in 1936 he gave away a house (donated by a builder and furnished courtesy of a department store). His park's capacity was just over nine thousand, and three times that many people showed up for the drawing. So he roped off the outfield, packed in fans twenty-deep behind the barricade and froze his supply of baseballs, making them so heavy there was little danger any batter would hit one into the crowd. (It was not someone getting beaned that worried him; he just didn't want to lose any balls.)

Another time Engel sent a female softball pitcher to the mound in an exhibition game; she promptly struck out Babe Ruth, Lou Gehrig and Tony Lazzeri. He also auctioned off the Lookouts' radio announcer before thousands of cheering women. The winner got to use him for a day, doing dishes, mowing the lawn and taking care of household chores. And once Engel traded one of his players, Johnny Jones, for a turkey, saying the turkey had had a better year. (The Johnny Jones turkey sandwich remains a popular item to this day in the deli at Engel Stadium.)

Sadly, baseball has no more Joe Engels and Bill Veeck, and probably never will, though I think El Paso's Jim Paul belongs just behind that top echelon of creative promoters. Their absence will deprive us of laughter and fun.

Baseball today is money-driven, and as minor-league franchise values have soared, local ownership increasingly has sold out to wealthy businessmen from distant cities who have no stake in the community. What they bring to baseball is the same no-nonsense business approach they used to make millions in banking, law firms and real estate companies. But the practitioners of the outrageous and the innovative have little place anymore in a sport-business that disparages nonconformity and feels not at all comfortable in unchartered waters. At the bottom line, safety is more important than originality. As Bob Beban, a former salesman, Pacific Coast League umpire and pro golfer who runs the Eugene Emeralds, one of the minor league's most successful franchises, said, "I never had an original idea, but I worked hard at what others had perfected."

The day after I got to Chattanooga, Rick Holtzman rose at 4:00 A.M. in his Chicago home, drove to O'Hare and caught the American Airlines flight to Chattanooga, via Nashville, to spend a weekend with his investment at Third and O'Neal, down by the rail yards. An outsider to baseball, he had gone on a $7 million shopping spree in '87 and '88, purchasing five minor league teams—the Lookouts, Tucson Toros, Midland Angels, Quad City Angels and Columbia Mets—and now owned more clubs than anyone else in the country.

Not yet forty, Holtzman moved with the confidence of a man who had made a lot of money and made it early and, being a newcomer to the game, being a Northerner in the three Southern cities where he owned teams, was treated with a degree of aloofness by the establishment, which wanted assurances he wasn't a speculator. What made some people uneasy, I think, was that Holtzman played hardball business: Though a passionate fan and aficionado of baseball history, he believed profit was the best motivation for a successful owner, and he made no promise of being the shining knight who had come to save baseball for any particular town. Fix up the stadium, he'd tell a mayor, or I'll move the team. The approach was almost un-American considering that the subject was baseball, but it worked.

Talking with one recalcitrant mayor a week before his bid for reelection, Holtzman outlined his list of needed improvements at the ballpark and said that if his demands weren't met he'd move the team and hold a press conference saying the mayor was responsible for the relocation. "He came around quickly," Holtzman said. "There's no politician in the country so popular he can run against professional baseball."

The American Airlines flight got Holtzman to Chattanooga in time for a Southern buffet lunch at Penny's—barbecued ribs, stuffed peppers, corn and homemade bread pudding—and afterward he headed out to Engel Stadium, which he had saved from demolition and, with $2 million of city and county money, had remodeled as a replica of a 1920s ballpark. "I'd wanted to tear it down at first, too, until I found out how much of baseball's history had passed through Chattanooga," Holtzman said, his foot-long cigar in hand. So Engel Stadium became a shrine to the past, and a registered historical landmark, with brick walls, awnings, wrought iron, antique lamps in the concourse and the deepest center field—471 feet—in all of baseball. Only Harmon Killebrew ever cleared the fence in dead center.

"Well, lookit here, it's the boss," outfielder Chris Jones said, spotting Holtzman in the dugout during batting practice. His voice teased and he assumed his cockiest stance, leaning against the railing. "You know, boss, these pants on the uniform are too short. They keep pullin' up, and that shouldn't be. And I haven't got my bats yet. I ordered 'em maybe six weeks ago. Another thing. I need an off-season job, three-fifty minimum. That shouldn't be a problem, should it, three-fifty? And that water that was in the dugout the other night, we gotta do something about that."

"Hey, Jones," yelled groundskeeper Tony Ensor, "if you were getting more hits, you wouldn't have so much time in the dugout to notice those things."

"I hit a home run tonight and I got that job at three-fifty, right?" Jones said, ignoring Ensor. Holtzman looked at the outfielder with a bemused smile and nodded his head in a way that implied nothing at all. His first time at bat that night, Jones hit a screamer against the right-field wall, missing a homer by inches.

Jones had been a member of the '88 Lookouts team, an affiliate of the Cincinnati Reds, that had brought Chattanooga its first Double-A Southern League championship in twenty-seven years, and the celebration that rocked Engel Stadium the September night they defeated Greenville, 13–2, to clinch the flag was like a collegiate victory party, a joyous union of fans and players that would have had no place in a major league park.

At the moment of triumph—a third strike thrown by Mike Smith—Chris Hammond set off a string of firecrackers in the bull pen and the Lookouts raced onto the field to embrace not only one another but the fans as well. They hoisted their most boisterous booster, seventy-five-year-old Hubert Quarles, onto their shoulders. Fans poured out of the stands, and the players, rather than retreating to the privacy of the clubhouse, sprayed them with champagne, then passed them their bottles to raise in toast. Channel Nine interrupted its network broadcast of *Dynasty* to announce the Lookouts' victory, and in the booth behind home plate, where Charlie Timmons, a Chattanooga fireman with a university degree in music, sat under an elegant chandelier he had purchased himself, the Hammond organ boomed out, "Happy Days Are Here Again."

For thirty minutes the infield was a swirling mass of raucous celebrants. Said the Lookouts' oldest player, twenty-nine-year-old Hedi Vargas: "This is my first pro pennant. It will be in my heart always, for the rest of my life."

Holtzman, a Vietnam vet and college dropout, who had parlayed his life's savings of fifteen thousand dollars into Chicago's largest apartment-management company, had gotten into baseball after tiring of real estate and sixteen-hour days. "I decided to do only the things I enjoyed doing," he said. "I also wanted to find something profitable. If being involved with baseball wasn't profitable, I'm afraid it would have made my love of the game less." He had read that the minor leagues were prospering and contacted Baseball Opportunities in Scottsdale, Arizona, the only company in the country whose sole business is brokering baseball franchises.

For more than a year he shopped before settling on the Midland Angels in the Texas League, which was on solid financial footing, had a good general manager in Bill Davidson and a well-maintained ballpark. Flying back to Chicago after signing the papers, his attorney said to him, "Now, let me get this straight. You just spent $1 million for the right to sell hot dogs, right?"

"Yup. I guess that's about it," Holtzman replied.

Indeed, all he now owned, outside of a couple of typewriters and a rickety desk or two, was the franchise rights to do business. He didn't own the stadium (the city of Midland did); he couldn't depreciate and didn't own the players (the California Angels did). He didn't even get any bats and balls or an old Cub tractor to drag the infield with. Reasonable enough, he thought, then went out and bought four more teams. Holtzman had discovered what others before him already knew: that over the past decade minor league franchises had become one of the best investments in the country, better than the stock market, residential real estate, gold, fine art or collectible postage stamps.

Opportunities to buy into baseball used to be limited. Ever since the Rickey era, minor league clubs had been owned by major league teams or local civic leaders who cared little about the profit-and-loss statement. They were badly run and most—perhaps 75 percent—lost money. Then in the post-Vietnam seventies, with attendance falling, expenses rising and baseball's popularity slipping in a nation that felt betrayed by all its institutions, owners began unloading their debt-burdened teams, sometimes for a dollar. It was the steal of the century. Baseball was on the brink of a bonanza that would explode with the nation's rediscovery of a nostalgic appreciation for the past. The result would be television subsidies reaching into ten figures and new attendance records year after year.

And the minors rode the coattails of the majors into prosperity.

The West Palm Beach franchise sold for one dollar in the seventies and was valued at half a million dollars in the eighties. The Durham Bulls, a $2,500 investment a decade ago, would be worth $4 million today, maybe more. The Harrisburg Senators were dumped for $45,000 in 1980 and appraised at $1.5 million nine years later. Holtzman paid $1.1 million for the Lookouts, which had sold for $280,000 three years earlier. The Oklahoma City 89ers, with the worst attendance in the American Association, changed hands for $4.8 million, the most ever paid for a minor league franchise. Even short-season rookie-league teams were fetching several hundred thousand dollars. (No less spectacular—and artificially inflated—was the appreciation of major league teams: Edward Bennett Williams paid $12 million for the Baltimore Orioles in 1979; in 1988 his estate sold the team for $70 million.)

"It's simple supply and demand," Holtzman said. "They're not creating any more of these things and there are a lot of people who want one. All of my teams are worth more today than what I paid for them, and if I wanted to sell, I'd get two hundred inquiries tomorrow morning."

Owning a team became the trendy investment of the eighties— "It's still cheaper than buying a second home and it's a lot more fun," said one California investor—and into the ownership ranks came a host of celebrities: actors Bill Murray, Billy Crystal, Mark Harmon and Robert Wagner; athletes Don Drysdale, Roman Gabriel and the Brett brothers, George, Bobby, Ken and John; singers Jimmy Buffett, Conway Twitty and Tony Orlando; author Sidney Sheldon; Hollywood director-writer Tom Mankiewicz; Brandon

Tartikoff, president of NBC's entertainment division. There were also college professors, journalists, retired labor negotiators and a documentary filmmaker.

What the minors lost in entering the big-money sweepstakes was a touch of innocence and a mom-and-pop ownership fastened to the roots of small-town America. Maybe there's nothing wrong with that. The monied owners have brought stability to minor league baseball—no circuit has folded since the Northern League in the Dakotas went under in 1971—and Holtzman and other owners give fans better value for their dollar: The ballparks are better, the entertainment is better, the food at the concession stands is better.

Only the game remained as it was.

Chapter Ten

Antiquity! I like its ruins better than its reconstructions.

—JOSEPH JOUBERT

I kept crossing paths with a photographer named Jim Dow in the ballparks of the South, and when I got to Birmingham, sure enough, he was there, too. I would see him ambling around the outfield of empty parks and studying the design of walkways and overhead rafters and standing alone in the grandstands, his head buried under a black cloth, as though he, the Deerdorf camera and the tripod all belonged to the same body.

Dow was an architectural photographer from Boston. For the past four summers he had traveled the country, recording on eight-by-ten panorama panels a relic of Americana—the old downtown minor league ballpark. Before getting to Birmingham, he had stopped off in Huntsville, taken one look at Joe W. Davis Stadium and huffed indignantly, "What is *this*?" It was new, in the suburbs, made of concrete, and he left without taking a shot. I asked him what he liked artistically about the old parks. "They're quirky and funky," he said. In Birmingham, the home of Rickwood Field, he had come to the right place.

Situated in the city's decaying West End, Rickwood Field had been abandoned after the '87 season, and the Birmingham Barons—a Southern League affiliate of the Chicago White Sox—had moved to a new $12 million stadium in the municipality of Hoover, ten miles away. Hoover was what the West End had been eighty years earlier: white, middle-class, residential.

The Barons' new home, imaginatively named Hoover Metropolitan Stadium, was plopped in an empty rural expanse, just off the interstate and far from the heart of humanity. You couldn't walk there from anywhere and city buses didn't go there and there was not another building in sight: not a home, not a tavern, not a hint of anything man-made except the stadium itself. Baseball happened there in isolation; it could have been Kansas or the Carolinas. That, though, was my prejudice, not the fans', and they had taken to the place as if it were a shopping mall. Attendance had nearly doubled the Barons' first year in Hoover, most of the skyboxes—$17,500 per season on a five-year lease—had been let, and the Barons had outdrawn every team in Double-A baseball.

On the desk of Art Clarkson, the Barons' CEO and general manager, was a sign that said, BABE RUTH STRUCK OUT 1,330 TIMES. KEEP SWINGING. Clarkson got into minor league baseball via the jewelry business in Los Angeles and the failed World Football League and, unlike many of his colleagues, didn't believe in giving away free or discounted tickets to pump up attendance figures or turn a bigger profit at the concession stands. "You start giving away thirty-thousand-dollar Cadillacs for five grand and what's the public's perception—that it's a cheap car, right?" he said. By his reckoning, everything at Hoover Stadium, from the clubhouses to the press box, was major league, just smaller, and I didn't doubt that his park was functionally superior.

"Rickwood had real character," he said, "but the neighborhood there got old, the park got run down, the housing projects got tough. They chased me away. I don't know how many times my office was broken into. My market was moving away from me. Baseball is like the fast-food business; you've got to go with your market and that market today is in the suburbs."

Being in Birmingham made me appreciate Chattanooga's sanc-
tum for Joe Engel all the more. But the old parks were dying fast
across the country and the facilities that replaced them were soul-
less things, look-alike concrete doughnuts that were as appropriate
for rock concerts and football as they were for baseball. They were
called stadiums, not parks or fields, and were usually named for
municipalities instead of people. Their outfield dimensions didn't
vary much, and they had none of the odd features—who could
imagine Fenway Park without its Green Monster, Wrigley Field
without its ivy walls or the Atlanta Crackers' Ponce de Leon Field
(where a Sears store now stands) without its magnolia tree in center
field?—that had once stamped each ballpark with its own personality.

In the early days, when ballparks were built downtown, their
shapes were determined by the presence of existing apartment
houses, businesses and warehouses. Some were crammed so tightly
into their surroundings that in 1884 baseball set its first distance
rule, mandating that outfield fences had to be at least 210 feet from
home plate. Because there were obstacles and strange shapes and
varying dimensions—baseball is the only sport whose field mea-
surements aren't standardized—managers fashioned teams to take
advantage of their park's characteristics, perhaps concentrating on
speed and defense in spacious Engel Stadium and on power in the
bandbox parks of the crowded North.

Those first ballparks symbolized America's transformation from
seventeenth-century Puritanism, which considered popular recreation frivolous, to the industrialization of the eighteenth century,
which wanted freedom from the factory and the pleasures of shared
leisure. Baseball surpassed horse racing and boxing as the nation's
most popular spectator sport in the latter half of the nineteenth
century, and its parks became an expression of the city itself, just
as today's stadiums reflect contemporary society, with concrete
edifices anchoring huge parking lots reachable via roadways that
have been McDonaldized.

Jim Dow poked around Hoover Metropolitan Stadium, but
didn't take any photographs. He had made arrangements with
Birmingham's recreation department to open Rickwood Field for
him the next morning and invited me to go along. So I decided

to spend an extra night in Birmingham and returned to a mammoth shopping mall that had been my home for two days. It was Sunday. The Barons were on the road. The bars were closed. The mall was locked up. The multiacre parking lot was empty. The pay phone I tried to call Sandy on didn't work. Bothered by my aloneness for the first time in weeks, I opened a can of beef stew and went to sleep reading Neil Sheehan's *A Bright Shining Lie,* remembering Vietnam and forgetting to turn off my radio. The next morning as the mall's army of workers was arriving for duty I awoke to find Forty-niner's battery dead and its right front tire leaking air.

"I wouldn't be leaving your van on the street if I was you," the man from the recreation department said, unlocking Rickwood Field's wire gate. "Better to park in here where it'll be safe, then I'll lock up behind you."

He swung open the gate, and Forty-niner, its battery now recharged and its tire inflated, eased into the empty ballpark. The green paint on the façade outside was peeling and smeared with graffiti—"Tameka + Arriel Was Here," one scrawled message informed—and the lettering had started to chip away on the sign that said HOME OF BARONS BASEBALL. I parked in the shade of a dark concourse whose wall was decorated with nine white flags. Each bore a year, from 1906 to 1983, commemorating one of the Barons' championships.

Rickwood Field was low and airy with a single deck and a wooden outfield fence. It opened in August 1910, just hours after construction was completed, and ten thousand fans showed up that afternoon for the Barons' game against Montgomery, walking and riding the streetcars to the park that had replaced Slag Pile Field down by the Alabama Great Southern Railroad tracks. This, they thought, was the first step in bringing major league baseball to Birmingham, and Rickwood had been designed so it could be expanded to meet big-league standards.

The Barons' roster included right fielder Bob "The Speed Merchant" Messenger of Farmingdale, Maine, who, the program said, "in the off-season usually runs a foot race with a deer before breakfast just for exercise." There was also a catcher from Rock Island, Illinois—Harold "Rowdy" Elliott: "Another year's seasoning will fit him for the majors, and here's a prediction that there will be a merry scramble to land him." And Harry Coveleski from Shamoykin, Pennsylvania, who had pitched for the Philadelphia Nationals, beaten New York three times in a single week, and forever more been known as Harry the Giant Killer.

Dow set up his camera in left field, resting his tripod in grass the city still cut every week as though the Barons were only away on a road trip. The advertising signs on the outfield fence behind him had survived two winters and urged me to eat at Arby's, stay at the Radisson Hotel and buy at Jim Burke's Buick. I wandered into the home-team clubhouse and found a light that worked. Bare lockers lined the wall like skeletons. A cardboard box full of athletic tape and cans of shaving cream and a discarded baseball shoe sat on the trainer's table. By the light switch was a note from manager Rico Petrocelli, saying that batting practice would be at 5:00 P.M.

I sat for a long time in the bleachers, thunderclouds swirling overhead, and let the ghosts come floating back. The stands filled and I could see blurry faces in the red rooftop press box across the field. Lumbering Walt Dropo stood between home and first, watching his soaring drive clear the clock in deepest center. . . . There was Babe Ruth rounding second with mincing steps, his ball settling in a moving freight train that did not stop until it got to Nashville, two hundred miles away. It was said to be the longest home run ever hit. . . . Norm Zauchin chasing down a foul ball, crashing over the railing at first and landing in the lap of a fan named Janet Mooney, whom two years later he would marry. . . . And at short, bending low in anticipation of the pitch, my brother Ernie, who had always wanted to play pro ball but never did. He was as lean and graceful as I had remembered him before the fatal accident on the Maine Turnpike; at the crack of the bat, he was gliding to his left, and, in one fluid motion, gathering up the ball and throwing out the runner by a stride at first. From somewhere in the grandstands a solitary voice called out, "Thataway to play, Ernie!"

Baseball ended its seventy-eight-year run at Rickwood Field on a rainy September night in 1987, when, at 10:54 P.M., Rondal Rollin—the Barons' all-time home run hitter—swung and missed on a third strike in his last at bat in baseball. Before the game and before every other game for as long as anyone could remember, the Barons' starting lineup was written on a chalk board for the fans to see as they went through the turnstiles. I walked over by the shuttered concession stands. The board was still there, the names as distinct as if they had been chalked in yesterday: "Pino, 2b; Bertolani, ss; Thomas, rf; Rollin, lf . . ."

Vandals had left their calling cards everywhere in Rickwood Field, defacing walls and snatching up whatever they could carry away, but the epitaph of the final game had been spared without so much as a mark to smudge the names of those last nine men. It was as if even vandals recognized the sanctity of baseball's past.

In the days of segregation, when the Barons went on the road, Rickwood Field became the home of the black Barons. The team drew well, as did the black Lookouts and most of the clubs in the old Negro leagues, whose rosters held players of major league superstar quality. "If I'd been pitching to Ruth and Gehrig," said Satchel Paige, who didn't get to the majors until he was forty, "you could have knocked a few points off those big lifetime batting averages."

But baseball did not lead the country in matters of race, it followed, and ballparks were as much a symbol of racial inequality as were park benches. As recently as 1966 the (white) Barons had to leave Birmingham for a year and play their schedule in Mobile. The reason: city ordinance did not allow blacks and whites to play together. The Barons returned the next season after the ordinance was scrapped and a black outfielder named Reggie Jackson led them to the pennant.

The fact that black teams had drawn so well, that an exhibition game starring Jackie Robinson would bring out a full house of blacks, interested me because at no minor league game, in the North or South, did I see any more than a handful of blacks in the stands. Nor did I see a single black in any front office, except for a receptionist with the Las Vegas Stars; in fact, as far as I could determine, there were no black executives in the minors, period, even at the lowliest levels. Black managers were almost as rare and were nonexistent above the Double-A level.

The Atlanta Braves, for instance, had eight minor league clubs and a farm director, Hank Aaron, who was among the most outspoken critics of baseball's white monopoly. Yet Aaron, the last great graduate of the Negro Leagues, had appointed no black managers and only three of his seventeen coaches were black. Part of the reason may have been that Aaron was not a man for detail and didn't spend a great deal of time at his job. Asked by a friend why he never seemed to be in the office, he replied, "Why should I be for what they pay me?"

Curiously, while major league clubs had been under great pressure to increase their minority representation (which by 1989 had reached 9 percent in the front office and 15 percent on the field), the whiteness of the minors wasn't even an issue. Their games weren't on television, their teams weren't located in media capitals or political power centers, their collective decisions drew only local attention. What happened in Tidewater or Dunedin or Batavia didn't really matter from a national perspective, and as long as attendance was up and profits were good, the last group that intended to rock the boat by challenging long-standing inequities was the minor leagues themselves.

I asked a lot of people about the minor leagues' racial imbalance and was surprised how many, including black players, said they hadn't noticed it. When someone did offer an explanation, it usually dealt with economics: Why would a black college graduate want to start his career as a four-hundred-dollar-a-month intern in Kenosha when he had so many better opportunities? Why would a black athlete choose playing in poverty and obscurity in Pulaski or Wytheville over a basketball or football scholarship at a prestigious university? Why would a black family of six spend its limited discretionary income going to a ball game when it had so many other choices?

Each point had merit, but I think other forces were at work, for baseball culturally is marketed to a white male audience. General managers drum up support in the off-season with speeches at Rotary and Lions lunches but wouldn't know where to find the heart of the black business community. The signs on outfield walls advertise white-owned companies, and a white player is more likely than a black to grace the cover of a team's annual souvenir program.

Newspaper ads for special promotion nights—free helmets, bats or whatever—are placed in the sports section, a section few women read. But who makes the decision on how a family will spend its leisure time in the increasingly predominant one-parent black household of the inner city?

Calvin Griffith was once nearly run out of Minneapolis when he owned the Twins for saying that blacks don't support baseball. He was, of course, right, at least in terms of numbers at the ballpark. But what seems unusual is that an industry as pervasive as baseball doesn't know why. Nabisco, I'm sure, can tell you who eats Wheat Thins and Procter & Gamble knows who brushes with Crest, but baseball has no idea who comes to its parks, why they come (or don't come), when they decide to come, where they come from, what they want to find once they get there, or whether they liked being there. It doesn't know because it never bothered to ask. Baseball, after all, is the national pastime and, the reasoning goes, its draw is mystical and beyond the realm of ordinary market surveys. The premise is a dangerous one if baseball expects to compete for leisure dollars in the decades ahead.

One explanation for the absence of blacks was offered by a white postgraduate college student at Engel Stadium who was studying the demographics of Lookout fans: "This isn't racist because I've got black friends and white friends, and I know whites who are trash and blacks who are trash, but a lot of the Negroes are stupid, and they'd rather stay home and fuck and drink. They look on this as whitey's park."

Another explanation came from an old man I saw every night in Chattanooga, sitting on the top row of the grandstands with a cluster of elderly blacks. "I've been coming out here fifty years, since the days all us coloreds had to be over there, in the left-field seats, and there was a special gate for us to come in at. Does my grandson come out? No. No, he don't. He says he got other things going on. Myself, I can't understand it, but that's what he says. He says, 'Gran'pappy, what I want to go out there and sit with those old people for?' "

Chapter Eleven

We've overblown sports in this country. We've made
them bigger than they should be, the overemphasis on
winning, the puffing up of false images, the lying. It's like
in ancient Rome, when the circuses were more important
than life itself.

—FRANK LAYDEN, *on retiring as coach of the*
NBA's Utah Jazz

Every two weeks or so I'd ob-
serve what came to be known as Maintenance Day. This was
quality time and I would plan it carefully, scouring *Trailer Life
Campground & RV Services Directory* for a good place to spend a
couple of days. A typical listing would say something like: "RAIN-
BOW PALM PARK. Level grassy flatlands. 107 gravel sites, 35 ft avg
width, some shaded, full hookups (20 amp). FACILITIES: Restrooms
& Showers, dump station, pay phone, laundry, limited groceries,
ice, RV supplies, LP gas, BBQ. RECREATION: Catfish fishing, shuf-
fleboard, horseshoes. Last year's rates: $10 to $11. MC, Visa." The
campgrounds were huddled along the heavily traveled routes like
twentieth-century stagecoach stops, and they offered a welcome
respite from the dusty road.

Checking in was similar to registering at a motel, except that you
asked for a "space" instead of a "room." The clerk would then
inquire if you wanted full hookups, which was similar to someone

at a motel saying, "Do you want water and electricity in your room?" I would always say yes, because it was nice to turn on my lights and air conditioner without having to run the noisy generator, and hooking into the park's water supply meant that I didn't have to deplete my own tanks. The offices usually closed about 8:00 P.M. and anyone arriving after that checked in on the honor system: You took any vacant space and paid in the morning, a practice that might have produced some interesting results for Holiday Inn or Great Western.

The campground I found on a nameless stretch of road south of Birmingham was particularly good. It was set against a stream and had a large truck stop across the highway, where I could tend to Forty-niner's minor ailments and get him vacuumed and scrubbed. (It may have been my imagination, but his engine ran smoother after he had been washed.) Maintenance Days, though, were mostly for me. By the time I declared them my provisions were running low, my laundry bag had grown to unmanageable proportions, and I had begun dreaming of standing under a hot shower, instead of pressing myself against the wall of Forty-niner's tiny bathroom, holding overhead a nozzle that trickled chilly water. Then, too, there were my notebooks. They needed periodic emptying into my laptop computer, and if I didn't take care of the chore faithfully, I would find myself wondering. Now, let's see. Was it in Memphis or Little Rock that that happened?

Although truckers and RVers have different missions and don't mix much, I found myself drawn to the truck stop across the highway. The twenty-four-hour restaurant specialized in biscuits, mashed potatoes and hamburger steak swimming in heavy brown gravy ($4.95 on the dinner special) and had a large store of supplies, including a display of paperback books, all of which had been written by Louis L'Amour. Normally the truckers did not strike up conversation with me, preferring the company of fellow drivers to that of some tenderfoot in a pea-sized pleasure craft. But if I sat at the counter wearing my cowboy boots and the Barons baseball cap Art Clarkson had given me—attire that vaguely identified me as a trucker—conversation came easily and my advice would be sought on road conditions and the cheapest place to buy diesel fuel.

The parking lot behind the restaurant was fenced off in an attempt to control the access of prostitutes and drug dealers. It was the size of two or three football fields and by midnight would be filled with several hundred trucks. They would sit there, headlights off, their shapes dimly outlined by marker lights, the rumble of their idling engines shaking the night as though an armada of tanks was assembling for combat.

On the CB, strangers whose lives passed in the darkness at 60 mph found unseen, unnamed friends, shared intimate secrets, then moved on, switching channels, until a new voice and a new friend were within radio range. It was a friendship without risk or commitment.

"This is Horny Devil and this story's the truth," said a voice that could have come from the parking lot or out on the highway, "I was in a cathouse the other night. They charged by the half inch, and it cost me thirty bucks. Ronnie was with me and I heard he only run his bill up to seventy-five cents."

"Horny Devil?" said a woman. "Not often you get to talk to someone with that handle."

"Nope. I believe I'm the only one around. The handle used to be Preacher Boy, but I changed it 'cause there was too many people using that name."

"Where you at? Is that you over there in the red rig?"

"Nope. I'm sitting up here, third row back, with the interior lights on. I got air conditioning and a double bunk you can stand up in. You might want to come over and give me a back rub before I get moving. Gotta go in about thirty minutes."

"I appreciate that offer, Horny Devil, I really do. But I've got to be in Tallahassee by breakfast, so I'm just going to sleep here for a couple of hours before. . . ."

He interrupted her in an excited voice. "My God, there's a pretty truck! The one just pulling in. The red, white and blue Peterbilt. Look at that beautiful shine."

"Yup, that's pretty all right. I'll tell you, someone asked me one time, 'If you was to have your own truck, what would you have?' What I'd want is a baby-blue-powder truck with a picture of an Indian maiden on one side and a cowgirl on the other. And I'd want a double bunk system, air conditioning, and I'd want it to have a long nose. Not too long, though, and not too short. Just a pretty nose, a real pretty nose."

"Yeah, I heard that, Cowgirl. I'm going down to Florida, too, so maybe we'll do that back rub down there. How'll I know you?"

"You can't miss me. I'm the white Ford cab-over with marker lights that light me up like a Christmas tree."

After two days, my life was back in order—notebooks empty, laundry done, cabinets restocked, Forty-nine refreshed—and I entered God's Waiting Room through the rear door, following Route 231 that sneaks out of Alabama and slips into Florida just north of a town called Cottondale. My memories of Florida were mostly of escaping the University of Maine's snowed-in campus during spring vacation to party until exhaustion in Fort Lauderdale, so mentally I wasn't quite prepared for the gruesome heat and humidity of Florida's summer or for a place where a FOR SALE sign on a home led to the immediate assumption that the occupant had died.

Aging and tourism were Florida's most important industries, though drug smuggling provided much of its capital investment. Except along the borders of Alabama and Georgia, the Old South was gone and Florida was a land of exiles: farmers from the Midwest, poor Jews from New York, drug dealers, Cubans, retirees, sunbirds who sought refuge in communities with names like Frostproof and Paradise Isle. The influx of migrants had left Florida with a middle class of limited productivity and transformed a once rural backwater into the country's fourth most densely populated state.

Baseball happened twice each year in Florida. First, there was spring training for the majors, which brought $300 million into the state and, for six weeks, employed 8 percent of its work force; then, in early April, the seventy-year-old Class-A Florida State got down to business, taking over the ballparks vacated by the major league clubs. The league, though, was but the echo of spring training, and fans who had seen Don Mattingly and Nolan Ryan in March were distinctly blasé about the likes of Ken Luckham and Doug Duke in June. When Roger Angell called baseball the Summer Game, he could not have been thinking of Florida.

So oppressive were the evenings that teams often had to cancel batting practice and do their pregame stretching in the air-conditioned clubhouse rather than on the diamond, where heat waves radiated off the artificial turf like pillars of steam. Players wore double layers of socks to protect their feet from blisters, and pitchers seldom threw more than sixty or seventy pitches before their managers showed mercy and sent them off to a cold shower. Catchers sometimes lost ten pounds in a game, and when fans stood for the seventh-inning stretch, their seats would bear sweat tattoos shaped like buttocks.

Just the same, players and farm directors counted the Florida State League among the best in baseball. It was the only nonrookie league whose teams were all within one state, meaning that travel was less expensive and less demanding, and its fields were maintained to major league standards in preparation for the annual return of spring training. But everything that made baseball a fan's game in places like El Paso and Chattanooga—an old park, a relationship between town and team, crazy outfield dimensions— was alien to Florida. All the teams were named after their major league affiliates, the parks' outfield distances were nearly identical and more than half the clubs had been in the league for five years or less. Somehow the Osceola Astros and the Charlotte Rangers just didn't inspire much wonderment.

The headquarters for the minors—the National Association of Professional Baseball Leagues—is in Florida, on the bayfront at St. Petersburg. Since its humble beginnings in 1901, when the seven league presidents got together in Chicago to prevent player raids by the majors, the NAPBL has grown into the world's largest professional sports organization, overseeing an industry that generates $200 million a year and has over four thousand athletes working in Mexico, Canada and the United States. Yet, largely because of its dependence on the big leagues for players and subsidies, the association has surprisingly little power and has traditionally been the majors' obedient stepson, responding when spoken to with polite yes, sirs, and no, sirs. If the minors ever got too uppity, they would awake one morning to find that the majors had cut off their noses.

The relationship between the majors and minors is testy at best, a marriage of necessity. Many major league executives don't know the names, much less the faces, of the men who own and run their minor league affiliates. The California Angels don't even invite them over to the general manager's suite for a drink during base-ball's annual winter meetings and offer no apologies for ignoring them. (It's worth noting that the Los Angeles Dodgers host a sit-down dinner for their minor league people at the meetings, and it's no coincidence that a position in the Dodgers' "family" is one of the most sought after in baseball.)

During the summer of my journey the San Francisco Giants became increasingly concerned that the ownership of their Mid-west League affiliate, the Clinton Giants, wasn't spending sufficient funds to maintain a first-class operation. San Francisco dispatched vice president Al Nelson to Iowa to meet with Clinton's manage-ment. Nelson, no doubt sensing this was the time to make a good organizational impression, took everyone to lunch—at Taco Bell.

Predictably enough, the source of the mutual distrust between the majors and minors is money, mixed with a bit of snobbery. Major league clubs each spend around $7 million a year on their scouting and farm systems, which at today's rates gets you not much more than a couple of thirty-eight-year-old Dave Winfields for a season. But they consider the minors ingrates, already on a generous dole, and they keep wondering if it wouldn't be a lot cheaper to abolish the low-classification leagues and let each orga-nization put its young players in one Florida complex, where it could run three or four games a day throughout the season. "That would teach those hicks some manners," said one major league executive, only half in jest. For their part, the minors see the majors shelling out millions of dollars for drug rehabs and sore-armed pitchers who couldn't win a pennant for the Billings Mustangs. "Wait a minute," they say. "Let's split up this fat baseball pie equitably."

The minors' hole card is TV money—which, in their own greed, they signed away rights to when life wasn't quite so prosperous. The agreement that governs the informal relationship between the majors and minors still contains a provision written in the early days of television: No big-league team can televise its games within fifty miles of a minor league team's game. Thus a Cincinnati Reds game could not have been broadcast into Columbus while the Clippers were at home. But minor league schedules frequently aren't completed until February, which made it difficult for the networks to sell major league airtime to advertisers who plan months in advance. So the minors traded their blackout rights for a slice of TV revenues. That slice, referred to as "special compensation" by the majors and "hush money" by the minors, is worth twenty-five thousand dollars a year to each Triple-A club, and about eleven thousand by the time it trickles down to a Single-A team. It didn't sound like a bad deal for the minors in the days when a major league team got thirty-five thousand dollars a year from television. Today each receives $15 million.

I stopped off at the NAPBL offices, my clothes clinging to me as though I had just stepped out of a shower. Compared with the major leagues, where Commissioner Fay Vincent, a Yale Law School graduate and the former president of Columbia Pictures, works out of a palatial seventeenth-story office on New York's Park Avenue and earns $450,000 a year, the minors' setup is modest and unpretentious. Its ground-floor office is in the remodeled clubhouse of the old Al Lang Field, and its president, Sal Artiaga, who makes seventy-five thousand dollars a year, is the product of a working-class life. He had labored as a youth in the lettuce fields of the Southwest and the humblest jobs in minor league baseball and had told friends many times, "I don't want to ever fail." His parents were descended from New Mexico's early Spanish and Portuguese settlers. His father was a draftsman and plumber, his mother a doctor's secretary. After high school, where he was voted the friendliest student in his class, Artiaga took his first job in baseball, as assistant general manager (a euphemism in the minors for gofer) for the El Paso Diablos, at a hundred dollars a week. Aggressive, serious and occasionally hot-tempered, he worked his way over two decades through the Cincinnati Reds organization and up to the minor leagues' top elected job. As NAPBL administrator in 1987, Artiaga ran the association while his predecessor and close friend, Johnny Johnson, was dying of cancer. Artiaga was the only person, other than the immediate family, that Johnson let visit at his bedside. "After he died . . . if I had to go dig ditches for the rest of my life, I had no qualms with that," Artiaga told an interviewer. "Because I felt that I did the best I could under the circumstances."

· · ·

There were fourteen teams in the Florida State League, and the one that piqued my curiosity was the Baseball City Royals, outside Orlando. Any town named Baseball City could be no ordinary place, and when I approached the stadium at noon—seven hours before the Royals were to play the Dunedin Blue Jays—I was surprised to find the huge field that served as a parking lot already teeming with vans and pitched tents and wandering herds of fans. Well, why not? I reasoned. This was, after all, Baseball City and the Royals were locked in a heated pennant race with the Lakeland Tigers. The parking-lot attendant was a wholesome-looking young man, and I asked him where I should park Forty-niner.

"Welcome, brother," he said. "Are you here for Jesus?"

"I beg your pardon."

"Are you here for Jesus? The Jesus Festival?"

I recovered quickly and said, yes, I was just in from California, fearing I would be banished if I admitted otherwise. I parked next to a blue tent where a family of four sat on a blanket, reading the Bible, and rechecked my *Baseball America's Directory* I had not misread the schedule; the game with Dunedin was to start at 7:05 P.M. I made my way over to the Royals front office, passing people whose T-shirts read, "Love God, Hate Sin" and "God's Love Is Deep." Normally minor league parks are very informal. If I arrived well before game time, I could just wander in through open gates and I never needed press credentials. But the sign on the Royals' plate-glass window said, MEDIA MUST SIGN IN. No sooner had I done so than someone ordered me to put out my cigarette and someone else fastened on me one of those wristbands that patients wear in a hospital. "Don't remove this for any reason," the man said. "You'll need it for admittance." He went on: "We have some of the top entertainers in the world playing here. Carmen is tonight and Mike Cavanaugh is speaking on 'God and the Single Adult.' If you'd like to interview them, we can arrange it and get you a media escort."

The man had never heard of the Royals and said he didn't think the stadium was used for baseball anymore. I walked out into the grandstands, utterly perplexed. Black drapes were being hung over the Miller Lite scoreboard, a stage was going up in center field, and the clubhouse had been turned into a shower room, serving men and women on alternating shifts. If I had not found a chubby little groundskeeper wearing a baseball cap, who told me what was going on, I might have been disoriented forever: The Body of Christ had rented the ballpark and the Royals had headed up the interstate to play their weekend series in Daytona. The team didn't have any hometown fans anyway, he said, so probably no one but me had been inconvenienced. That was my first clue that I had landed with baseball's most bizarre franchise.

Several thousand families from around the country had converged on Baseball City for the Jesus Festival. I took down the BEWARE OF DOG! sign I had posted on Forty-niner's door to discourage thieves, thinking it both unnecessary and inappropriate in my present setting. This was a gathering where you didn't see a beer can, smell a joint, hear a cuss word or pass a stranger without saying hello. I walked into the seven-thousand-seat stadium that evening and sat in the stands, eating a Nathan's hot dog. I had come to Baseball City expecting to see Jeff Conine at first, Dave Howard at short and Francisco Laureano at second; what I found instead was Jesus at every position. Legions of kids sprawled across the infield, listening to Josh McDowell tell how his commitment to Christianity had helped him overcome stuttering, teachers who beat him in the second grade for using his left hand, an alcoholic father and an inferiority complex.

"I used to think God expected me to be perfect," he said from the stage, located in front of the camouflaged Miller Lite sign. "Then I realized he didn't call me to be perfect. He called me to be obedient."

Jesus was big business in Baseball City and most of McDowell's thirty books and fifty-five audio tapes were on sale at the vendors' tables outside the stadium. So were hundreds of other items—T-shirts (Be A Soulwinner) for $8, rubber stamps (Stamp Your Mail for Jesus) for $5, bumper stickers (Jesus Hits a Homer Every Time) for $3, buttons, games, books, caps, records, posters, earrings and key chains.

"The first time I heard Josh McDowell was last year and he blew me away," said a red-haired girl, who had just bought two of his books. "The nice thing is he doesn't keep any of the money. He gives it all away."

When the vendors shut down their booths sometime after midnight, they just walked away, not bothering to secure their merchandise. This was a theft-free society. I went back to Forty-niner, drew the curtains tight and, feeling wicked, poured a stiff whiskey. Except for the blue tent next to me, I had parked in an open expanse of field to ensure an easy exit. Throughout the night I could hear cars arriving and the *tap, tap, tap* of hammers pounding tent pegs into the ground. I awoke the next morning in a sea of tents and cars and sleeping bags that rendered me immobile.

The Jesus people packed up Sunday morning, and the Royals returned that night. Their new $15 million stadium was the winter home of the American League's Kansas City Royals, and the junior Royals liked playing in a park of major league caliber, even if their fans rooted for the visitors as often as not and reporters seldom showed up to cover their games, Baseball City having no newspaper. Most of the players were no longer distracted by the rattling *whooosh* and bloodcurdling screams that emanated from behind home as the roller coaster flashed by every ten or fifteen minutes.

What made this franchise so peculiar was that the Royals were part of an amusement park, a team without a town because Baseball City wasn't a city at all. It consisted of a couple of motels, including a Great Western that Ted Williams had just bought, several family-style restaurants, a truck stop, two gas stations, one street named Home Run Boulevard, but no homes and no post office. The big attraction was something called Boardwalk and Baseball, which brought together in one Disneyland-sized complex a minor league baseball team, a miniature Hall of Fame with memorabilia borrowed from Cooperstown and thirty rides, ranging from a mile-long roller coaster (which Michael Jackson rode for hours on end when he would rent the entire park at night) to an old-fashioned carousel.

The owner of this quirky combination was the publishing company Harcourt Brace Jovanovich, Inc. It believed that baseball and boardwalk amusement parks had a related appeal, drawing on nostalgic images of rural America and the cotton-candy aroma of bygone summers, and thus considered the marriage a natural one. For twenty dollars you could spend the day at the park and in the evening take in a game without extra charge. The Royals didn't assign seats at the stadium or sell season tickets and never could quite figure out if the fans on a particular evening had come out to ride a Ferris wheel or see a ball game.

(Because visiting clubs don't share in gate receipts, as they do in the majors, home teams often take liberties with their attendance figures in the minors, hyping them substantially. The higher numbers enabled them to charge advertisers more for a spot in the program or on the outfield wall. But the larger the numbers, the more the insurance companies wanted for their premiums.)

I stayed for the Sunday-night game after the Jesus people's departure and it was a good one, with the Clearwater Phillies winning 8–6 in eleven innings. About 250 fans were on hand and they clapped politely when Bobby Moore cleared the bases with a triple in the fifth for the Royals, but otherwise didn't show much emotion. The Royals remained in first place despite the loss, which meant that general manager Karl Rogozenski had to once again deliver on his promise to manager Luis Silverio and the two coaches: free pizzas after every game the Royals were on top in the Central Division in the Florida State League.

The next morning I checked several local papers looking for an account of the game. None carried any mention of it. But they all had prominent stories about another Florida child being shot accidentally by a handgun. A different child had been killed or wounded every day I was in Florida, and at first I thought I was reading the same story over and over again. The latest victim was four-year-old Evie Hagan, whose brother had been playing with his father's gun. The bullet remained lodged in her brain stem, and her parents had spent Sunday at her bedside and had attended two church services. A reporter asked Evie's father if he still thought it was wise to keep guns at home. He said yes: "I'm a true-blooded American and I do not feel like it's right for us to take weapons away from people."

Chapter Twelve

Our deeds follow us, and what we have been makes us
what we are.

—SHAKESPEARE

Charleston is to a Southerner
what Jerusalem is to a Muslim or Jew—a spiritual capital. Gentile
and gracious, it is the embodiment of the Old South. The planta-
tions and aristocracy and stately mansions predating the Civil War
all are comforting reminders that the Miamis and Atlantas are but
orphans of the Southern soul, and as if to make the point, Charleston's people seem to stroll, not walk, and steep their accents in vats
of honey. The city is crowded into a peninsula, bounded by two
rivers and a harbor, and it was here, in 1946, that black workers
adopted from a white Baptist hymnal a theme song for their strike
against the tobacco industry, "We Shall Overcome."

I poked along up Florida's Atlantic coastline and arrived at
College Park in Charleston on an afternoon so blistering that even
the magnolias looked drained of life. The Rainbows' general manager, Kevin Carpenter, dressed in shorts and a T-shirt and
drenched with sweat, was on a ladder in center field, replacing

bulbs in the scoreboard. "I ought to be done up here in an hour, if the heat doesn't kill me first," he called down. Carpenter, who was twenty-five, had been at his job long enough to know there was no executive privilege in the low minors: general managers counted the night's receipts, put toilet paper in the men's room, and helped spread the tarpaulin when it rained; assistant GMs sold advertising space in the scorecard, then sometimes had to walk through the stands selling the scorecard, too; concession managers cooked hot dogs and any owner worth his salt knew how to take tickets, pound down a pitcher's mound and handle a broom.

The Rainbows in recent years had been best known around the Sally League for having an abundance of twenty-five-cent beer nights (with free tickets on Saturdays) and a plenitude of drunken fans, most of whom sat behind third base giving each other beer showers. Families were no more likely to show up for an evening at the park than they were at the local tavern. It got so rowdy that South Carolina revoked the Rainbows' liquor license, and with that, the drunks stayed away as well. Carpenter's job was to put the Charlestonian civility back in College Park.

Discount beer nights were gone, and the Rainbows had begun a Good Sport campaign, sponsored by Anheuser-Busch, the beer company. Good Sports, the program reminded fans, wore shirts and shoes, never used bad language and knew when it was time to drink a Pepsi instead of a beer. In little more than a year College Park had been transformed, and the wolves in the third-base grandstands had sobered up and become the guardians of decency; if someone's language got foul, a fan wearing a Good Sport button would say, "There's no cussing allowed in the park," and the offender would fall obediently silent. Try that in the bleachers of Boston's Fenway Park, and the fan with the button would be bounced on his head down the concrete steps, but in the folksy setting of the minor league South, a call to rectitude still stirred an old-fashioned community response.

The park was not crowded my first night in Charleston, and I found a seat behind home plate, a few rows from the wives of the half-dozen married Rainbows. Being a minor league wife, I had decided, was the toughest job in baseball. They lived with another's dream, so distant in Class-A cities like Charleston and Savannah and Sumter that it seemed little more than a fantasy. Unlike their husbands, they accepted, even expected, the prospect of failure, and what they saw in the years ahead was not stardom and mega-buck contracts but merely another season in another city, another five-month tour of duty without a job or a conversation unrelated to baseball or a paycheck big enough to raise a family on.

There was, to be sure, a certain pride in coming through the pass gate, dressed more for a Long Island cocktail party than a ballpark, and hearing someone say, "She's a ballplayer's wife," but that was a shaky foundation on which to build a life and an identity. Still, there wasn't a "baseball wife"—a term of reverence players use to describe the most loyal of camp followers—who would demand that her husband quit before he had played out his fantasy and ridden the dream as far as it would carry him.

"You tell people what you do and they envy you," said Carmen Murdock, whose husband, Joe, had attended Southern Arizona University and was off to a 5–0 start with the Rainbows. "That's the funny thing. They think you've got a great life and actually it's pretty horrid. You're in places you don't want to be and you're not paid enough to survive. The average salary here is what, a thousand a month? But the apartment and renting furniture cost four hundred. Then the husbands come home like kids with dirty laundry every day and you can spend eight dollars a week just on washing."

Her friend Laura Tucker said, "I thought like everyone else at first: How lucky we are. Then we got the first paycheck." Laura was eight months pregnant, her husband, Vance, had an earned run average that nearly matched his shoe size, and the Tuckers were dipping into their savings to meet expenses. "We're paying to be here," she said.

"The only thing I don't like is the insecurity," said Beth Lester, the wife of player-coach Jimmy Lester. "They can release you to-morrow if they want. They just sent four players down to Spokane last week, and you know it has to go through every player's mind, That could have been me."

"You do think about that: Are we going to be here tomorrow?" Laura said. "You know the chances aren't very good of even getting out of the minors. And if you do make it to the majors, how long are you going to last? Of course, if Vance ever makes a million, I take back everything I said."

"I went out to a picnic at our apartment the other day," Carmen said. "I was sitting there at the pool with a bunch of people. Just to talk to someone who didn't talk about baseball was so refreshing. They were discussing other things and I said, 'Wow, there is another world out there besides baseball.' "

For the Rainbows' seventy-two home-game schedule, Carmen Murdock would observe the unwritten Code of Conduct for Minor League Wives: She would serve a hot meal at midnight when Joe got home from College Park, allow him to fidget around the apartment half the night, switching the cable TV dial incessantly in search of baseball, and rise the next morning in time to return to the park. She would attend every game (though players' wives seldom arrived before the first pitch), and she would remain stoic if fans booed or taunted Joe for a bad performance.

For several weeks Carmen had been saying, "Please let's do something, Joe, anything, different some morning. The beach. Visit a plantation. *Anything.*" Her husband finally relented one day I was in Charleston and said, "OK, wake me up at ten o'clock."

The next morning Carmen jumped out of bed, excited, and cooked a big breakfast. "Come on, honey," she said. "Breakfast's almost ready and we're going to the beach." It took a while before he responded: "What if I don't *want* to get up!" She set breakfast on the counter, where it soon grew cold, and stretched out on the sofa. "Oh, shoot," she said.

Joe arose at one o'clock, spent an hour reading the news from the Class-A leagues in *Baseball America* and left for his nine-hour shift at the ballpark.

"See you at the game, honey," his wife said.

Charleston was a special stop because it was one of the cities on my journey Sandy wanted to see, and she flew in from Los Angeles for a four-day weekend. She had never been taken with baseball and viewed the sport as I did fishing: It certainly looked boring but if that many people loved doing it, maybe they knew something I didn't. What Sandy saw when she looked at the field was nine men standing around, waiting for something to happen, and I suppose

I could understand her bewilderment. I tried to explain that there was so much going on, it was a wonder the pitches came as rapidly as they did, but that was like telling a tea drinker that coffee is a tastier beverage.

We went to a Rainbows' game Sandy's first night in Charleston. In fact, she insisted we go. She wanted to share what she could of my summer, as we both were aware that the little universe I had fallen into pulled us in different directions, and she was delighted when I said we were staying at the Howard Johnson motel—in the parking lot. She brought a bagful of the past month's mail and pictures from home and greetings from old friends, and we lounged about Forty-niner as though it had always been our home.

Sandy had joined me earlier in Tucson and would later catch up with me in Montana. These times were my holidays in a vacation. I would put away my notebook and leave the ballpark behind me and we would slip away as tourists to explore old Charleston and wander down the road to Savannah. When I took Sandy back to the airport, I always wished not that I was going home with her but that she was staying with me, here on the road.

The only other place I ever felt as attached to as I now did the highway was Woodstock, Vermont. Just after World War II, my parents bought, for ten thousand dollars, an old farmhouse there that sat on one hundred and fifty acres of meadows and forest. Woodstock was the most perfect New England town you could imagine. The country inn looked out on a village green and the boards on the covered bridges were brown with age. Charlie Clough's pharmacy had a soda fountain where the druggist himself made the sundaes, and Gillingham's sold a wondrous array of implements I had never seen in any city store, from peaveys to scythes. At first the locals viewed "the Lambs from Boston" with suspicion, because we were outsiders and the assumption was that anyone from a big city was probably not entirely trustworthy.

My brother Ernie, harboring major league dreams, hooked on with an informal baseball league that played once a week, on Sunday afternoons. The other players were farmers, and, Ernie's priorities being what they were, he could not understand why they cared more about their hay crops and how much milk their cows gave than they did about perfecting their rough-hewn baseball skills. "If I was the manager," he once said, "I'd tell them, 'I want every swinging dick on the field for practice as soon as your god-damned cows are milked.' " The field where Ernie's team played was on a wooded hill at the edge of Carl Lewis's farm and had been cleared and leveled and built by the local families during the eve-nings of a summer in the mid-fifties. It was the center of our community. We picnicked there on Sundays, before every game, a cluster of neighbors spread out on blankets, swatting ants and eating cucumber-and-onion sandwiches and talking about the weather. There were tall maples and pines behind home plate and if you ran too far in left field, you would disappear down a grassy knoll and into a pasture. The team held no practices and none of the players wore uniforms. As I recall, Ernie was the slickest fielder, and the forty-year-old catcher, Ora Lewis, who had one of the largest dairy herds in Prosper, was the most feared hitter.

Our Woodstock home was on a dirt road, a couple of miles from the hilltop ball field, and each morning I awaited with great anxiety the bearer of the previous day's baseball scores. The mailman's name was Hal Maynes, and he usually came by about 9:30 A.M., which was an intolerably long time to remain ignorant of Mil-waukee's pennant pursuit. The Braves had become a superb team in 1957, two years after my stint as the *Journal*'s teenage columnist. Their lineup included four future Hall of Famers—Warren Spahn, Eddie Mathews, Hank Aaron and Red Schoendienst—and a sup-porting cast with no apparent weakness.

I would see Maynes's green Jeep with its canvas sidings coming down the road, past the stone bridge that spanned a brook, and I would wait for him at the collection of six mailboxes. Without even being asked, he'd unwrap someone's *Rutland Herald* and turn to the sports page. Milwaukee was clinging precariously to first place in early August that year, and day after day the wire-service story of the Braves' game seemed to start with the heroics of a career minor leaguer who had just been called up to fill in for the injured Billy Burton: "Hurricane Bob Hazle homered in the tenth inning to give the Braves . . ." one story would say. Or, "Hurricane Bob Hazle's bases-loaded double rallied the Braves . . ."

"I've never heard of this guy," Maynes said one day. He turned off the ignition, something he did only on rare occasions. Standing by the Jeep's open door, I stuck my head over his shoulder so we could both see the *Herald*'s sports page. "But look at this. He won yesterday's game, too, with two homers against the Phillies. Who the heck is Hurricane Bob Hazle?"

Somewhere between Newberry and Joanna, a couple of hours out of Charleston, the road winds north through tired mill towns and hills of honeysuckle and kudzu. Bob Hazle reached down to the floorboard of his '82 Buick Regal for his mug of coffee, grown cold in the miles since home. He started singing softly to himself, accompanying The Platters on station WEZY:

> "You've got the magic touch. You make me glow so much.
> It casts a spell, it rings a bell, the magic touch. . . .
> Here I go reelin'.
> Oh, oh, I'm feelin' the glow,
> but where can I go from you?"

"That mist burns off and we're going to have a beautiful day," he said. Hazle was gray-haired and fifty-eight, only nine years my senior, though he had always seemed so much older when I was young. When I had called him from Charleston to introduce myself and ask if I could drop in for a day or two, he was reluctant. "Shoot," he said, "I'm just a back-roads whiskey salesman. You'd be wasting your time, really." But I was insistent, and now we were headed toward the little one-room liquor stores scattered through the South Carolina countryside where Hazle was born and raised and which he had never left except to serve in the army and play ball.

"This isn't a glorified job. It's just a living," said the man who led the Braves into the only World Series they would ever win in Milwaukee. "The same faces week after week, the same conversations, the same miles, it gets wearisome. But don't get me wrong. I like my work, even though you tell some people you're a whiskey salesman and they frown."

Hazle had achieved in his life what few of us ever will: for one brief shining moment he was the Hemingway of his profession. Then it was gone. His life became ordinary again, and he had to find contentment, or at least acceptance, in learning how to live with his blessings instead of his regrets. It was a lesson he understood well after a heart attack had nearly killed him in 1981: Forget what might have been and be thankful for what is.

"I woke up in intensive care when I was having the attack and I couldn't see any heartbeat on that machine I'm hooked up to," Hazle said. "I thought—this is crazy—'Lord, here I am. Here's Mr. Hazle.' They called in Mary Webb, the chaplain. 'Mary,' I said, 'don't worry about me. I believe.'

"The surgery changed my values. The first thing it taught me was the value of money, which is nothing. If you don't have your health, what good is all the money in the world? All of a sudden Pat and me found we didn't need all those things you're always buying and saving for.

"And I must say, I'm not the go-getter I was. I mean, I asked myself, what is this? You push yourself, all the time trying to meet quotas and get ahead, and you push yourself right into a heart attack. Well, I figure now, go ahead, do the best job you can. Take pride in what you're doing. But don't die for something that doesn't really matter."

Most of the privately owned liquor stores on Hazle's seven-hundred-mile route were hardly bigger than a rabbit's den. On an outside wall of each was painted a huge red dot, a mark intended to inform illiterates that the store dispensed alcohol. Hazle knew every owner along the way. He knew their ailments, their spouses' names, their favorite fishing holes, their golf handicaps. As soon as he set his foot inside their door, he was a man onstage, relaxed, attentive, a friend of Southern charm come to visit.

"Hey, Ray, what's up?" Hazle said, walking into J. R. King's in Clinton, his eyes instinctively sweeping the dark little shop to check the placement of his brands. "You're looking good today. You must have been out fishing this morning."

The shelves were stocked with Heaven Hill vodka, Fighting Cock bourbon, Red Rooster (The Wine for the 21st Century) and Thunderbird (The American Classic). Ray was dressed in bib overalls. He looked up from behind the cash register as he snuffed out his cigarette and said, "Sheeet."

"Ray, I know the Black Velvet's going good and you'll need

more of that. It's on special. I figure you're due for a big order today. I know you don't need the money."

"Sheeet," Ray said. "The price of whiskey's going up, taxes are going up, utilities going up. You ask me, inflation's coming back, too. I wouldn't be surprised to see it hit twelve or fourteen percent by the end of the year."

"Just do me a favor. Keep your eye on that Black Velvet. It can do it. It's getting hot."

Ray nodded and said, "Sheeet."

Hazel got back in his secondhand Buick. He allowed himself only one nonbusiness diversion on his Tuesday route and that was a cup of coffee in Newberry with John Carbosco, who ran Trader John's. The cluttered shop was full of old locks and guns and signs and antiques and also had an extensive baseball-card collection of players from South Carolina. Carbosco was pouring the coffee as we walked in. I asked if he had any Bob Hazle cards. He produced several wrapped in plastic, offered at one dollar each.

"Here's South Carolina's only .400 hitter," he said. "You want to know my opinion, Hurricane Hazle's one of the best ballplayers ever come out of these parts. Right up there with Lou Brissie."

Back in the forties, when Hazle was growing up in the Carolina hills, all the textile mills had baseball teams and most of the town would turn out for every game. If you were big and strong and fast afoot, the mills would give you a summer job and ask you to do not much more than stroke hits or throw strikes. Robert Sidney Hazle—six feet tall, 190 pounds—could bang the ball clear to Greenville. He was a mill reed-cleaner by day and a local hero by night, and after a winning hit, whiskey-breathed men with a twenty-dollar bill in their palms and a gambler's glint in their eyes would shake his hand and say, "Nice game, son."

Hazle—who had earned sixteen varsity letters in high school and been captain of the baseball, basketball and football teams his senior year—went on to play in the minors for the Cincinnati and Milwaukee organizations, but with a chipped anklebone, a wrenched knee and a history of being a first-ball streak hitter, he wasn't high on anyone's list of prospects. With Wichita in 1957, his seventh year in professional baseball, he had started the season in a horrible slump, then gotten hotter than a prairie fire. On July

The author at age fourteen (1955).
The portent of a life.

Author (left) and friend John
Sherman at Milwaukee Country
Stadium, 1959. Rescued by the
Cookie Lady.

Angel Delgadillo on abandoned Route 66. "We been bypassed."

SANDY NORTHROP

The author in Forty-niner during Maintenance Day.

Milwaukee Brewers' minor league spring-training clubhouse in Peoria, Arizona.

Spring training in Arizona.

The Ports' Bobby Jones, Steve Monson, Dan Fitzpatrick.

The Voice of the Stockton Ports, Buddy Meacham.

El Paso's Dudley Dome, where every night is a carnival.

Warren Spahn, the winningest left-hander in history.

Liquor-store owner Don Buddin, a former Boston Red Sox shortstop (left), and Hurricane Bob Hazle.

Hall of Famer Eddie Mathews: living life his way.

Chuck Tanner, at home in New Castle, Pennsylvania, for the first summer in forty-two years.

Former shortstop Johnny Logan, the only one of the original Braves who still calls Milwaukee home.

Miles Wolff, with good reason to smile. His Durham Bulls are among the top franchises in minor league baseball.

Steve Dalkowsky, "the fastest pitcher who ever lived."

Fred Koenig, manager of the Pulaski Braves.

The magic of the Salt Lake Trappers. From left, owner Van Schley, infielders J. D. Ramirez and Mike Grace, manager Barry Moss.

Shortstop Charlie Montoyo signs autographs at Billy Hebert
Field in Stockton.

Stockton Ports celebrate another division championship.

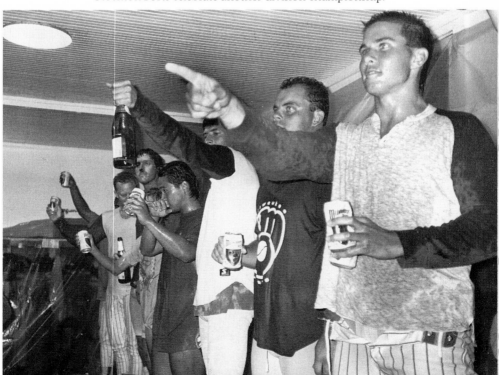

28, while the team was in Denver, his general manager walked up to Hazle at breakfast. "Pack your clothes," he said. "Milwaukee's just called you up."

"Tell me another joke," Hazle replied.

He flew out that night. "I promised myself one thing," he said. "That if I failed, it wasn't going to be for not trying." What the twenty-six-year-old rookie did to National League pitchers was roughly equivalent to what the tropical storm Hurricane Hazel had done to the South Carolina coastline in 1954—he destroyed what stood in his path. For eight fairy-tale weeks he was the mightiest slugger in baseball. With a bat borrowed from teammate Chuck Tanner, he won game after game with extra-base clutch hits. He couldn't explain what had happened. He wasn't doing anything differently and suddenly his touch was magic. The ball looked as big as a grapefruit as it floated toward the plate and seemed to spin so slowly he could discern every seam. There were moments he would wake up in the morning fearing he had been dreaming.

"I suppose he'll cool off," second baseman Red Schoendienst said as the Braves drew close to the pennant, "but right now this kid is Musial, Mantle and Williams all wrapped in one."

The Braves, who had let the 1956 pennant slip away on the final weekend of the season, led the National League by half a game on July 31, the day manager Fred Haney sent Hazle to right field against the Pirates for his first starting assignment. He doubled once and drove in a run. In his second start, he banged out two hits against Brooklyn, then a few days later devastated the second-place Cards in a weekend series, collecting four hits and driving in two runs the first game and adding three more hits and three RBIs in the second. The Braves won the first ten games in which Hazle played.

"Hazle . . . did everything but sweep the poor Phillies out of Connie Mack Stadium," the *Milwaukee Journal*'s Bob Wolf wrote on August 26. "He hit two three-run homers, added a single and a walk and was a one-man wave of destruction as the touring Braves continued pennantward." At the end of his first month with Milwaukee, the Hurricane had stunned the baseball world: He was hitting .507 and had knocked in twenty-one runs and scored sixteen.

The Braves traveled to Wrigley Field in early September and clobbered the Cubs, 23–10, with Hazle doubling three times and singling once. Four days later his homer helped the Braves beat the Cubs again, and on September 22 he homered in the tenth inning to defeat Chicago once more. The next night the Milwaukee Braves clinched their first National League crown. A sportswriter telephoned Hazle early in his hotel room. "Why did you wake me?" asked the Hurricane, who ended the season with a .403 batting average. "I was having such sweet dreams."

Hazle smiled at the memory as we pulled into another liquor store, his twenty-third stop of the day. "Gosh, that was a good life," he said. "But I tell you the truth, once I left the game, I never thought about going back, managing, coaching or whatever. What's done is done. Besides, the way it ended, I left with kind of a bad taste in my mouth for baseball."

His Braves teammates voted only a two-thirds share of the World Series bonus for the man who had won them the pennant (because he had played less than a full season). "I'd liked to have gotten a full share, naturally," he said. "I've heard of players getting full shares for doing a lot less than I did." Then the Braves' general manager, John Quinn, having promised to boost Hazle's six-thousand-dollar salary with a handsome dividend after the Braves beat the Yankees in the seventh game of the World Series, mailed him a thousand-dollar check. Hazle returned it, saying he needed the money, but not at the cost of his pride.

In 1958 Hazel was hit twice by beanballs—spending two weeks in a St. Louis hospital on one occasion. Before he had even recovered, Quinn sold him for thirty thousand dollars to Detroit, where he played a few games, was struck in the eye by a fungo one of his coaches hit and was sent back to the minors. After two marginal seasons, bouncing around West Virginia, Arkansas and Alabama, though still convinced he was a major league ballplayer, he retired at the age of thirty-one and went home to South Carolina to sell granite for tombstones, then whiskey.

"It seems like everything went wrong in '58," he said. "Just everything. It was quite the opposite of '57, when everything went right. I told the wife it was time to wrap it up. The end had come.

Please appreciate, I'm not griping. I had my shot. It's just that in the majors you have that vinegar, that intensity, and it gives you strength. Back in the minors I just couldn't get hyped every day anymore."

We drove slowly through Woodruff, Hazle's boyhood home-town, whose entire citizenry had signed a good-luck telegram to him before the World Series and honored him with a parade after the Braves triumphed. There was a FOR SALE sign on the little weathered house on North Main Street that once belonged to his parents, and he wished he could have afforded to buy it and fix it up, if only for old times' sake. We passed the cemetery—"That's where Mother and Dad are, over there next to the trees"—and turned down by the cotton mill. The ball field was still there, even though there had been no mill teams in South Carolina for years. The bleachers were gone and the outfield distances had been short-ened for the benefit of the youngsters who now used the field. He could still remember walking home from the park, his bat and glove over his shoulder, and hearing his mother say, "We might not have much but we can be clean for supper. So put on a fresh shirt and scrub your face."

Not far from Woodruff, Hazle pulled into Tommie and Sophie Axson's liquor store, his last stop of the day. Their ten-year-old son, Shane, was in the gin section, examining his albums of base-ball cards. He asked me if I had ever collected cards, and I said yes, I once had shoe boxes filled with them, but my mother had thrown them out years ago.

"You should start again," Shane said. "I think you ought to begin with the Sheffields and McGwires. They're going to make you money. Here's a Rickey Henderson that goes for two dollars. Mark Grace is worth three. See this Dale Murphy? If it was printed backwards, it'd be worth *forty-five dollars.*"

He thumbed through the pages, fixing a value on every player. I told him I had a very valuable card in my wallet and showed him the Bob Hazle I had gotten at Trader John's. Shane looked skepti-cal, checked his *Becketts Baseball Card Monthly,* and announced, "He isn't listed. So why's the card valuable?"

"Because he's in your store," I said.

Shane furrowed his brow. "Is it *you?*" he asked.

"No, not me. It's the big guy by the counter talking to your father."

Shane went over to the two men, held the card at arm's length and circled Hazle like a painter studying his subject. His eyes traveled from the picture of the left-handed hitter, bat cocked over his shoulder, to the face of the whiskey salesman, dressed in a white shirt and tie.

"Nah," he finally said, giving me back the card, "it's not him."

We didn't get back to Columbia until nearly 7:00 P.M. Bob and Pat Hazle lived in a ranch-style house on a cul de sac. Their home was full of laughter and friends, either theirs or those of their four grown children, and dinner always started with joined hands and a prayer. The bar was stocked with a bucket of fresh ice and ample drinks, and as often as not, a barbecue was being fired up on the porch near the swimming pool the Hazles had built three years ago. When it rained, Hazle grilled with an umbrella held over his head.

"People'll say to me, 'You played ball. You ought to be retired,' " Hazle said, mixing a drink. "And I say, 'Do you know what you're talking about, fella? We didn't make any money to amount to anything then. I got to work to pay the bills like everyone else.'

"I guess if I made a mistake, it was dropping out of college after two semesters. My three brothers were the smart ones. They got a good education at Clemson. They're retired now and they're not hurting for anything. They've moved far beyond me. But I couldn't see it. I was too young, too loose. I was going to make a mint playing ball. Aw well, what the hell. We've had fun, haven't we, Mama?"

"A .400 hitter, Bob," Pat said. "Can you imagine what you'd be worth today? You just came along at the wrong time."

There was a brochure on the kitchen table that had arrived that day. It was from a Milwaukee promoter who was organizing a reunion of the '57 Braves and their fans on a Caribbean cruise. The Braves superstars—Spahn, Mathews, Aaron—would be there, their promotional presence exchanged for free passage; for anyone else, the cost was $999 to $1,600, too prohibitive for Hazle to consider. "But wouldn't I love to see those guys like Nippy Jones again," he said. "I wonder if Nippy's going."

Hazle's white Milwaukee uniform with No. 12 on the back still hung in his closet, safeguarded in plastic. I asked some of the young minor leaguers I met during my trip if they had ever heard of Hurricane Bob Hazle. None had. But the legend he symbolized was what sustained them all. It was what they dreamed of, to step from the bush-league shadows of a wicked slump and stand for even a fleeting moment in the spotlight of major league stardom.

Hazle plopped into a chair next to Pat, a glass of Black Velvet whiskey in hand. He massaged his temples, trying to get liquor stores and quotas and brand names off his mind. His two daughters dropped by and his granddaughter jumped into his lap to give him a kiss. Pat took rib-eye steaks out of the refrigerator. They freshened up their drinks and Hurricane Bob Hazle poked the coals on the grill and said that this—coming home, being home, staying home—was the grandest reward that work could offer.

"The Hurricane these days," said Pat with a wink, "is just a gentle breeze."

Chapter Thirteen

I'd rather drive a bus in the minors than be an attorney.

—TONY LARUSSA, *attorney and Oakland
Athletics' manager*

T he last two winters of the dec-
ade were kind to major league players. Superstar salaries soared
past $4 million a year, and any player who couldn't command a
million-dollar salary—as one in four did—probably needed a new
agent or new glasses so he could hit better than .250. "Did we
overpay?" asked Cleveland president Hank Peters after rescuing
aging, injury-prone Keith Hernandez from involuntary retirement
with a $3.5 million two-year contract. "Yes."

Some of the salaries, such as Orel Hershiser's $7.9 million three-
year deal with the Dodgers, did not seem out of line with either
the athletes' accomplishments and their ability to generate income
for their teams or with the tenor of the times. After all, the same
week Hershiser struck gold in Los Angeles, a jury across town
awarded Marc Christian $14.5 million because his lover, Rock
Hudson, had exposed him to AIDS.

"We're entertainers in the same sense that Frank Sinatra and

Bruce Springsteen are," Hershiser said, "but the fact that they get fifty thousand every time they sing a song doesn't get the exposure we do. And every time they negotiate a contract, it isn't regarded as a sentimental attack on a team and a city."

That's a good argument except for one point: There is no longer much relationship between performance and remuneration in baseball, as there is in other professions. The top-paid five players in 1988—Ozzie Smith, Gary Carter, Jim Rice, Mike Schmidt and Eddie Murrray—had a composite batting average of .264, with fourteen homers and sixty-three runs batted in. Cecilio Guante, released by the Texas Rangers, went to the Cleveland Indians for $650,000 a year. Seattle's Steve Balboni, a lifetime .231 hitter, was awarded $800,000. After going 1–13 in 1989, Zane Smith signed on with Montreal for $660,000. The Pirates' Walt Terrell, who had lost nearly twice as many games as he had won over two seasons, locked in $3.8 million on a three-year deal. When Baltimore finally managed to unload Freddie Lynn (who earned $1.5 million for hitting .246 and wanted a raise) to Detroit after a marathon bargaining session, the Orioles' general manager, Roland Hemond, alone in his office at midnight, danced a jig around his desk.

Babe Ruth was reminded in 1930 that President Hoover made less than the $80,000 he was asking the Yankees for. "I had a better year than he did," the Babe replied. Ruth eventually got his money, a salary that was eighty times greater than what the average American workingman then earned (about one thousand dollars a year). No one doubted he was worth it. Today the Yankees' Pascual Perez earns ninety times the average American's salary ($21,000). He completed two of the twenty-eight games he started in 1989, lost thirteen of twenty-two decisions and has a history of drug and alcohol problems.

Mediocrity had become not only acceptable but something generously rewarded.

For years players had no bargaining power. A "reserve clause" in their contracts bound them permanently to their clubs, denying them the right to seek another job within the profession, as can, say, an IBM technician who wants to go to work for Apple. Baseball was a legal cartel, exempt from antitrust laws thanks to a 1922 U.S. Supreme Court decision that baseball was not a business. (Is

General Motors a sport?) Owners paid whatever they choose. "I sent back my contract once, holding out for a few more dollars," said former journeyman catcher Bob Uecker. "And [General Manager John] Quinn mailed it right back to me with a note saying I lacked thirty-one days to be eligible for a pension and saying, 'If I were you, I'd sign.' Did I sign? Hell yes. I had a family to support."

In 1975 Dodger pitcher Andy Messersmith challenged the reserve clause. First an arbitrator, then the courts, backed him, ruling that he—and all baseball players—were free agents. The decision should have put a restraint on salaries by providing a constant surplus of players on the open market. The players' wily union rep, Marvin Miller, a former chief economist for the United Steelworkers of America, recognized this, but the panicky owners apparently did not, and Miller offered a "compromise:" Players would need six years' service in the majors to be eligible for free agentry. Thus he put in place a mechanism to regulate supply. If half a dozen teams wanted a third baseman, they would probably find only one or two available in any given year. In outbidding one another for his services, the owners would drive up not only his pay but that of every other third baseman. The horse was out of the barn and all hell broke loose.

Miller ran the Major League Baseball Players Association from 1966 to 1983, and what he left behind was the best package of benefits any industry had ever known. Players are fully vested in their pension plan the first day they get to the majors and need only forty-three days' service to draw eventual benefits; with a salary of half a million dollars a year, a player who lasted ten years in the majors would get $1,973 a month at age forty-five, or $8,548 a month if he waited to cash in until he was sixty-two.

It was, of course, not without envy that I noted baseball was the country's second-best-paid job, exceeded only by professional basketball, and perhaps my grousing was just sour grapes. After all, The Job Rated Almanac listed "book author" as the second-worst-paid job at $5,873 a year; only migrant farm workers earned less.

In addition to the huge salaries, which were the result of a TV-contract bonanza as well as free agentry, major league baseball paid in 1988 more than $26 million to players whose employment had been terminated because of injury or incompetence—damning testimony to management's own ineptitude. But as much money as there was floating around the majors, there wasn't even any talk of improving conditions or salaries in the minors. Players were still paid like authors, umpires scoured back streets for the cheapest rooms a town had to offer, and assistant general managers hustled the phones, hoping to meet their rent from the commission on a group ticket sale to some church or department store.

Bruce Throckmorton, Mark Wohlers and Dave Dickman had found a shopping-mall steak house in Pulaski, Virginia, where four dollars got a man a six-ounce hamburger steak (precooked weight), gravy, potatoes, an unlimited salad bar and dessert. Even by the standards of the Appalachian League, where salaries ran about two hundred dollars a week, before taxes, that was an excellent deal, and the three of them were squeezed around a corner table, plates piled high, discussing their entrée into the world of professional baseball. The New York Yankees had announced that day they were cutting their two-game winner, Pat Dobson, and would pay him the rest of his $800,000 salary for the year.

"I got lucky," said Throckmorton, at twenty-three the oldest member of his team. "Three of us are sharing a private room in a lady's house for twenty-five dollars a week. She said the economy's so bad around here, having twenty-five or thirty ballplayers in town really helps."

"Four of us had a trailer just over the mountain last year," said Dickman, who wore a Notre Dame jersey and was the archetype of a young athlete: handsome, dark-haired, broad-chested and bubbling with confidence. "It was so small you could just about turn around in it. But I figure this teaches you how to budget. When you get to The Show, then you get the benefits."

"What's the minimum salary up there now?"

"Sixty-eight five, I think," said crew-cut Wohlers, a teenager just out of high school.

Dickman whistled in appreciation. *"Sixty-eight five! Not bad!* Have you noticed how people don't really understand what the minor leagues are all about? You tell people what you do, and they say, 'When am I going to see you on TV?' You just have to say, 'I'm working my best to get there.' "

"You know, the first pitch I threw in professional ball, I gave up a home run. A *home run*! Damn," Throckmorton said.

"That's nothing," Dickman said. "My first pitch, I hit a guy in the head. I said, 'Oh, Christ. What am I doing here?' "

"The way my wife and I figure it," Throckmorton said, "we'll look at what kind of a year I had at the end of the season. If we think this is as far as I can go, I'm not one to waste time. I don't think you should be living a dream that's never going to come true."

"If I work my butt off, even if things don't pan out," Dickman said, "I know that one day my kid can say, 'Hey, my old man played a little ball and he got paid for it.' Everyone at this table can say that and we'll always be proud of it."

"Can you get free seconds on the pie?" Wohlers asked.

The Appalachian League was a short-season league, one that started in June and spanned seventy-two summer nights. It was the bottom rung of the professional ladder, a sort of graduate course for rookies just out of high school or college. Stretching through Tennessee, North Carolina, West Virginia and Virginia, the seventy-seven-year-old Appy was a throwback to the days when teams were run by the community and no one much cared about the bottom line. The league was among my favorites, so rural and antiquated that in its little coal-mining towns I half expected to find municipal offices adorned with pictures of President Eisenhower.

Throckmorton, Wohlers and Dickman played for the Pulaski Braves, who averaged the smallest crowds in professional baseball—389 a game. The Braves' press box and part of the grandstands had been swept away in a flood the previous year, and the team was without a radio station to broadcast its games, the sponsoring station having gone bankrupt over the winter. The Braves rattled around the mountains in a chartered school bus, and when I got to Calfee Park, the team was climbing on board for the two-hour ride to Bluefield.

"I'm going to the grocery store. Do you want anything?" Diane Koenig asked her husband, the manager.

"Yeah," Fred Koenig said. "A third baseman."

Koenig, who was fifty-eight and had spent ten years in the majors as a coach and twice that many in the minors coaching and managing, took the front seat on the passenger side. His wife had urged him several times to hook on again with another big-league club and he had always replied, "They're too spoiled up there. I'd rather be down here where the kids still want to learn." To Koenig's left, dressed in designer jeans and a white windbreaker, sat Phil Niekro, a roving instructor for the Atlanta Braves, whose 318 major league victories had made him a millionaire and a certain Hall of Famer. The uniformed players eyed Niekro respectfully and quickly as they filed past him but said nothing. They plopped into the metal seats, opened their copies of *Baseball America* or put on Walkman headsets blaring hard rock. The bus rumbled down Pierce Street. "OK, let's go kick some ass," growled Pulaski's rookie coach, Phil Wellman.

The road the bus followed to West Virginia had been punched through the mountains and laid across the spine of wooded ridges. It skirted townships whose striking miners had not brought home a paycheck in ten weeks. There were no strangers in these quiet, tidy towns. Families in need turned to one another, and soot-faced men who had spent their working lives in the bowels of the earth rejected the thought of welfare or food stamps as undignified, even in the toughest of times. "I may have lost my bank account, but not my pride," one miner told me. Dave Dickman watched the isolated splendor of the miles drift by his window, the valleys and sharp peaks, dark forests reaching out as far as the eye could see. "America, the beautiful," he mused. "For someone from the North like me, Appalachia is what you'd call an exercise in cultural awareness."

We arrived at Bowen Field in Bluefield ninety minutes before game time. The Bluefield Orioles had the longest affiliation in the minors (thirty-one years with the Baltimore Orioles), and the team's president, general manager and booster-club director—eighty-year-old George Fanning—was at the gate to meet us. A retired high school chemistry teacher and baseball coach, Fanning had been with the club since 1954 and was its only staff employee, though "employee" wasn't quite the appropriate word because he worked for free. Other than giving away an occasional bicycle and a few batting helmets, he didn't believe in promotions, and in a town with few diversions other than bowling and drinking, he drew a steady twenty-five-thousand fans a season simply by offering a pleasant evening of baseball.

"People tell me I'm crazy not to do promotions, but I know I'm not," he said. "If I promote, the damn federal government's just going to take that much more anyway. I get people to keep coming back because I don't rob 'em. I don't charge but two bucks for admission, and if someone doesn't have any money, heck, I let 'em in for free."

I asked if he ever got inquiries about selling the team, not realizing that the franchise was owned by the Baltimore Orioles, not the local booster club. Fanning apparently had the same misconception.

"All the time," Fanning said, "but I don't talk to 'em. Those outsiders come in, and in a couple of years they'll have drained off all the money and they'll be gone. Hell, over yonder in Martinsville they're charging four dollars for admission, and that's pretty near major league prices." He spoke softly to make the next point confidentially. "You see those helmet liners over there in the concession stands? You know what Baltimore charges for them? Five dollars. You know what they cost? Sixty-five cents. The majors are taking their fans for a ride."

A moot point perhaps, but Fanning did offer good value. The cost of going to a major league game—admission, parking, a hot dog, beer, soft drink and bag of peanuts—ranges from a low of $11.75 for the Cincinnati Reds to a high of $22 for the Chicago Cubs. The same evening at Bluefield's Bowen Park, minus the beer, which was not available, cost $3.75.

Bowen Field, built on the site of the old fairgrounds, was fifty years old. It sat in a hollow, surrounded by thick woods, and at dusk the lights of the few houses down the dirt road shone through the tall trees, and from the grandstands you could see kids riding their bicycles toward the flickering beacons of home. Beyond the outfield fence, on land owned by the local Baptist college, a steep hill rose. Miners too poor to afford the price of a ticket used to watch the games from there in the fifties, lighting small fires to keep warm. The elms and maples were shorter then, and to fans inside

Bowen Field the silhouettes of the miners huddled around their burning logs were almost as distinct as that of the ballplayers themselves.

"Up here in the mountains, you're in God's country, you know. Make no mistake about it—God's country." Jack Waters loved his mountains with a religious fervor. He had sold peanuts as a twelve-year-old boy in Bowen Field the day the park had opened. He was still here, half a century later, and on this night was setting up a table from which to hawk a statistical history of the Appalachian League that someone had put together over several long, lonely winters.

"Most of the time," Waters said, "the boys Baltimore sends us fit right in and we make 'em feel at home, though I noticed last year some of the players we got were not so socially acceptable. That whole outfield, top to bottom, was *homo*sexual, the way they looked to me. Course, that's nothing I can prove. It's just an opinion.

"You know what our crime rate is in the mountains? 'Bout zero. Some bad checks, a few rapes, a little drunkenness. That's 'bout it. You know why it's zero? To answer that, you have to know the state motto—*Montani semper liberi.* Mountaineers are always free. We shoot the sunnabitches that cause crime.

"There's a fourteen-year-old boy that was stealing from my property. I caught him, goaded him in the balls and stuck my .358 magnum right here"—Waters pointed to his throat—"and what stopped me from pulling the trigger, I honest to God don't know. He goes to court and the judge's lecturing him and the boy interrupts and says, 'Oh, Judge, don't you worry 'bout my getting in trouble no more. I ain't never goin' near Mr. Waters' property ever 'gain.' "

The gate to Bowen Field opened to the public at 6:00 P.M. and Fanning's wife stood in her booth, dispensing tickets from a roll similar to those used in old-time movie houses. The park had no reserved or box seats; all were first-come, first-serve. Fanning, wearing a baseball cap, palms on his spread knees, surveyed the early arrivals from a bench outside his tiny office. He had already gone to the bakery to buy its daily supply of surplus buns—three dozen for a dollar, which enabled him to sell hot dogs for seventy-five cents each—and now there was nothing to do but wait for the man from the recreation department who had promised to bring the American flag for the center-field pole.

"Bill, the flag's not here and they're raising hell about that," he said when Bluefield's city manager showed up to buy his ticket. "It doesn't look right out there with no flag."

The park filled quickly. Entire families came, sometimes three generations in a group. There were old men in suspenders who chewed tobacco and miners' widows who brought padded cushions to soften the bite of cement bleachers. Teenage boys with slicked-back hair and freshly ironed shirts came, too, leading their girl-friends by the hand to the semiprivacy of the uppermost row.

From the steps of the first-base dugout, Bluefield's rookie pitching coach, Chet Nichols, watched the fans stream in. He had white hair, a paunch and, just shy of sixty, was old enough to be the starting pitcher's grandfather. The program didn't offer any background sketch of him, but I knew his résumé by heart: he was the lefty who had had the top E.R.A. in the National League for the 1952 Boston Braves and had moved West with the team for Milwaukee's glory years.

Nichols had left baseball almost thirty years earlier and risen to the vice presidency of a bank in Rhode Island. Then he tired of making loans, tired of the pressures for profit, and when an old friend from the Milwaukee days, Roland Hemond, who now ran the Baltimore Orioles, called, asking if he wanted to ride the bush-league buses through God's country, he had traded in his pin-striped business suit without a second thought. "I'll come and visit," his wife had said, "but I'm not going to stay there for the season." Nichols was living alone at a cheap motel up the road from Bowen Field and cherishing every precious second of his second chilhood.

"Baseball's like riding a bicycle," he said. "You don't forget the fundamentals. I hadn't thrown a ball in five years and now I'm out here throwing these kids BP [batting practice]. I hope one of the things I can teach them is that there is life after baseball, that they have to prepare themselves for something else."

The game that night was not an artistic success. Players were still nervous and overly eager, and balls careened off infielders' gloves and batters were easy outs trying to stretch routine singles into doubles. Pulaski's seventeen-year-old Tab Brown, making his first professional start, gave up seven runs in three innings and left the mound looking as though he were about to burst into tears. The catcher kept rising out of his crouch on breaking balls, putting him off balance and denying Brown and his successors a good target. Fred Koenig, watching his team destruct, jotted himself a note. It said, "Shoot the catcher."

Koenig was a burly man of infinite patience and good humor. He'd put on his cap backwards to look goofy, drop his trousers in the clubhouse to show what he thought of a poorly played game and take a player aside, put an arm around his shoulder, and explain how a play should have been executed. When his young third-base coach let a batter swing away instead of bunt after a rain delay, he met Wellman walking back to the dugout between innings and said quietly, "I understand what you were thinking, Phil, but the grass is wet, the pitcher may not have settled down and that's a good time to lay one down." Koenig was like a marine sergeant major, unflappable, knowledgeable, as fair as he was demanding; the Pulaski recruits would have gone to war for him.

The Braves rallied from a 9–1 deficit in the eighth and ninth innings, but fell short by a run. The fans crowded around Phil Niekro for autographs, as Bluefield did not get many celebrity visitors, and the trainer, Mike Cerame, took dinner orders from the players. "They're keeping the concession stand open for us," he announced, noting each player's request on a yellow scratch pad. "A hot dog and a soft drink are a buck and a quarter."

"*A buck and a quarter? Geez!*" said one player. "How much is just a hot dog?"

It was nearly midnight before we left Bowen Field. Diane Koenig, being a true Baseball Wife, had driven to Bluefield after going to the grocery store—she never missed a game—and followed our yellow bus home in her Chevy van. We drove slowly through the darkened streets of Pulaski, named for Count Casimir Pulaski, who was killed during the siege of Savannah in 1779. The main thoroughfare was deserted, and in the night it was difficult to see the plaques, each bearing the name of a deceased local resident, that had been placed by the elm trees lining Washington Street.

The players piled off the bus, lugging their equipment bags into the clubhouse at Calfee Park. Cerame collected their uniforms, underwear, jockstraps and socks and stuffed them into the two washing machines. Koenig and his two coaches retired to the privacy of the adjoining manager's office. Koenig, sitting naked at his desk, reached into the refrigerator for a beer and Niekro poured a Jack Daniel's. They talked for more than two hours about nuances of baseball strategy I didn't really understand. Koenig, still naked at his desk, reaching for another can, said, "I better tell my wife we're apt to be late or she'll be mad."

"Has she been sitting out in the parking lot all this time waiting for you?" I asked. He supposed she had.

My staying power had weakened over the years, and having the convenience of living in the parking lot just outside Koenig's office, I turned in. "You'll be fine here," the policeman who worked the Braves' games had told me. "I'll tell the night man and he'll put you on his patrol and look in on you from time to time." The team bus was to leave for Johnson City, Tennessee, at eight-thirty the next morning, and when I awoke a thick fog hung in the valley. The players had already started to arrive, walking over the hill from the little town of Pulaski, carrying Egg McMuffins in white takeout bags and the local Sunday paper whose page-one headline read: "175 Dogs Missing in Pulaski Country This Year."

They came in groups of two and three, mumbling, "Mornin', guys," to one another. Only the third baseman, John Kupsey, walked in alone and silently. He had, his teammates said, an air of New Jersey arrogance that did not sit well, particularly in light of his .118 batting average and forty-two-thousand-dollar signing bonus. On top of that, word had gotten round that Kupsey's father had made a dreadful misjudgment during the Braves' preseason instructional league, calling Koenig to complain that his son had gotten a big bonus and ought to be playing regularly. "He plays for himself, not the team," Koenig had replied coldly. "Besides, he can't hit and he can't field. What do you want me to do with him?" Kupsey stood now off by the edge of the parking lot. The others milled about.

Thirty minutes passed. Then an hour. The chartered bus for Johnson City was nowhere in sight. Koenig was on the phone in his office, calling motels in the area. "Do you have a big yellow bus in your parking lot and a driver asleep in one of your rooms?" There would be a pause while the clerk checked. "No? OK, thanks, I'll try someplace else."

It seemed a good time to leave the Appalachian League. Durham—home of America's most famous minor league team, the Durham Bulls of movie fame—was a day's drive away, and I left the Pulaski Braves, wondering if their bus would ever show up. They had been the only players on my journey who had called me "sir," and when I would suggest they use my first name instead, someone would invariably say, "Sure, I'll be glad to, sir." As I pulled out of Calfee Field, a large, bearded man in bib overalls bounded off the porch of his clapboard home across the street, waving me down. He wore a fierce scowl, and I thought he was going to complain about my leaving Forty-niner parked overnight in the neighborhood.

"Anytime you got a game," he said, "you come on over here and set up in my driveway. You'll get better shade that way. Anytime at all. Just drive on in."

Chapter Fourteen

Baseball is a dull game only for those with dull minds.

—RED SMITH

The more I learned about base-
ball, the less I understood, because the deeper the complexities ran.
It was like peeling away the layers of an onion and never quite
reaching the core. But slowly, almost imperceptibly, I was introduced to a game different from the one I had known at the beginning of the season. My mind began seeing things that earlier had
slipped unnoticed by my eyes.

There was the secret language of the umpires as they spoke to
one another on the field with a roll of the finger and a rub of the
cap, acknowledging who would cover what base so that one of
them would always be moving ahead of the play. There was the sign
language flashed from the dugout to the third-base coach to the
players that, even to some highly paid major leaguers, remained no
less bewildering than Chinese. "You know I'm not too good on
these signs," Milwaukee's Cecil Cooper used to tell his first-base

coach when he got on base, "so just give me a wink if I'm meant to run."

I no longer saw outfielders merely catching the ball. I'd see them "read" the swing of the hitter, the sound of impacting horsehide on wood and the arc of the ball. On a ball headed toward the fence, the most skilled ones would drop the foot on their glove side, bring the opposite leg across the body and take off in position for an over-the-shoulder catch. Stealing a base didn't seem a matter of chance anymore but, rather, depended on the runner's awareness that he had to get from first to second in less than 3.2 seconds—the combined time it usually took the pitcher to stretch and throw the ball to the catcher (1.8 seconds) and the catcher to fire to second (1.4 seconds). I learned to appreciate the infielders who were always in position and a catcher with "soft" hands who never stabbed at the ball and made every pitch appear to be a strike. Plays that had once seemed routine now unfolded as minidramas, a practiced art in which mind and body worked as one.

"Under stress, tension, fear, you revert to reflexes and old habits," Buzzy Keller, the Pittsburgh Pirates minor league field coordinator said one day, leaning against a batting cage where his charges hammered away at the pitching coach's down-the-middle fastball. "My wife teaches typing and she pointed out that to unconsciously hit the 'a' with your little finger, you've got to think 'a' three hundred times to put that movement in your mental system before it becomes part of your reflex. Well, in baseball, I read there are over eighteen thousand different situations you have to react to without thinking. That's why the game is so mental, so complex. Hell, if I hadn't ruined my arm, I'd still be out here at age fifty-five trying to hit that damn slider."

More than any sport, baseball is a game of the mind, as much as of the body, because failure is the norm. The best major league teams lose one of every three games, the finest hitters fail seven times in ten. Babe Ruth struck out twice in a single inning a record thirty-two times, Hank Aaron grounded into more double plays (328) than any player, and Nolan Ryan, the all-time strikeout leader, has lost more games than all but seven pitchers in major league history. That's the essence of baseball—dealing with failure, both personal and collective.

Baseball is also tough mentally because failure comes in streaks, each individual defeat feeding on the one before it. Finally, as a slump deepens, the player's mind begins to focus on what has gone wrong—he falls asleep replaying his error or his three strikeouts—and in a game situation his nervous and muscular systems go through the sequence of past failure, reinforcing the likelihood of more failure and less confidence. For some, the goal of getting to the majors is so intense that once the challenge is conquered and the big dollars secured, failure is accepted as it never was before. The players' habits and attitudes change, even though none would ever admit it, and their motivation slips away. What got to them to the top in the first place—trying to be the best they could be every day—is replaced by a willingness to just survive.

"This is the first year I haven't felt motivated," a player with a new million-dollar contract told Jack Curtis, who does motivational counseling for professional and Olympic athletes. "Every other spring I've been scared as hell coming to camp and busted my tail to make sure I had a job. This year I know I can fail and still be set for life."

I got intrigued with the mental aspects of baseball after stepping into Dave Butts's nightmare in Durham. Butts was the Bulls second baseman, a blond-haired young man who, you knew without asking, had been voted best athlete, most popular student and senior-class president in high school. He had grown up on a farm in Kentucky, learning how to drive a tractor sitting on his grandfather's lap. When he veered too far to the left or right, his grandfather would bring him back on track with a gentle slap on the side of the head, as though the old man were holding the reins to a team of horses.

Butts took up baseball at the age of four, competing against two uncles he was determined to outplay. Each night his mother had to drag him in to supper. During bean harvest, he would return from high school practice at dusk and work in the fields until midnight, and when he went away to college, he became the only Cadiz High School player to make his college team in fifteen years. Later, an Atlanta Braves scout said, "We'd like to give you a fifteen-hundred-dollar bonus, seven hundred a month and send you to Idaho Falls," and Butts replied, "Where do I sign?" The signing of Cadiz's first pro athlete ever was page-one news in the weekly *Record*, and for a hundred miles around, Dave Butts was a local hero. Kids asked for his autograph and his three younger brothers thought he had hung the moon.

"Dave's said that the hardest part of being released or however it ends will be going home, because they won't understand," Lezlie Butts said one night at Durham Athletic Park as her husband came to bat. "What they won't understand is how far he's come and what a long, hard endurance test this is."

During the off-season Butts had taken batting practice every day but five in an indoor cage and had spoken to Bobby Dews, who ran Atlanta's farm system for his often-absent boss, Hank Aaron, about his future with the organization. Dews hemmed and hawed and finally said the feeling was Butts might one day make the majors as a utility infielder. In the Bulls' season opener, Butts, starting his third pro season, homered.

Then he hit no more. First there were liners that should have fallen for hits but didn't; then pop-ups and easy grounders and finally the futility of strikeouts. At one point he managed only seven hits in sixty-one at bats. His average shrunk to .080 and the manager dropped him to eighth, then ninth, in the batting order. "Hitting this low, at least the worst I can do today is go oh for three or four," he said to himself. He went from not believing this was happening to him to believing he really wasn't much of a player. He looked for positive reinforcement, but his teammates remained distant, not wanting to say anything to hurt him and not knowing what they could do to help him. "Players stay clear of someone going through temporary insanity," the manager said. "He might throw a bat or take down the bathroom door or drown himself in the shower." At the plate, knowing he was going to make an out, Butts's eye would be distracted by the movement of an umpire or would focus on an outfield sign he had never even seen when his concentration was working.

"If I ever talk about quitting," he said to Lezlie one night, "don't let me do it. Please!"

The toughest part of the week was calling home and talking to his thirteen-year-old brother. The boy thought of his idol as a college star with a .350 batting average—indeed, the second baseman had come to expect that of himself, too—and it was difficult for Butts to sound upbeat when life as a pro was so miserable. He decided not to call home again until he got his average up to at least .240. During a much less severe slump in his rookie year, Butts's manager had told him: "Leave the game at the park. Your marriage will last a lot longer that way." He had not always heeded the advice and Lezlie remembered him coming home one night, drinking too much beer and being "hateful"—an adjective that to me seemed entirely out of context with Butts's soft-spoken, gracious demeanor. He had apologized to her after she said, "Look, I'm not the one who's in a slump." After each game, they would eat a hot meal at midnight, stay up talking for a couple of hours and at six-thirty the next morning Lezlie would struggle out of bed for work at the bank. It was a relief to her when the team went on the road.

One week Butts would show up at the park early for extra batting practice, the next he would stay away as much as possible. Nothing helped. Pitches flashed by him as a blur. "It's like I've lost my vision," he said. One of Atlanta's hitting instructors, Willie Stargell, came to Durham. Butts was alone in the park, working out, and Stargell walked up to him and said, "Here, let me help you." For a long time the overweight black Hall of Famer with twenty-one years' major league service stood in his street clothes in front of the mound, patiently throwing "slow pitch" after "slow pitch" to the young white athlete with the furrowed brow. "Bat back, level swing, drive the bat right through the ball," Stargell would say. "Thataway. That's good contact."

A deathly hush fell over the crowd when Butts came to bat, and the three daily papers that covered the Bulls began asking why he was even playing. "Don't worry about Butts," manager Grady Little would say. "He'll get his hits." Which, in fact, he finally did. Butts attributed the slump's end to Little telling him to relax and take a deep breath before every pitch. A more likely explanation was that the TV announcer, Steve Shelby, sitting in the dugout before a game one night, offered to take the hex off Butts's bat. He rolled the barrel of the bat around his bald head, said a secret blessing and lo, the wooden stick was heavy with hits again.

Taking a deep breath, Butts banged a solid single to right his first time at bat that night. The next time up he singled to center. Then he doubled up the alleyway. He didn't dare celebrate, for fear the curse might return, but in the days ahead, *knowing* he was going to get a hit, every ball he struck seemed to fall safely on some patch of grass. A terrible burden had been lifted. He started having baseball dreams again almost every night—good dreams in a World Series setting—and he began calling home to talk to his teenage brother. Once more, he was the dream keeper of a baseball life.

I could not imagine what it would be like to endure a slump in my professional life as Butts did in his—to go out on assignment after assignment for my newspaper and write stories that were not good enough to be printed, to feel my colleagues becoming distant and know my editors were whispering, "Don't send Lamb. His stuff is second-rate." I think my confidence might have been permanently bruised, and knowing what a great motivator the fear of failure is, I can only hope that I, like Butts, would have had the courage to stick around for a few more swings to prove the skeptics—and perhaps my own self as well—wrong.

My arrival in Durham, the last week in June, represented an anniversary of sorts. It had been exactly thirty years ago that my pal John Sherman and I had left Boston, holding out our thumbs and a sign that said CALIFORNIA. Route 66 and the other roads West were loaded with hitchhikers in those days; now there were virtually none. I felt a traitor when I sped by one of the few I encountered, standing alone on a long stretch of highway, but my wariness was not unjustified. The Arizona Highway Patrol had made a random check of a hundred hitchhikers: eighty-four had criminal records and twelve were runaways.

John flew down to Durham, from the country inn he and his wife ran in rural Virginia, to spend a few days with me and see his first minor league games. Thirty years earlier we had traveled in poverty, sleeping in highway ditches and making pledges to Jesus in exchange for meals at Salvation Army soup lines. Forty-niner's comforts now felt almost improper, though we both agreed it would be difficult to revert to the hardships of past wanderings. Our reunion was a good one, two old friends coming together to celebrate a summer's bonding. It was a friendship that made no demands and encompassed no expectations, the kind of friendship you made only when you were young.

Unfortunately, John did not see Forty-niner at its best, for he arrived when the toilet was broken and the generator had become cranky. When this happens, you don't just call a plumber or pull into a garage; you have to find an RV specialist and in Durham I could find no such creature. I would have to live with my misfortune until I headed north to a larger city, perhaps Richmond or Baltimore. After a night of breathless heat in a motel parking lot, John was sweat-stained and tired of pouring water from a tea kettle into the toilet, hoping it would flush.

"Christsakes," he said. "Can't we just check into the motel? It's *twenty* feet away. It's probably got toilets. It's probably got air conditioning, showers, everything." Though I had resisted such temptations since leaving California, the suggestion was a good one. Never had a drab motel room felt so luxurious. Its amenities restored our spirit—and appearance—and a few hours later we set off to check out Durham, where the restored bat of Dave Butts had helped lift the Bulls into first place.

Durham is in the heartland of minor league baseball. Within three hours' driving time there are ten teams, and instead of obscenities written on men's-room walls in these towns of the Carolina League, one sees love messages to sports: the top five NBA draft choices encircled with a heart or an ode to the Duke Blue Devils or the words "Long Live the Bulls" inside an American flag.

Less than twenty years earlier, when baseball was slipping out of the national consciousness so rapidly that the commissioner's office retained the consulting firm of Arthur D. Little, Inc., to study ways to reverse the trend, no one in Durham much cared about the Bulls. The team took out an ad in the local paper for the last game in 1971, announcing "the final game of a long, disastrous, just plain awful season." Only 330 fans showed up to see Durham lose to Rocky Mount, 4–2. That winter the franchise moved, leaving behind a run-down Durham Park and the scattered ashes of

Buck Weaver, a pitcher from the forties whose final request had been granted in front of a full house.

For eight years Durham had no baseball. But a North Carolinian named Miles Wolff was roaming the country in an old Toyota, looking for a team. Wolff had spent three years as general manager in Savannah, had written two books (a novel and a historical account of the early civil rights movement) and looked more like a dentist than a baseball man. He was young, articulate and intelligent, rare qualities among the old men who then ran—and ran badly—most of the teams in the South. When the Carolina League expanded in 1980, Wolff bought a franchise for twenty-five hundred dollars and set off for the downtown corner of Corporation and Norris streets, where Durham Park was tucked among a cluster of row houses and tobacco warehouses. Almost everyone agreed he had made a lousy investment.

But from day one, thanks in part to extraordinarily good timing, the reborn Bulls were a smashing success, a team destined to break all Class-A attendance records and become the centerpiece of Durham's downtown restoration. First, the nation's cyclical interest in baseball was on the rise again, a revival Wolff dated to Carlton Fisk's dramatic World Series home run off the foul pole for the Red Sox in 1975. Then Duke University law students discovered the Bulls, and fifty-year-old Durham Park became trendy, the in place to spend a summer's evening. Finally, there was the hit movie *Bull Durham*, written and directed by former minor leaguer Ron Shelton. So many orders for Bulls souvenirs poured in from around the country that Wolff had to open a concession's outlet in a shopping mall. Wolff also bought two other teams, in Butte, Montana, and Burlington, North Carolina, and purchased and became publisher of *Baseball America*, the cult paper of minor league aficionados. But the flagship of his $5 million mini-empire remained the Durham Bulls, as grand a team as you'll find anywhere in baseball.

The Bulls parking lot had space for no more than 150 cars, a throwback to the days when fans walked to games from their downtown jobs. I couldn't find room for Forty-niner, so John and I parked near a sports bar ten blocks away. A large crowd had already formed outside Durham Park. "Come on, Miles," shouted an elderly woman at the head of the line, shaking the gate. "Open up. It's six o'clock."

Durham's crowds, every one a sellout while I was in town, were electric and were the only ones I found in any park other than Milwaukee County Stadium that actually sang, instead of mumbled, the national anthem. Out by the shallow right-field wall, a huge bull snorted smoke to mark hometown heroics, and during rain delays, a retarded kid from the neighborhood would prance across the outfield, arms raised in imaginary triumph as the theme song from *Rocky* echoed through the park. The Bulls had adopted Willie and gave him clothes and food. What made the fans special at Durham Park was that they weren't just baseball fans; they were *Bulls* fans. They treated the players like visiting dignitaries, and the team in turn gave them reason to snub their noses at the other two rival cities in the Triangle. Sure, Raleigh had the capital, and Chapel Hill had the university, but in Durham they had the Bulls.

"This is a lot more fun than a major league game," John Sherman said one night, and I agreed. John was rediscovering a passion for baseball that he had set aside years ago and was so content that I had trouble getting him out of the ballpark.

"Let's take off and have a drink and get a real meal," I said in the fifth inning of one game.

"OK, but after the seventh," he said. "I'd like to see a couple of more innings."

The Bulls didn't need promotions to attract capacity crowds, though Wolff, largely out of a sense of loyalty, continued to give an occasional night's work to two showmen who had helped him build a following in the early years. The two were the antithesis of each other: one a shy five-foot-three Greek-American and notoriously cheap tipper, Ted Giannoulas, who as the Famous Chicken was baseball's most popular (and most expensive, at up to seven thousand dollars per appearance) promotion; the other a long-necked, loose-limbed, marathon-tongued man twice the Chicken's age, Max Patkin, who had been riding the buses and commuter airlines from town to minor league town for more than four decades as the Clown Prince of Baseball.

Giannoulas started his career handing out Easter eggs for a San Diego radio station at two dollars an hour. He had few friends inside baseball and seemed a lonely man once he took off his chicken suit. A one-man corporation, he traveled with his own Famous Chicken souvenirs, and his mother made his costume, turning out one head a month. The seventy-year-old Patkin, a minor league pitcher in the forties, had few friends *outside* baseball and traveled with only an old suitcase. A good many years earlier a journeyman outfielder, Sam Meale, had told him, "Max, you're the funniest-looking fucking thing I ever saw," and Patkin had taken it as a great compliment, because it calmed his gravest fear— that he wasn't really funny. Patkin's fee was negotiable; usually fifteen hundred dollars secured his services, maybe a little less when you threw in a night's lodging. If Giannoulas was comfortable alone in a motel room, Patkin was most at ease in a clubhouse surrounded by the people he understood best, baseball people. Neither the Famous Chicken nor the Clown Prince much cared for the other.

Patkin shuffled into the Bulls' clubhouse, carrying a uniform with a question mark on the back. He was tall and stooped and had only one tooth in his upper gums. Manager Grady Little greeted him at the door. "Hey, Max," he said, "you gettin' any pussy?"

"Nah, I'm too ugly. Tell you the truth, I haven't been laid on the road in fifteen years. I know fat guys who're getting more than me. Maybe I'm not trying hard enough. There must be some lonely woman out there who'd like an ugly old man.

"I booked too many dates this year—seventy-five, I got seventy-five dates and I coulda gotten more—and even with all those dates, I'm not getting anything. Just Monday I was in . . . I was in . . . Now, where the fuck was I Monday? Can you believe it, I can't remember where the fuck I was Monday. Where the fuck was I Tuesday? Unbelievable! I can't the fuck remember that either. Monday. Monday. I gotta figure this out. I'm in the Carolina League, right? I must be getting punchy. Martinsville! That's it . . . No, Martinsville was Thursday. This is Friday and I'm here, so where the fuck was I Monday? Maybe it was Charlotte. Jesus Christ, who cares?

"I'm doing all these cities and that Chicken is making all the fucking money. You know he doesn't leave a penny for the clubhouse guys. I only leave a five- or ten-dollar bill, but they appreciate it. You'd think that Chicken'd give the minors a break. He ought to show a little compassion instead of taking everything out of baseball, maybe give a free show or something for some team that can't afford him. He gives the best show in baseball, I'll say that, but he's a cheap little prick. People think I'm picking on him for sour grapes. Bullshit. I don't begrudge him all his money. His manager called me one day and said if it wasn't for the Chicken, I wouldn't be making the money I'm making. Can you imagine that little shit saying that? After I've been performing for forty-four years."

Patkin worked slowly at getting into his uniform. He put on his cap sidewards. The manager and the players had gone out onto the field. The clubhouse was empty except for the two of us. There was no one to perform for yet, and he never knew what his audience would be like until he went out in the third inning. He hoped there would be a lot of kids in the stands tonight. They were the ones who appreciated him the most.

"This is the hard part, right now, sitting here waiting to go out," he said. "I get lonely, I get depressed. I've had problems that nearly gave me a nervous breakdown. I was having problems with my wife before the divorce and I was catching her with other men. Then she committed suicide. That nearly cost me my sanity. Many nights I'd go out there and I could hardly do the show. Then hanging around the motel all day, that'll kill you. Look, I never regretted it. I met every great player who ever fucking played—Ruth, Greenberg, Teddy, Robinson, Cobb—but the nights are tough. You come back to the parks year after year and you feel the same eyes are watching you. Lots of nights I feel the crowd's not with me, like they're saying, 'Get the fuck out of here.' When I get down on myself like that, I cuss myself under my breath and say, 'Work, you son of a bitch! Work! There are *kids* out here who want to laugh.' I tend to cuss a little anyway. Cussing stimulates me. Don't ask me why. Bill Veeck said I had a little gutter in me. I don't know, maybe he's right.

"In 1969, I was in Great Falls, Montana, and there were four fucking people in the stands. *Four fucking people!* You know why? That was the day the man walked on the fucking moon for the first

time, and afterwards, the general manager comes over and thanks
me for working so hard. I never worked so hard in my life. I did
a really good show. I was loose.

"You should have seen me in the old days, when I had my weight
down to one fifty. I had this skinny neck and long nose and as soon
as I walked on the field, they'd laugh. I didn't have to do a fucking
thing except show up to make them laugh. Batters would step out
of the box they were laughing so hard. I don't know, I guess I was
always skeptical about being funny. I never really had that confidence you need. Every night when I first went out there, I was
scared to death. I don't mean nervous. I mean scared to death.
Now I just get on edge. If there are families and kids out there, I
got a shot. But if it's just the die-hard fans, they say, 'Oh, shit, I
seen him before and he's doing the same old shit.' "

Patkin walked onto the field in the third inning to a ripple of
applause. His gags were goofy and fun. He stood behind the first
baseman, mimicking his between-inning tosses to the other infielders as though he were the player's shadow. He chased himself
around home plate and did a zany job coaching at third. He
couldn't move as agilely as he once did, and because of age and
injuries and illnesses, he had had to eliminate 40 percent of his
routine. There were spurs in the arches of his feet and he had had
prostate problems. He had also undergone surgery for a herniated
disk; three weeks after the operation he was in Nashville, performing as scheduled. Patkin worked hard that night in Durham, standing still for nary a moment, and the fans gave him a hand when
he left the field after the seventh inning.

"How'd I do?" he asked as he walked back into the security of
the clubhouse. "Do you think they liked me tonight?"

Two innings later, in the bottom of the ninth with two outs,
Brian Deak homered over the left-field fence to give the Bulls a 4–3
victory. The five thousand fans cheered wildly and the Miller Lite
scoreboard flashed its call to arms in large, bright letters: "HOW
SWEET IT IS!" Miles Wolff opened one of the concession stands
after the fans had left and about twenty members of the Bulls
family—a couple of players with their girlfriends, a few ushers and
vendors, a local sportswriter, the front-office staff and the PA

announcer—stood about for an hour, pulling free beer from the tap. Max Patkin leaned against the counter, telling baseball stories. The harder people laughed, the faster he talked.

The groundskeepers finished their work on the infield and the concourse lights went out. Patkin was the first to leave. "Well, good night, fellas," he said, "I'll see you at the winter meetings. I need some sleep. Tomorrow I've got to go to . . . to . . . oh, fuck, would you believe it?" He walked toward the open gate, and as he disappeared in the darkness, I could hear a voice saying, "Martinsville? No, I was just there. It can't be Durham. I'm here. This is just fucking unbelievable!"

Chapter Fifteen

Being a hero is about the shortest-lived profession on earth.

—WILL ROGERS

Where are our heroes?

It seems the land was full of them when we were young. They were the creations of our own willingness to believe, the chosen few we viewed through one-dimensional lenses; we did not want to know of their frailties and deficiencies, and even if we had been curious, there would have been no one to tell us, because in those days journalists were protectors of the myths. Have our heroes left us simply because, as we grow older, we exaggerate the feats of remembered men? Or is it that today we have only moneyed celebrities, living in the glare of constant media exposure that builds, then destroys? We see their faces so often on television, we read so much about the life behind the manufactured image in gossipy magazines that it's hard to think of them having any more mystique than our next-door neighbors. Soon they become tiresome, because once the image is stripped away, there is nothing much of interest left. We look for elements of ourselves in the men we elevate to lofty heights, but how do we relate to an All-Star pitcher who makes $3 million a year and complains about having to carry his suitcase from the team bus to his hotel room?

"Show me a hero," F. Scott Fitzgerald once said, "and I will write you a tragedy." He may have been right, though I would rather have a few flawed heroes around than none at all. In my cowboy era (which preceded my baseball era), Randolph Scott was my first Great American Hero. I wrote him fan letters (they went unanswered) and saw all his Westerns, my favorite being the last one, *Ride the High Country*, with Joel McCrea. Once in Los Angeles, not too many years ago when I came home from an assignment in Africa, my wife gave me one of the grandest surprises of my life— lunch with a mystery guest who turned out to be Randolph Scott. He was in his early eighties then, still strikingly handsome and very gracious. I was thrilled to be in the presence of the man who had made so many cattle drives and won so many gun battles. He was beyond destruction, and two subsequent books that spoke of his past secret life in Hollywood as an effeminate gay did not make me feel deceived. To me, Randolph Scott would always ride off alone into the sunset, having brought justice to another frontier town.

Eddie Mathews was also indestructible. Even when he snubbed me in the Braves' clubhouse, he was no less an idol to me. After all, he had hit forty-seven home runs his first year in Milwaukee, and he and Hank Aaron were in the process of becoming the most productive home-run-hitting teammates in history, outdistancing Mays and McCovey, even Ruth and Gehrig. He was young and tough and talented, my chosen symbol of the Braves' phoenixlike rise from unworthiness, and I rated his perfection as falling some-where between that of God and of Randolph Scott. I followed Mathews's career through to his retirement in 1968, then lost track of him, until a steamy day in Durham when the Bulls took on the Lynchburg Red Sox.

Alone at the end of the dugout, he sat with his head cupped in his hands, sweating profusely and chain-smoking. Eddie Mathews had a thundering hangover. He wore dark glasses, shorts and tennis socks that were curled up over the ankles. Like Willie Star-gell, Mathews was a hitting instructor for the Atlanta Braves, and on this day, with the afternoon heat and humidity hanging in the nineties, it was only a sense of duty that pulled him to his "office" behind the batting cage. "I've got a cold beer in the RV if you want one," I said. His stomach churned audibly at the suggestion. "That would kill me," he mumbled.

Mathews didn't look as big or as powerful as the young slugger who had been on the inaugural cover of *Sports Illustrated* in August 1954. He was nearly sixty now, balding and bad-backed, and he treated every day as an unexpected bonus—a bonus denied his father, who had died of tuberculosis during Mathews's second year in the major leagues. "You gotta slow down, Eddie," Hank Aaron had said to his friend not long ago, and Mathews had laughed and replied, "And have no fun? Shit, no!" The name of his fourth wife, Judy, was tattooed on his forearm. His nose had been broken four times—twice by baseballs and twice in barroom fights. The sculpted metal bull he had bought in a bar and had delivered as a prank to Durham Park was mounted over the hot dog stand. And when Mathews's eighty-three-year-old mother, whom he loved dearly, would pick up the phone and hear heavy, wordless breathing on the line, she'd say immediately, "Eddie? Eddie? Is that you?" Mathews would respond with a hearty laugh and they would talk for an hour.

The Bulls finished batting practice. A stream of perspiration ran down Mathews's chin and hit the dugout floor in steady drips. "I got to get out of this heat," he said. His mouth was so dry the words came with a smacking sound. He got up and walked through the stands to the parking lot, a Hall of Fame third baseman unrecognized by the fans he passed. He got into his rental car and sat there limp, the air conditioner on max.

In the late forties, owner Lou Perini started rebuilding the aging Boston Braves, assembling a group of remarkable teenage athletes, who a decade later would bring a world championship to Milwaukee. Carrying twelve Boston sportswriters, his plane, dubbed the Rookie Rocket, flew around the country, and at each stop a new player would be signed at an elaborate banquet, attended by the player's high school coach and friends. In Fullerton, California, Del Crandall came on board; in Santa Barbara, Eddie Mathews signed and was introduced as the Braves' third baseman of the

future. The positions were, in effect, handed to the recruits pending a successful apprenticeship in the minors. The veterans on the
Braves seethed.

Before reporting to the minor league club in Thomasville, North
Carolina, Mathews was told to spend a few days with the Braves.
It would be a chance to meet his future teammates, the farm
director said. He flew to Chicago, where the Braves were playing
the Cubs, and walked into the clubhouse carrying his glove, spikes
and jockstrap in a paper bag the hotel maid had given him. Bob
Elliot, the man whose job the seventeen-year-old Mathews eventually would get, took one look at him and said: "I've seen some
country bumpkins in my life, but, rookie, this is the big leagues.
You don't have to bring your lunch to work."

Mathews drifted over to a corner where a group of players were
gathered. "Get that mother-fucking asshole out of here!" second
baseman Eddie Stanky bellowed. Manager Billy Southworth suggested that Mathews go out and take a few swings. The rookie
reached for a bat. "Get your goddamn hands off that bat," pitcher
Red Barrett said. Mathews bent down to pick up another one.
"Get your goddamn hands off that one, too," Barrett said. Finally
in possession of a bat, Mathews stepped into the cage. The first
three pitches were aimed for his ear and sent him sprawling.

That night he walked around the corner from the hotel and,
although not old enough to drink legally, entered a bar. After a few
minutes the bartender brought him a beer. "This one's on the two
gentlemen over there," he said. Mathews looked down the bar and
saw the Braves veterans, Vern Bickford and Walker Cooper. He
nodded in thanks, feeling a touch of redemption. The bartender
leaned over to Mathews and added, "They said to drink up and
get the fuck out of here."

The era Mathews played in—and still belonged to in his heart—
was vastly different from today's. It was a time when drinking hard
was a baseball ritual; players hung around the clubhouse for an
hour or two after a game, just talking, and men shared a loyalty,
to one another and their organization. Achievements were rewarded, albeit stingily, a year at a time. One season, after Mathews's home-run production dropped to thirty-seven, the general

manager said, "What are we going to do with your contract after a year like that?" and Mathews replied, "I'll take a five-thousand cut," which he did. There were no teams west of St. Louis in 1955 and the Braves traveled mostly by train, along with the beat sports-writers, who, in sharing a kinship that disappeared with jetliners and stratospheric salaries, were considered family members instead of adversaries. Aaron, being black, was not allowed in the dining car; if he wanted a meal, Mathews was among the players who would bring one back to his seat.

"Looking back," Mathews said, "it makes me angry that I didn't stand up and be counted and say, 'What's this shit?' I was a chicken shit not to have said anything, but we didn't even think about it then. *They* didn't think about it. It's just the way it was. Fuck. And I didn't say a word.

"Hank does a lot of agitating now, but you have to understand where he's coming from, what he's been through." Aaron received so many threatening letters from white racists as he closed in on Babe Ruth's home-run record that the FBI assigned agents to open and read his mail. "Sometimes his agitating gets to me, though. I've told him, 'Hank, I wake up in the morning and I see white and that's OK. If you wake up and see black and that pisses you off, that's your problem.' "

Mathews traveled between the Braves' teams in Greenville, South Carolina, Durham and Richmond, usually with his wife, who packed a cooler with cold cuts they would eat in the motel. "Having her along keeps me out of the bars," he said. Despite a rebellious exterior, Mathews was a shy, private man who hated addressing the assembly of minor leaguers in spring training. But on a one-on-one, the Bulls' players considered him an excellent teacher; he was patient and knowledgeable in the mechanics of hitting and offered as much encouragement to a NP—a player the organization considered "no prospect"—as he did to one being groomed for a place in Atlanta. "You see a kid who's twenty-five and still in Durham, and you just wonder if he realizes he isn't going to go very far," he said. "But you can't just walk away from him." What surprised me was that the young Bulls didn't really know who Mathews was or appreciate his greatness as a player.

They seemed no more impressed being tutored by an Eddie Mathews or a Willie Stargell than they would have been by a Max Patkin.

They had heard Mathews was good—a few even knew he was in the Hall of Fame—but almost no one knew if he had hit left-handed or right-handed, whether he had played third or the outfield, when he played or what his role with the Braves had been. "What do you mean he played for the *Milwaukee* Braves?" one asked. "There's no Milwaukee Braves." To his generation the past had never happened. Another Bull asked me what Mathews's top salary had been, and I said it was sixty-five thousand. "Come on," he replied, "that's less than the minimum."

"I've been here three years and I get shocked when they say, 'What position did you play?'" Mathews said. "It's like they fell off a turnip truck. If they don't know who I am, what stats I put on the board, then why are they going to relate to what I tell them? I talk to Dave Justice [a Richmond Braves outfielder] and he just gives me a big grin and keeps making the same mistakes. He doesn't hear me, like he's sealed up inside. I don't know if he figures I can't help him or if he just looks at me as a old fucker telling him what to do. It's so totally frustrating because I'm sure I've never hurt anybody, and I think I've helped a few."

I asked Mathews if he remembered my visit to Milwaukee as the teenage sportswriter. His response was only a chuckle, so I suspect he didn't and I did not press further. But I think he was pleased to find someone who valued his accomplishments, who knew that his '57 Braves had been one of the century's twenty-five greatest teams (an accolade I can hang on the *Sporting News*, not just my own prejudices). Mathews was headed north to Richmond for the weekend and so was I, still hoping to get Forty-niner's toilet fixed. The Richmond Braves, Atlanta's Triple-A International League club, were playing a rare day game and we agreed to meet afterward for dinner.

Richmond is the start of a megalopolis stretching five hundred miles up the Eastern seaboard to Portland, Maine. Take away the sweet accents, and the city felt Eastern, not Southern, though any Virginian would surely consider such an observation blasphemous. I dropped by the Braves' new stadium, The Diamond, just off I-95, across the street from the Greyhound station. A visiting college professor from California sang "The Star-Spangled Banner" and someone from Napa Auto Parts threw out the first pitch. The Braves won in the eleventh inning. Dave Justice went 0 for 5. Good accommodations were difficult to come by in Richmond, but I finally settled on a cheerless Holiday Inn a few miles from the park because it had a covered parking lot and nice public rest rooms off the lobby. About an hour later, as I was typing notes into my computer and drinking coffee, there was a squeal of tires outside Forty-niner and a loud banging on my door. Eddie Mathews stepped inside. His eyes surveyed my tidy living quarters quickly. "Now wait a goddamn minute!" he said. "You got any bourbon in this thing?"

Settling for a Canadian whiskey, he plopped down at the table by the rear window. I think he prided himself in being outlandish, a member of the old guard who disdained conformity and liked the dangers of standing at the cliff's edge. "I know I'm a ding dong," he said, "but in my day, if you hit .330, it was OK to be a ding dong." If many of today's ballplayers were cut from the mold of corporate executives, Mathews's ilk was that of the rodeo rider, men who drank and brawled and raised hell. He held his wallet together with a rubber band and carried an honorary deputy sheriff's badge from De Kalb County, Georgia, a gift from former Braves pitcher Pat Jarvis, who was now the sheriff. Mathews, the only man who played for the Braves in Boston, Milwaukee and Atlanta, hadn't just worked for a team, he had been part of a family that had stayed together for a decade. The former teammates he cared the most for were the ones whose names he prefixed with the most expletives.

"We had so much fun, I can't believe it," he said. "We thought it would last forever." But by the mid-sixties, the Braves had new owners, a new general manager and a new home, Atlanta. Its aging stars had been cut adrift, one by one. Mathews got a call New Year's Eve, 1966, as he was leaving home with his wife for the evening. A sportswriter was on the line. How did Mathews feel about going to Houston? he asked. Mathews had spent fifteen years with the Braves and no one from the organization had bothered to call to say he had been traded. "I knew I wasn't hitting like I was supposed to, but there had been no hint a trade was coming," Mathews recalled. "I've always thought of myself being pretty macho but I cried like a baby."

Mathews knew a little place for dinner up the road from the Holiday Inn called the Wiggly Attache. It looked like one of the taverns that are on every neighborhood corner in Milwaukee: dim lights, a long bar and a jukebox, a row of booths. We took a booth whose seats were covered in red Naugahyde. Mathews ordered a bourbon and asked the waitress, "You like older men a little, don't you? Just a little?" His tone was teasing, not threatening, and she blushed and seemed to like the line. Mathews usually ate lunch alone at Wiggly Attache's bar when he was in Richmond. He remembered the bartender and a couple of waitresses, but they didn't recognize him, so I assumed he was not one who sat around advertising who he was or what he had done. He may have wished the young athletes he tutored had bothered to learn he was no journeyman .220 hitter, but outside the ballpark he did not sing for his supper. He had, I thought, a pride in what he had done and a modesty about who he was.

We drank at a fearful clip for a couple of hours. The stories he told with each new bourbon were ones that will be buried with his generation of ballplayers. There was Max Surkont tossing fire-crackers out the window of the team bus in Pittsburgh . . . a waiter at the team hotel in Philadelphia refusing to serve Warren Spahn and several teammates because he knew Spahn wouldn't tip. "Spahnie just didn't believe in tipping," Mathews said. "He'd say, 'I don't tip gas station attendants, so why should I tip waiters?'" And there was the night drinking with pitcher and former para-trooper Bob Buhl at a rooftop hotel bar in St. Louis when four men at a nearby table kept repeating, just loud enough for Mathews and Buhl to hear, "The Braves suck." "We listened to this shit for fifteen minutes," Mathews said. "Then Buhl got up, as though he was walking out, and I got up and stopped behind a big pillar. They didn't know I was there. The next time they said 'Braves suck' we came up behind those motherfuckers and beat them zingy." Math-ews and Buhl pulled the biggest one by the hair into an elevator, stripped him naked and let him off at the second floor. Then they went back and finished their drinks.

Mathews wondered what had happened to Hurricane Bob Hazle and I told him he was a liquor salesman in South Carolina. "That's the guy who won the '57 pennant for us," he said.

"Then why did you only vote him a two-thirds share of the World Series money?" I asked.

"Were we really that cheap?" Mathews looked surprised. "Damn. That's awful. We couldn't have won without him."

Fortified by a steak and more drinks, we left the Wiggly Attache past midnight for the perilous drive back to the Holiday Inn. Mathews's white Sprint bounded across a raised lane divider outside the restaurant—we decided the divider had been built during dinner, because we were sure it hadn't been there earlier—and sped down Broad Street. My obituary flashed to mind: "Eddie Mathews, one of baseball's greatest home-run hitters, and a passenger were killed early this morning when their car . . ." It would be a lengthy article, which would wrap up my life in a single paragraph, probably the fourth or fifth.

"You wonder what makes things fair," Mathews had said back in the restaurant. "I know a guy who gave up drinking, smoking, chasing women and he got run over by a beer truck. And Don McMahon. Never drank or smoked. He dropped dead on the pitcher's mound.

"I'll tell you the truth, if I went South tomorrow, I wouldn't have many regrets. I wished my father had lived to see what I did with the Braves. That's about it. I've had a hell of a lot of fun. People say, 'Slow down, aren't you afraid of dying?' I tell them, 'I just want a week to apologize to everyone before I go.' "

Like Randolph Scott, Eddie Mathews will always be etched in my mind's eye: *It is the last of the ninth at Milwaukee County Stadium, score tied, No. 41 at bat. Mathews swings and the crowd's roar swells. The right fielder is going back, back, looking up from the base of the green wall. I am on my feet. . . .*

Mathews was not one of Andy Warhol's fifteen-minute celebrities. In an age of media hype that values flash more than consistency of excellence, Mathews's virtues had spanned seventeen seasons. A strange thing to say about an old hero, but he reminded me of what I had been like in spirit when I was young: rambunctious and challenging the fates, drinking with gusto because you had much more fun with a buzz than you did sober, believing you needed a few laughs every day. I envied him for clinging to youthful notions I had lost in Vietnam.

Maybe our heroes, stripped of their shining moments, are no more and no less than we ourselves are. Yet Mathews's place in my personal hall of fame remained undiminished. He was of an era that is no more, an era when ballplayers were a lot like us.

Into Upstate
New York and Across
the Heartland
July 4–July 29

Chapter Sixteen

If only I could of thrown strikes.

—THE LEGENDARY STEVE DALKOWSKY

I had family and friends scattered from Washington, D.C., to Maine, and when I got to Maryland, I was tempted to ride I-95 right back into my old backyard. But the momentum of the journey had overtaken me. The thought of retiring from the road, of returning, even briefly, to a world of normal conversations and concerns was unsettling, and fifty miles from Washington I turned inland, away from all that was familiar.

The rain fell in pounding sheets, and I slowed, wiping the fogged windshield with my hand and squinting to keep track of the road. Eighteen-wheelers rushed by. Forty-niner swayed in their wake, as though struck by a giant fist. "I fooled you. I fooled you. I got all pig iron," sang a raspy voice on my CB radio. And from somewhere out on an invisible highway came the singsong reply, "And the Rock Island is a mighty good line. . . . This is Good Time Charlie wishing you all a happy Fourth of the Juuuuly."

. . .

I followed the Susquehanna River north, stopping in Harrisburg, where the Senators of the Double-A Eastern League had an Independence Day doubleheader scheduled with the Williamsport Bills. The Senators park is on a wooded river island, at the edge of town, and two thousand people were sitting there under umbrellas, waiting patiently for the skies to clear. They never did, and, after a couple of false starts to the game, the two young umpires pawed and kicked at the soggy infield turf and one of them held out his hands as though to say, What can we do? It was the Senators' twenty-first rainout of the season, enough to destroy the profitability of any minor league team. I decided to weather out the storm in the parking lot. I brewed some coffee and devoured the last of my doughnuts, which, remarkably, were still as fresh as the day I had bought them two weeks earlier in Pulaski. I checked the package, curious about the ingredients. Among those listed were: "bleached flour, thiamine mononitrate, dextrose, gelatinized wheat starch, guar gum, sorbic acid (a preservative), sodium casinate, titanium dioxide, artificial color (contains FD&C yellow #5)." Having sustained myself on ballpark franks for three months, I had no complaints and thought them delicious.

The rain slackened and summer showers trailed me into the Dutch county of Pennsylvania and upstate New York. The two-lane road crisscrossed the Susquehanna, dipping and climbing through forests and plunging hills that reminded me of Oregon. It wandered past little towns with roadhouses and old-fashioned diners. I wondered if the people knew, or cared, that diners had fallen out of style years ago. Or that more recently they had been revived as trendy nostalgia, and restaurateurs in California were spending fortunes to build new ones that looked just like the old ones that had stood along this road forever.

Two days out of Harrisburg, I reached Elmira, an old New York railroad town. Mark Twain had married an Elmira girl and written there for a while, and a walking tour of the town included a stop at Cleo's Bridal Shop on Church Street, which, visitors were told, had been the home of a nineteenth-century major league player named Daniel Richardson. Other than that, I had trouble learning much about Elmira. The only book I found on the town was titled *Elmira Trolleys* (they had disappeared decades ago), and every time

I asked someone about local history, they immediately began speaking of the flood of 1972, which had nearly washed away the town and still spooked everyone. "It could happen again, you know," they would say.

The industries had pulled out in the sixties, and between their departure and the flood, the town had had to struggle to stay alive. The lunch counter of the downtown five-and-dime was quiet, even at lunchtime; many businesses had failed, and the Greyhound didn't go much of anywhere besides Scranton, Rochester and Binghamton. Given the choice between promoting growth and development and protecting Elmira's character as a small, pleasant place to live, the populace clearly favored the latter.

If one was looking for historical continuity in Elmira, baseball was a likely starting point. Elmira had had a minor league team since 1888 and had won championships while affiliated with three big-league clubs that no longer even existed: the St. Louis Browns, Brooklyn Dodgers and Washington Senators. Elmira's Dunn Field was where infielder Don Zimmer (now the Chicago Cubs manager) was married, with the preacher toeing the pitcher's mound and potted plants adorning the infield; where Pete Rose played his first professional game and Wade Boggs had his worst season (.263 in 1976). It was also where a fireballing lefty with a million-dollar arm and a ten-cent head became a legend and made his name—Steve Dalkowsky—synonymous with the dreams and nightmares of every player who ever toiled in the minors.

Dalkowsky wouldn't have found much changed in Elmira in the twenty-five years he had been gone. To get to Dunn Field, he would still have to drive down tree-shaded Maple Avenue, passing the Victorian home of Virginia Dean, who had been taking in ballplayers as boarders every summer since her husband died ("They're here three months, I got to Florida for three months and that only leaves six months to be alone," she said), and would turn left on Luce Street by Ward's Grill. The park was a quarter mile away, on the banks of the Chemung River and set among the homes of a modest neighborhood, where the sound of lawn mowers filled the weekend afternoons of summer. Dalkowsky might even have recognized Daniel Donahoe, a retired judge, sitting in the same first-base box seat he has held since 1958.

The Elmira Pioneers were in the fifty-year-old New York–Penn
League, the oldest continuously operating Class-A circuit in baseball. The investor group that owned the team was headed by Clyde
Smoll, a former Philadelphia labor negotiator, who seemed unusually conscious of the bottom line. Broken bats were taped back
together and offered for sale at $3.50 in the concession booth.
Busted batting helmets went for $5 and players' used stirrup socks
for $3. "Lock that gate and don't let anyone in unless they pay a
buck and half!" he shouted to an attendant in the tenth inning of
one tie game—a time when most teams open the passageway and
let kids drift in free. Umpires complained they had trouble getting
enough game balls from him and whenever a foul ball disappeared
into the night, Smoll appeared visibly pained.

In the grass-covered parking lot outside, fourteen-year-old Jerry
Butler made a nice summer living chasing down foul balls and
selling them back to Smoll, a dollar for a game ball, fifty cents for
a batting-practice ball. "I could get more from my friends," the boy
said, "but I like Mr. Smoll." Jerry always knew if a righty or lefty
was coming to bat, and he moved with every hitter, expertly positioning himself where the balls were most likely to land.

"When's the last time you were in Elmira?" Jerry asked me one
evening. I said this was my first visit. "You've *never* been in *Elmira?*" he replied, figuring he had met the world's biggest yahoo.
I told him I was writing a book on baseball and would only be
around a few days. The next night he spotted me across the parking lot and yelled, "Hey, you finish that book yet?"

The president of the Pioneers when Dalkowsky played in Elmira
in the early- and mid-sixties was an optometrist, Art Wellington.
Now retired, Wellington still attended every game and remembered
having had to bail his pitcher out of jail one night when the
downtown lampposts he and several teammates had climbed in
celebration of a pennant-clinching victory bent like paper clips.

"Dalkowsky had all the marks of success," Wellington said. "He
was an amazing young man who threw so hard one of his pitches
tore right through the screen behind home plate. His name still
comes up from time to time. I think he went back to California.
You wish his story would have a happy ending, because everyone
liked him, but I don't see it ending that way. I'm sure I'll pick up

the paper someday and see that he's died of sclerosis or some disease like that."

Steven Louis Dalkowsky was born in New Britain, Connecticut, the son of a hard-drinking electric-tool-plant worker. His left arm was the gift of God, an arm so powerful he could throw the ball harder and faster than anyone who ever lived. That, at least, is what everyone said who saw him pitch. He was faster than Ryne Duren, faster than Koufax, sometimes reaching speeds of 115 mph, the old scouts said, and the day he graduated from high school, in June 1957, scouts from every major league team except the Cleveland Indians were on his doorstep. "They were wonderful fellows," his mother told writer Pat Jordan. "Their cars were lined up all the way down Governor Street. Big, beautiful cars. One came with a chauffeur. I couldn't even concentrate. And oh, how they were dressed! Rubies and diamonds! They were big shots."

Dalkowsky signed with the Baltimore Orioles scout Frank McGowan for a thousand-dollar bonus and was sent to Kingsport, Tennessee. He was not a big man. He stood five foot ten, had unusually thin wrists and wore glasses as thick as a Coke bottle. In sixty-two innings at Kingsport he struck out 121 batters, including twenty-four in one game. One inside pitch was thrown so hard it tore off part of a batter's ear. The next year, in Wilson (North Carolina), Aberdeen (South Dakota) and Knoxville, he fanned more than two hundred, and one night threw a fastball that the catcher missed entirely. It struck the umpire in the face mask— knocking him eighteen feet, chest protector over whisk broom, according to local newspaper reports.

But if his speed was a gift of God, his control was the curse of Satan, for Steve Dalkowsky was wilder than a northeast gale. His fastball would explode in the stands—a hundred feet off target— and knock batters out of the on-deck circle. Batboys cowered in the dugout. He gave up more bases on balls in a single season than anyone in the history of the California League, and once in Stockton threw six wild pitches in a row. In Aberdeen one night he struck out seventeen and walked sixteen.

"Hey, Dalkowsky, you pitchin' tonight?" a fan yelled after three warm-up pitches missed the screen behind home plate and splintered box seats. Dalkowsky mumbled yes and the fan shouted back, "Then I'm getting the hell out of here, and I'm taking my kids with me."

His managers tried everything. They had him warm up for an hour before the game, hoping fatigue would induce accuracy. They took him to a psychiatrist specializing in behavior modification. The doctor showed him ink blotches and asked what he saw. "I don't see nuthin'," Dalkowsky replied. They built a wooden target, extending six feet on either side of a strike-zone-sized hole, but his pitches demolished the two-by-fours before one found the hole. Baltimore brought in its pitching coach, Harry Brecheen, to stand behind the mound and it put a right-handed and left-handed batter at the plate simultaneously. Dalkowsky threw perfect strikes. But as soon as Brecheen was no longer there to calm him, his fastball became helter-skelter again, and by the second inning of every game, even in the chill of South Dakota nights, his uniform would be soaked with sweat, as though some demon controlled his body.

"Everywhere I went," Dalkowsky recalled, "people'd say, 'Geez, there he is,' like I was a freak or something. It drove me crazy."

It wasn't until he got to Elmira that he started throwing strikes with consistency—he led the league with six shutouts in 1962— and the next year the Orioles put him on their major league roster and invited him to Miami for spring training. Miss Ecuador was staying in the room next to his at the Miami hotel; he bought a drill and bored a hole right through the wall. On the field he showed flashes of brilliance. He threw a pitch by Ted Williams that Williams said he never even saw, and he struck out Roger Maris on three pitches. Rick Monday, who had signed for a $104,000 bonus, went down swinging four times in four at bats in a later encounter. Each time he fanned, Dalkowsky would yell, "A hundred and four grand, my ass." Although he was still lethally wild— in one exhibition game Cincinnati manager Birdie Tebbetts had his batters stand *outside* the box so they wouldn't get beaned and Dalkowsky had struck out the side on twelve pitches—Baltimore decided to bring Dalkowsky north as its short reliever. Ten days before the end of spring training, he fielded a bunt off the bat of pitcher Jim Bouton, fired to first and grabbed his arm in pain. A

knot the size of a golf ball swelled up in his elbow. The Orioles
shipped him out a few days later to Rochester, where he pitched
badly and ended up back in Elmira. "Everything seemed to come
unglued then," Dalkowsky said. "My arm hurt, and I really started
drinking."

Three years later, while working in the basement of professional
baseball, the California League, he was given his unconditional
release by the San Jose Bees. The *Sporting News* ran a brief story
with a seven-year-old photograph under the headline "Living Legend Released." Dalkowsky, not quite twenty-seven, had played for
eleven teams in nine minor leagues, and over his nine-year career
had won forty-six games, lost eighty, struck out fourteen hundred
batters and walked nearly as many.

"Nothing really worked," he told a writer. "Maybe it was because of the drinking. All I know is I would go drinking with guys
like Boog Powell or Musial, and they were so much bigger than me,
they could drink a lot more and not show it. Maybe the Lord
meant it to be that way."

He went back to Stockton, where he had played in 1960 and
1964 and married a schoolteacher, whose mother ran a pet store.
Dalkowsky married her, he said, for money, not love. His mother-
in-law thought he was a tramp, and all the dogs in the house drove
him nuts. "Do you know what it's like to get up in the morning
and find dog mess in your bathroom?" he asked. One day he drove
off in the family Thunderbird to get a pack of cigarettes and never
came back.

Steve Dalkowsky would place his bottle of red wine thirty or
forty feet ahead, then work his way toward it, chopping through
the row of cotton with his short-handled hoe. "I'm just trying to
work hard and forget the past," he said. He'd stop to take a slug
of wine, occasionally sharing his reward with one of the migrant
Mexican pickers. Then he would walk down the row, place the
bottle firmly upright and begin chopping again. He labored ten-
hour days, sometimes twenty-five or thirty days in a row, stooped
and sweating, the heat of the San Joaquin Valley so brutal that it
left no strength to remember.

One day in the mid-seventies, the Bakersfield Police Department
called Chuck Stevens, baseball's Good Samaritan, and said a man

named Dalkowsky was in the drunk tank. Did he want to help? Dalkowsky by then was nearly dead. Living in flophouses, he had been arrested for drunkenness dozens of times and could hold down nothing but a few drops of brandy. Stevens, who played first base for the St. Louis Browns in the forties, ran the Association of Professional Ballplayers of America, an organization that helps indigent former players. With the aid of Ray Youngdahl, a one-time Dalkowsky teammate who had become a California real estate executive, they began the process of mending. Dalkowsky was tied down and taken to the detox clinic to ride out his delirium tremens.

The last I heard of Dalkowsky, he was living in an apartment near Bakersfield with his second wife, Virginia, a strong woman who worked the counter at a bakery and tried hard to keep her man straight. Mostly he sat around, remembering the old days in Kingsport and Aberdeen and Stockton, drinking fifteen or twenty beers a day but never touching wine. Virginia had thrown him out more times than she could remember and always taken him back. "I love him and I feel sorry for him," she said. Dalkowsky told friends he would like to be a major league groundskeeper, but that would mean going back to start in a place he had already been—the minor leagues—and so he had never applied for the job.

Every now and then, Dalkowsky would go out to Sam Lynn Ballpark to see the Bakersfield Dodgers play, and people would still say, 'Geez, there he is. That's Steve Dalkowsky,' as he walked by, one hand on the railing to steady himself. I called the Dodgers from Elmira, hoping I could arrange to meet Dalkowsky when I returned to California at season's end. They said they hadn't seen him at the park all season, but someone gave me his number and I telephoned. The recorded message said: "You have reached a number that has been disconnected or is no longer in service. If you feel you have reached this recording in error, please try the number again."

I didn't call again, though I did later learn that Dalkowsky was still in Bakersfield, living on Virginia's salary from the bakery and a stipend from the Association of Professional Ballplayers. He charged for interviews, I was told, and viewed writers dimly because the last one he had talked to had promised to send a check but never did. But I think he would have been pleased to know that the young minor leaguers I met spoke of him with reverence, not realizing that the legend, as it usually is, was bigger than the man himself had ever been.

Chapter Seventeen

And stepping Westward seemed to be a kind of heavenly destiny.

—WILLIAM WORDSWORTH

Not far from Elmira, I turned left onto Route 6, the nation's second-longest transcontinental road, stretching 3,227 miles from Provincetown, Massachusetts, to Bishop, California, on the doorstep of Death Valley. For the first time in four months I was pointed back toward the Pacific. The very thought of the wide, handsome West excited me, and I floated along as if lifted by balloons. "When I crossed the Mississippi, I felt as though I'd shed a big burden," Ernie Pyle wrote to a friend in 1937, and though the river was still far ahead of me, I understood his sense of elation. I wondered if the Western dream would have lured me from Boston a century earlier, and I decided yes, I still would have gone. I probably would have tried one of the raffish towns—Tombstone or Dodge City or Bannack, Montana—and, not fitting in very well, would have eventually made my way to San Francisco.

Route 6 travels in an uncertain direction, disappearing for long

stretches, overlapping interstates, then heading off on its own
toward nowhere. It is a patchwork of old trails—the White Way,
the Lone Star Route, the Southwest Trail, the Greater Sheridan
Road—sewn together in the twenties when federal and state au-
thorities developed a numbered highway system. In the miles
ahead, I would leave it often, then in the emptiness of Nebraska
or Colorado or Utah, its signposts would reappear, beckoning me
like an old friend. "Come, we'll travel together," they seemed to
say, and as often as not, I complied.

The little towns were clustered close together in western New
York. They had village greens, and the American Legion post
usually occupied a prominent position on Main Street. I saw many
U.S. flags and one drive-in theater. The sweetness of the season's
first mown hay hung in the air. Roadside stands sold corn and
strawberries, and near a red barn whose side was painted with the
words "Chew Mail Pouch Tobacco. Treat Yourself to the Best"
several cars were parked and a couple of families had gathered for
an evening barbecue. The men stood together beside the grill,
holding cans of beer, and the women sat in lawn chairs that had
been pulled together in a semicircle. I realized I was hungry and
stopped across the Pennsylvania border for something to eat. I
found an excellent café whose menu was on a board over the
counter. The white stick-in letters said: ". . . old fashioned loin and
FF 2.50 . . . minute ST 2.00 . . . grilled ham and CH 1.65 . . . juices
45–65 . . . homemade pie ASK . . ."

Cafés, like neighborhood taverns, should be timeless and folksy
if they are to be gathering spots, and this one was. Packets of
Alka-Seltzer were displayed by the milk-shake mixer, and the glass-
fronted counter on which an old cash register rested contained Life
Savers, cough drops, pocket combs and nail cutters. News clippings of local interest were taped to the pine-paneled wall: bingo
at the Elks, a 4-H baseball game, several recent weddings. The two
plump, elderly waitresses brought customers coffee without being
asked and I never once heard them say, "Have a nice day." My
place mat showed a set of hands held in prayerful thanks and were
printed with Orthodox Jewish, Protestant and Catholic prayers.

Propped in a corner booth was a black-and-white TV with rabbit
ears, tuned to the Cubs game. No one was paying much attention.

Remarkably, Don Zimmer, the Elmira Pioneers' graduate, had his team in first, though everyone knew Chicago would fold by season's end, enabling the Cubs' omnipresent fans to enjoy another winter of self-flagellation.

The Cubs had been in the running twenty years earlier, too, at the same time the Weathermen where planning their Days of Rage. Two of the radical underground leaders, Bill Ayers and Bernadine Dohrn, met secretly one day with several other Weathermen in a Chicago apartment. Someone suggested the violent campaign should start in August, September at the latest. "No, what if the Cubs win the pennant?" Ayers said. "We have to wait until October." He had his priorities right: the pennant first, the revolution second.

In contrast to the pastoral gentleness of Route 6, the brick-faced railroad and mill towns that ran from Erie, New York, to Wheeling, West Virginia, cutting a swath through western Pennsylvania, were a world apart. Many of them were ethnic towns—Polish, Syrian, Irish, Italian—that had made steel and tin and had prospered because there was coal in the valleys. Boys who lived there thirty or forty years ago worked feverishly to develop their athletic talents with one goal: to escape a lifetime in the mines. It was no coincidence that the region's native sons—Johnny Unitas, Joe Montana, Dick Grote, Tito Francona, the Niekro brothers, Mike Ditka, Chuck Tanner—were good at their chosen trade and tough as bolts of iron.

Tanner was baseball's "Mr. Sunshine," the unrepentant thank-God-for-another-day-at-the-ballpark optimist. No one on the Braves had been nicer to me than Tanner during my summer visit to Milwaukee in 1955. Once he had yelled across the clubhouse, "Hey, Dave, come on over here and sit down. I want to talk to you." I had nearly burst with pride to be identified and summoned. For a good many years afterward, we exchanged occasional letters. "I have been in quite a mixed-up mood," he wrote in '59 after the Braves had sold him to the Cubs and the last-place Cubs had dealt him to Boston. "The Red Sox sent me directly to their Minneapolis baseball club, so I am going to have to work my way back up." He was then thirty years old. Tanner had lived his entire life in New Castle, north of Pittsburgh, a town that resembled a leftover from a fire sale.

The nearest daily newspaper of consequence to New Castle was the *Youngstown Vindicator*, "The People's Paper." The name sounded like the title of a Charles Bronson movie, but I liked the notion that a newspaper, in name at least, still fancied itself the guardian of the common man. Two page-one articles caught my eye in the *Vindicator* I bought from a vending machine outside a bar.

One was headlined "More Women Turn to Guns to Stay Safe" and quoted student Sherry Harp saying in a local gun class: "There's a lot of women alone, and with all the drugs and everything out there . . ." The other article reported that Sam Brown, owner of a northside restaurant called The Pit, had captured three robbers and had held them at bay with his .38-caliber revolver until police arrived. Ten years earlier, Brown had shot and killed a fifteen-year-old boy who had tried to rob his restaurant, the paper said. He told the *Vindicator*'s reporter: "There are wolves out there and they'll eat you up. I'm not going to let nobody, not nobody, come in here screwin' around and take this place away. I opened this little raggedy shack and fed my family the past twelve years. I've worked hard to put this business together. I'm not going to let nobody destroy it."

Chuck Tanner grew up in a small farmhouse, just outside New Castle, which, until he was in the eighth grade, had no heat, electricity or bathroom. Rent was five dollars a month. One day a neighbor came by and offered to plow the family field for forty cents, and his grandfather said, "Thanks just the same. We'll spade it." Tanner, wearing a big straw hat and clodhoppers, would sneak away from farm chores and join a group of older boys in pick-up baseball games that went on for so many hours he might have starved had his mother not shown up each afternoon with a stack of peanut butter sandwiches. "You'll be a bum," his grandfather said. "All you want to do is baseball, baseball, baseball." Everywhere Tanner went he ran: to his job at the brick plant, to his job washing dishes, to football practice, to the American Legion park and back up the hill to home. He became one of Shenango High School's finest athletes, and by the time the Boston Braves signed him to a minor league contract, the pressure of constant sports competition, of wanting so desperately to excel, had given him bleeding ulcers. Between innings he would sit on the bench of the Owensboro (Kentucky) Oilers, drinking milk.

In the minors he hit over .300 seven straight years. But with sixteen big-league teams then, instead of twenty-six, talent was not spread as thin as it is today and escaping the bush leagues was much tougher. Most American and National League clubs had thirteen or fourteen quality players, pitching staffs were deeper, and for every major league player there were twenty-seven minor leaguers waiting in the wings. (Today there are six.) Not until 1955, when in his tenth year of professional ball Tanner and his wife, Babs, were still living in a converted chicken coop in New Castle, did the Braves promote him to Milwaukee. (That was also the year Tanner drank his first beer.) On opening day he pinch-hit for Warren Spahn in the eighth inning and drove the first major league pitch he saw—a fastball from Gerry Staley—over the fence to help the Braves defeat Cincinnati, 4–2. If anyone had asked, I would have wagered Forty-niner's front axle that Tanner had been a superstar his rookie year, and I was surprised to check *The Baseball Encyclopedia* and see that he had been a part-time outfielder who had batted less than .250, with six home runs. His major league career, in fact, had been shorter than his minor league career.

"So you finally found out I was one of the donkeys on the bench," he laughed when I told him this. Tanner, a grandfather, had celebrated his sixtieth birthday on the Fourth of July and, for the first time in forty-two years, was out of baseball, having been fired (along with his coaches) as the Atlanta Braves manager the previous season. The Braves had cited "philosophical differences," which meant that general manager Bobby Cox wanted to put together his own cadre of loyalists whose allegiance would be to him, not Tanner. (Cox had replaced Tanner with Russ Nixon, the most consistent manager in baseball; in four years of managing Nixon had never finished anywhere but dead last.) We went downstairs into Tanner's den, and the first thing I saw was a picture of Willie Stargell with the inscription: "My life has been much better having you as a friend."

Tanner should have been in a state of depression, but wasn't.

Not only hadn't the phone rung with an offer of another manager's job—running the Atlanta Braves, a bad team that kept getting worse, was a professional curtain call for most managers—his sister-in-law had just died, his restaurant in New Castle had burned down, his prized thoroughbred, Majesty's Imp, had developed bone chips and had been scratched at the last minute from the Kentucky Derby. And through it all Tanner, a man of boundless enthusiasm and good cheer, kept thinking of how fortunate he had been: to have even gotten close to the Derby, to have managed eighteen consecutive years in the majors after his playing days were over, to have met important people and been an equal.

"Mr. Dan Galbreath, one of the world's greatest men, he's a friend," Tanner said. "And Gene Autry. Tommy Lasorda and I are like brothers. Shoot, I was in a room once and someone yells, 'Hey, Chuck, come on over here. I want to talk to you.' You know who it was? *Bing Crosby.* Son of a pickle. Bing Crosby! And I'm from *New Castle.*"

Tanner had played for Milwaukee for only two full seasons, and I had forgotten that, too, thinking he had stayed much longer. But I do remember that he used to dash everywhere at breakneck speed and would run so hard from left field to the dugout after each inning that he often got there before the first baseman, Joe Adcock. When a foul tip shattered his jaw, doctors wired it shut and he kept playing. Tanner bird-dogged managers and coaches, asking why they did this or what happens when you try that. In the twilight of his career, he had the choice of playing one more year for the Los Angeles Angels for eighteen thousand dollars or going back to the lowest minors to manage a team in Iowa for six thousand. He made an investment in the future and chose the latter. As a manager he had twenty-five rules, one for each member of the team, and what he did best was to make players believe in themselves and give of themselves. It took him eight years to get back to the major leagues. But long after Wes Covington and the other Braves he had subbed for were gone and forgotten, Tanner was still there, winning more big-league games than all but nineteen managers in history.

"I got everything out of my ability I could," Tanner said, which wouldn't be a bad epitaph for a man's headstone. I remembered

Steve Dalkowsky's lament—"If only I could of thrown strikes"—
and thought how sad it must be to start the summation of one's
life with the word "if." Tanner had far less talent than the Braves'
name players—the Mathewses and Spahns and Aarons—yet had
stayed in uniform longer than any of them and, with a salary of six
hundred thousand dollars a year from Atlanta, which he would
continue to collect for two years after his dismissal, had been the
only one to capitalize on the big money baseball now lavished on
its people.

Tanner had spent twenty-six years in the majors as a player and
manager, and in all that time had seen practically nothing of any
city except the hotel and the ballpark. Once, he got to the Statue
of Liberty and a couple of times during rainouts, he saw a Broadway show. Other than that, it had been only baseball, fourteen
hours a day, seven days a week. "I just don't feel normal till I get
to the park," he said long ago. Even in Los Angeles, where no one
walks, he would leave the Bonaventure Hotel on foot after a late
breakfast when his Braves were in town, head down Figueroa
Street, cut through Chinatown and hike up a hill to Dodger Stadium. He was always the first to arrive, about seven hours before
game time.

I asked him if he thought he might have lost out on anything
by seeing so much of baseball and so little of the world.

"Lost out?" He was incredulous. "Lost out? Hell, I've been one
of the lucky ones. I don't need a plane or a boat to be happy. All
I need is a ballpark. People say to me, 'Now that you've got the
money and the time, aren't you going to go to Europe?' What do
I need that for? I haven't even seen all the streets in New Castle
yet."

I left New Castle on a Monday afternoon, bound for Milwaukee.
Tanner said his interest in horse racing—he owned a small stable,
Batarasan—had helped overcome the withdrawal symptoms of
leaving baseball. But the separation was only temporary, he said,
and any day he expected to pick up the phone and and hear an
offer for redemption. "I'll be back," he said. "You'll see. I'll take
another team and make it better. I'd even consider going back to
Triple-A if the job was right." As I pulled out of his driveway I saw
Tanner in my review mirror, on the lawn, smiling, his hands braced

on the back of his hips, as though he were still standing in a third-base coach's box.

Ohio and Indiana slipped by in a blur of straight roads cut through golden corn fields. The corn was a foot shorter than it should have been in mid-July and farmers stood on their porches each dawn, coffee cups in hand, sniffing the air. But there wasn't even the smell of rain in the heavy, humid mornings, and each day their land become more parched and more cracked. Living in Southern California, where there is no weather, one tends to forget that weather dominates the lives of so many Americans and is discussed more often every day in small towns and big cities from coast to coast than any other subject. At home I knew the daily forecast without even opening the newspaper: sunny and 75, a forecast that was as perfect as it was boring.

I pulled off Route 30 in Ohio and drove into Delphos for groceries. The digital sign on the bank at Second and Main streets put the temperature at 98 degrees and the time at 3:02 P.M. Thirty minutes later the temperature had dropped twenty degrees and a wild wind descended on the town. The streetlights went on and black clouds swirled low overhead. Lightning and thunder cracked and the door of the little fire station attached to city hall opened automatically. Shopkeepers stood by their windows, peering out at the deserted street, then up at the sky.

"Those clouds are going every which way," a woman in the pharmacy said. "We're going to get it now."

"They're already getting it over in Putnam County, I can assure you that," said the pharmacist. "The storm's coming from the southwest. Worst possible direction. I'd say it's moving about five miles an hour, wouldn't you?"

The storm attacked Delphos like a tidal wave, and in a few minutes was gone. Clouds scraped the tops of grain silos, teasing with the hint of a rain that would nourish and not hurry off. Then they, too, were gone and the hot sun returned. Driving out of town, I saw gullies in the corn fields where the torrents had rushed through. The thirsty earth had drunk hardly a drop and the tasseled corn stood wilting and utterly motionless, row after row, to the horizon and beyond.

Chapter Eighteen

The whole history of baseball has the quality of
mythology.

—BERNARD MALAMUD

merican cities achieve recognition not because of their universities or think tanks or resident orchestras, but because of the success or failure of their professional sports teams. And in 1953—the year Marilyn Monroe posed nude for the centerfold of *Playboy*'s first issue, Ernest Hemingway won a Pulitzer Prize for *The Old Man and the Sea* and Dwight Eisenhower took the presidential oath in the first inauguration televised coast to coast—Milwaukee, a small Midwestern minor league city, became synonymous forever more with the romance of a people and its baseball team.

Milwaukee was one of those out-of-the-way places that, unless you lived there, you probably didn't know much about. Huddled against Lake Michigan, it wasn't a center of commerce like Chicago or even a transportation crossroads like Minneapolis. John Gunther hardly mentioned Milwaukee in his thousand-page book, *Inside U.S.A.*, written in 1947, and, in fact, dismissed the whole region in a brief chapter titled "More About Minnesota, Plus Wisconsin." The city had one television station, more bowling alleys and taverns than anyone could count, and an American Association minor league team known as the Brewers, who played in a creaky wooden park, Borchert Field, which eventually would be torn down to make room for a freeway.

Ever since the Great Fire of 1871 had destroyed Chicago's breweries, Milwaukee had been the nation's beer capital, the home of Schlitz (The Beer that Made Milwaukee Famous), Miller High Life and Pabst. Heavy-machinery manufacturers followed the breweries into Milwaukee, and the city evolved as a workingman's town, as decent as it was unsophisticated, a city of blue-collar ethnic neighborhoods where the people, like their German, Dutch and Polish ancestors, worked hard, shared a sense of community responsibility and expected good value for a dollar spent. (William Proxmire epitomized Milwaukee's frugal, traditional character; he spent $145.10 in his 1982 campaign for the U.S. Senate and won hands down.)

Although the alignment of the sixteen major league franchises had remained unchanged since 1903, it had become apparent by 1953 that cities such as Boston, St. Louis and Philadelphia could no longer support two teams, and on the afternoon of March 18, National League owners meeting in St. Petersburg, Florida, voted 8 to 0, albeit somewhat reluctantly, to allow Lou Perini to move his seventh-place Boston Braves to Milwaukee.

"It's too bad to have to move such a team to Milwaukee," one of the owners said after the vote. "Those Dutch will never support a second-division club. It's a bad psychological start."

Two days later, on Sunday, ten thousand fans drove out to the newly constructed Milwaukee County Stadium on South Forty-sixth Street. For several hours they sat in the grandstands, wrapped in rain slickers and blankets, looking out on an empty field and dreaming of what was about to be. They spoke in the hushed voices one hears in church before a service begins.

An entire city—indeed, an entire state—was falling in love with the same mistress. Mayor Frank Zeidler declared a week of celebration, and when the just-christened Milwaukee Braves arrived from their Florida spring training camp, they stepped off the train onto a red carpet that had been laid in the Chicago & Northwestern Station. They paraded through downtown in open cars on the raw gray day and thousands cheered them. At their hotel the players found their rooms stuffed with presents, and everywhere they went during the season there would be gifts and more gifts: free use of cars, free groceries by the bagful, free cigars and gasoline and neckties, free restaurant meals and free clothes, dry cleaning and beer. Fans gave Warren Spahn a new tractor for his Oklahoma ranch, Billy Burton fifteen hundred dollars for the down payment on a house and Max Surkont a year's supply of Polish sausage. (Surkont promptly ate himself out of shape and was traded the next year.) Even Esther Lynch, the wife of sports editor Russ Lynch, got cut in on the booty, with an expensive fur coat delivered one day to the Lynches' home. It was from the Braves' owner, Lou Perini. Lynch was on the phone to Perini the next morning. "You get that coat out of my house by noon!" he ordered. "We don't take payola at the *Journal*."

Restaurants renamed the hamburger a Bravesburger and a new high school athletic league called itself the Braveland Conference. One Beloit plant needing engineers advertised that the company was "only ninety minutes from Braves stadium" and a preacher in Portage, a hundred miles from Milwaukee, told his congregation, "I want you to support the Braves, but don't forget us. Collections are falling off." A few blocks from the church, a sign in the window of a one-man barber shop said, "I can't stand it any longer. Closed for two days. Gone to see the Braves."

Tickets were in such demand that the Braves stopped filling block orders and had to restrict window sales to one home stand at a time. The Milwaukee Road ran so many special trains—seven one Sunday alone—that it had to build a passenger platform where its rails passed the stadium. Fans appeared for games carrying sirens and bells and wearing gaudy hats and headbands laced with feathers. They cheered everything, even the walks and errors. Sometimes on a Saturday afternoon, an entire wedding party would show up, then rush off to the church about the fourth inning. Music-makers started coming, too—a singing trio, accordion players, a six-piece band—and the musicians' union complained that fans with instruments shouldn't be allowed inside the

park. But they were paying their own way and the union acquiesced.

The Braves responded to all the attention by giving the Brooklyn
Dodgers a run and finishing second. By season's end, Milwaukee,
with a metropolitan population of 870,000, had drawn 1.8 million
fans, more than any team in the seventy-seven-year history of the
National League. That would be the equivalent of today's New
York Mets drawing 37 million people.

Now you understand why I loved Milwaukee no less than Tootsie Weisenbach, why as a teenager in Boston I had allowed my
allegiance to travel west with the Braves. Other teams would
move—the St. Louis Browns to Baltimore the next year, the Philadelphia Athletics to Kansas City the year after that and the Giants
and Dodgers to California in 1958—but none ever captured the
imagination of a city the way the Braves had. And none ever will
again. The barber who closed his shop could stay home today and
watch the game on TV. The Braves Goodwill Ambassador, Hal
Goodnough, a retired Massachusetts high school teacher, who
toured the state in a red Nash Rambler emblazoned with a grinning
Indian head (an unacceptably derogatory symbol today) and the
words THANK YOU, WISCONSIN! THE MILWAUKEE BRAVES could do his
work by fax. And as for the intimacy between the fans and players,
the gifts and adoration, well, what can you give a millionaire?
Surely not neckties and a case of beer.

Milwaukee was laced with freeways and interstates that I hadn't
remembered, and several times I pointed Forty-niner in the wrong
direction and had to inquire where County Stadium was. I felt an
emptiness in my stomach, that twinge of sadness—or maybe a
longing is what it really was—you get when you return to your old
neighborhood after many years and see the house where you grew
up. It's not that the house looks bad or that the area has changed
much; it's just that nothing belongs to you anymore, and even if
you knocked on the door the occupants wouldn't know who you
were or understand why you had cared so much. Strange, I
thought, how what seems like an inconsequential gesture can shape
our lives; if I hadn't written that letter to Russ Lynch thirty-four
years earlier, there would have been no Milwaukee for me to return

to and probably no season stolen from my adulthood to wander a minor league trail.

The last time I had been in Milwaukee for more than a fly-through visit was in 1959, the year my friend John Sherman and I hitchhiked the country, and heading back to Boston, I had insisted we detour north to see the Braves play. "Come on, John," I said, "you'll get a chance to see Eddie *Mathews*, Johnny *Logan*. . . . It'll make the summer." He looked at me oddly, and I knew he'd rather have pushed for home. We were hungry and had not a dime between us. We reached Milwaukee without difficulty and slept the first night under a bush near the Menomonee River. When I awoke, I was on eye level with the polished boots of a motorcycle cop. He asked what we were doing and I said we had come to see the Braves play. His attitude softened. But our financial condition made us vagrants and he announced in a not unfriendly way, "Unless you've got someone you can stay with, I'm going to have to run you boys in."

My mind raced frantically and settled on the Cookie Lady. She was Gladys Baumbach, a legendary fan who brought the Braves homemade cookies before every game and who, I was sure, would remember me from my visit to Milwaukee four years earlier as the teenage sportswriter. The policeman gave us a dime and I found her number. Forty minutes later we were rescued, and Mrs. Baumbach was cooking us the first real meal we had tasted in days.

We stayed in Milwaukee for three or four games and someone introduced us to Lou Perini, the wealthy owner who ran a Boston construction company. He was intrigued that we had survived a summer on our wits and asked when we were returning to Boston. John and I dreaded the thought of the last, long stretch for home, thumbs again raised, empty stomachs rumbling. I said we'd probably leave in a couple of days.

"I'm flying back in my plane Sunday after the game," Perini said. "You're welcome to join me."

The highway where we had thought we would be standing appeared from the window of Perini's twin-engine prop as little more than a ribbon and it seemed curious to pass over it so effortlessly, a precise destination time assured. I sat next to the Braves owner for a good part of the journey, suggesting names of players I thought the team should call up from Toledo and Wichita and feeling for all the world like royalty. When we landed in Boston, the wire services had picked up a story Russ Lynch had written about our hitchhiking the country and our chance encounter with Perini. A page-one article appeared in the *Globe* under the headline, "Braves Fans Broke, Ride to Hub in Perini's Plane." I swear, every time I got close to the Braves, something wonderful happened.

The Braves played their final game in Milwaukee on September 22, 1965, before twelve thousand fans. The romance had lasted thirteen seasons. Eddie Mathews, the only surviving member of the original National League Braves, came to bat in the eighth inning and received a three-minute standing ovation. A bugler in right field played taps. Then the team that had never had a losing season in Milwaukee packed up and, drawn to the television dollars of a larger market, became the Atlanta Braves (the only major league baseball club that in 1989 drew fewer than one millions fans). It was the beginning of a new era in sports featuring gypsy franchises that abandoned communities in the dead of night; cities fought for the honor of hosting the displaced teams and in the process their taxpayers were hustled out of millions of dollars to finance public stadiums for private gain.

Milwaukee needed five years to get another team, this one the American League Seattle Pilots who arrived as the renamed Brewers. Milwaukee was still a good baseball town and the Brewers would draw well, but the city had used up its only miracle.

I parked Forty-niner outside County Stadium and took a few halfhearted swipes at the Indiana dust covering my counters and table. It was about time to declare another Maintenance Day. The two-tier park had been the newest in the big leagues when I had first seen it. Now it was almost forty years old, with inadequate parking, an undersized press box and no money-making skyboxes. The Brewers had said a new stadium was essential if the team was to remain in Milwaukee. Not much seemed to have changed, except that the decks had been extended in right field, obscuring the bleachers Lou Perini had built on the grounds of the Old Soldiers

Home beyond the fence. VA veterans used to pack the free seats in "Perini's Woods" for every game, but with nothing to see now but the backside of a wall, I assumed the bleachers stood empty or had been torn down.

Although old-timers in Milwaukee would occasionally slip and refer to the Brewers as the Braves, I was surprised that all the memories of a past I still cherished had been buried. Names of marginal contributors to the Braves' two National League pennants—Harry Hanebrink or Dave Jolly or Carlton Willey—drew no recognition at all, and when I asked a player if he had ever heard of Russ Lynch—without whom Milwaukee might still have been a minor league town—he replied, "I think so. He played second, or maybe short, right?" I found only two reminders in County Stadium of baseball's finest romance: one was a small bronze plaque in the concourse "To The Greatest Fans in All of Baseball." It was signed Louis Perini and dated September 20, 1953. The other was sixty-two-year-old Johnny Logan, who sat behind home plate with a radar gun, charting pitches for the Brewers, the only Brave from the early fifties who still called Milwaukee home.

Logan was born in upstate New York but he wore a made-in-Milwaukee label. He was earthy, blue-collar, tough, a superb shortstop ("I adopted myself smartly-wise," he said of his skill in always being in the right defensive position) who once had been knocked cold making a double play and had asked when he came to, "Did we get the guy at first?" Logan was a true Milwaukee burgher. He had the elegance and pretentiousness of a cafeteria. He was as genuine as a well-brewed glass of draft. "Hey, hey, heeeey, pal, how ya doin'?" he'd greet friends and strangers alike, putting an arm around their shoulders. Everyone in Milwaukee knew and liked Johnny Logan, and when people approached with a ball, he'd take out his pen with a smile, though as often as not these days the person would ask, "Can you get Robin Yount to sign this for me?"

If Logan had opened a sports bar in Milwaukee, he would have made a fortune, but he tried other jobs after the majors no longer wanted him. "When you're making big money, you live fast," he said. "When it comes down, it's tough." He went to Japan to play for the Osaka Hawks but only lasted a year ("You don't produce in baseball, it's sayonara in whatever language you talk"), then came home and spent two years on the Alaska pipeline, living in army-style barracks and working seven days a week.

"Did you feel any resentment after thirteen years in the big leagues having to go back to manual labor?" I asked.

"Manual?" he said, his mind seizing on the word "menial." "That wasn't manual. We were making fifteen dollars an hour. Besides, it was interesting how they curved that thing around the antelope."

Back in Milwaukee, he ran a tile company for a while, sold radio advertising, had a radio show and twice campaigned for sheriff. "I thought being a ballplayer, knowing how to get along with people, I could blend this in to the situation at the sheriff's department." he said. "I'm talking harmony." The trouble was Logan didn't have any law enforcement experience and his words always seemed to tumble out in a jumble, like the time he ordered apple pie à la mode and told the waitress as an afterthought, "And put some ice cream on it." The opposition distributed bumper stickers that said, "Do You Want Johnny Logan to Carry a Gun?" and the old shortstop with the fiery spirit and quick hands was roundly defeated.

Like Yogi Berra, Logan had his own language that went right by you, then made you question what you had heard. "Oh, Johnny, you look so cool," an admiring teenage girl gushed upon finally meeting her idol one sizzling summer day at County Stadium. "Well, you don't look so hot yourself," he replied. Logan was much in demand on Milwaukee's banquet circuit—even if he wasn't a scheduled speaker, people were always asking him to come up and make a few comments—and he worked hard to master public speaking. For a while the team's PA announcer, Bob Betts, wrote Logan's speeches, but the words invariably didn't come out quite as intended and Logan would end up throwing away the script and ad-libbing.

He told one audience how proud he was to share the head table with Stan Musial—"one of the most immoral ballplayers of all time"—and when given the award as Brave of the Year at an Elks banquet, he turned to Governor Warren Knowles and said, "Governor Known, I'm happy and abled to be here on this suspicious occasion. I accept the trophy proudly and will perish it forever."

I sat with Logan for a few games behind home plate. He had aged well. "My mind's sharp but it's not sharp, if you understand what I mean," he said. He had given up smoking the year before, never had a drink before 4:00 P.M., and didn't touch so much as a beer in the ballpark. "People'll say, 'Hey, he's not paying attention to his work,' if they see you with a beer," he said. His golf game was nearly good enough to get him on the seniors' circuit. Logan said he felt sorry for today's sportswriters who are often ignored in the clubhouse or find that players they want to interview are hiding out in the off-limits trainer's room. "The experienced player realized reporters had a deadline or a boss to make happy when I played," he said. "We tried to help them." And he wondered why players spent so little time discussing baseball these days and left the stadium so quickly after a game.

"In my time," he said, "you'd get five guys together and you'd talk about two things: one, the game; two, family problems. And three, I don't know what else we talked about. You got to come up with the word, 'cause I don't want to bring it out. Course, it's hard to compare players of my era with millionaires anyway."

Logan took his job seriously, measuring the speed of each pitch, then recording what kind of a pitch it had been and where it had been in relation to the plate. He sat among a group of stoic scouts, who said not a word, and yelled encouragement to the Brewers. I asked him if he was going on the Braves' reunion cruise to the Caribbean in the fall. "I talked to Pafko and a couple of the guys about it," he said. "You know what happens? Mathews, Aaron, Spahn, they go for free. And the rest of us got to pay. What an insult. You think I'm going? Hell, no."

It was true. Logan had not been among the titans on the Braves and his value on the baseball-card circuit—the measure of a retired player's worth in today's marketplace—was only five hundred dollars per appearance, about half of what Ralph Branca got for having thrown one famous (and ill-chosen) pitch. But Logan had played so beautifully. He had the heart of a lion and for a while there was no finer shortstop in the National League. He was the Brave you wanted at the plate with the game on the line, the infielder you prayed Snider or Kluszewski would hit the ball to in the last of the ninth.

Logan was more guarded than the other former Braves I had met and he didn't seem much interested in revisiting the past. Whenever I probed, asking about his life after baseball, wondering if he saw the same ghosts in County Stadium that I did, he would go back to concentrating on his radar gun.

"I got memories," he said, "but they're not really what you'd call memories, if you follow what I'm saying."

Milwaukee had a new fifty-story building downtown, a new hotel and a new pedestrian skywalk connecting the major department stores, but still looked essentially as I had remembered. It had the character of a town and the appearance of a city. It was a place where aging couples danced to jukeboxes in the dark corners of neighborhood taverns, and families arrived at the Brewers games early, setting up their beer coolers and portable grills in the parking lot. Milwaukee had fifteen hundred taverns and twice that many bowling lanes, and although the breweries were in decline—Schlitz had changed its brew, slipped badly and closed its plant on Third Street—Wisconsin still drank more beer per capita than any other state.

"Let me show you something you won't see anywhere else in baseball." Harry Dalton, the Brewers general manager, was speaking. He got up from his desk, stood on an armchair, the toes of his shoes carefully inserted beneath the seat cushion so as not to dirty the upholstery, and parted the blinds in order to peer out of the small office window. It was two hours before game time. The listless Brewers were sputtering along in seventh place, and the vanguard of a crowd that would number forty thousand, despite the threat of rain, had turned the parking lot into a huge tailgate party. Frisbee and volleyball games stretched to the farthest corners. Tents had sprung up for private catered parties. Groups sat around in lawn chairs and on blankets, opening containers of potato salad and cooking hot dogs. Long rows of RVs stood bumper to bumper and there was a party in each. A man in a golf cart navigated his way through the sea of fans, peddling beer and soft drinks.

Dalton, who was usually in his office by six every morning, even after a night game, had been a general manager for twenty-three years, longer than anyone else in baseball, and had put together teams that had won four pennants and two World Series. In Baltimore, Anaheim and Milwaukee, his philosophy had never wavered: You build champions the old-fashioned way, with a strong scouting staff and a good minor league system. Under Dalton the Brewers' farm teams had won more games in the eighties than any organization except the Yankees, and 48 percent of the Brewers had worked their way up through Stockton, El Paso and Denver. No team in baseball had a higher percentage of home-grown talent.

The Brewers were neither a wealthy nor a flashy organization, but after a summer in the minors I felt as though I had stepped from Burger King into the Ritz. In the press box, there was a free meal each evening (real food, not just hot dogs), free drinks, a daily twelve-page summary of statistics that made me wonder why reporters needed such stuff: The Twins had outscored the Brewers 76–33 in the eighth inning of their games during the season; the Brewers had won 26 of 48 games in which they had homered; Paul Molitor was 7 for 7 when bunting for a hit.

Eddie Wellskopf had catered the press room since 1956 and remembered when writers who covered the Braves had worn suits and ties and sat around drinking for a couple of hours after their game stories were filed. "They were boozers and I mean whiskey boozers," he said. Today quart bottles of soda pop line his bar. He keeps a supply of liquor nearby in case anyone ever asks, but no one does.

Forty-niner and I had taken up residence behind an abandoned factory—the accommodations proved superior to those in the bushes of the Menomonee River—and since I was never in much of a hurry to get home at night, I dawdled outside County Stadium after several games to watch a ritualistic performance that I myself had once executed with great precision, the pursuit of autographs.

After the last out each evening, several hundred young fans would gather in the darkened parking lot, clutching pads of paper, scorecard, gloves, balls, bats, anything that would bear a signature. Most were boys, in their early teens, but there were others, too: tots in the arms of their fathers, a few girls, several lone adults who appeared to be retarded. Almost all wore a hat or a T-shirt or a jacket with the emblem of a major league club. Several groups would form, as if by accident, and each seemed to float like a unit with a single mind, positioning itself for the sudden appearance of the ballplayers.

The players were easy to spot. They were taller and bigger than everyone else. Their hair was wet and recently combed. They wore polo jerseys and bright slacks. "There's Dan PLEEE-sac!" a squeaky voice would yell, and a hundred pairs of sneakers would pound across the pavement to surround him. Then from another exit would emerge Paul Molitor, and you could read indecision in the faces of the young boys: *Do I stay here trying to get Plesac or give up my position and go after Molitor? I'd rather have a Molitor autograph but I've got a better chance with Plesac.* The taller boys had a distinct advantage because they could bend their arms over the heads of the smaller children and wave their notepads directly in the players' noses.

Bud Selig, the Brewers' owner, walked through the milling kids unnoticed, chewing furiously on the gum that had replaced his smelly little cigars. This exercise was clearly not about influence or money. "There's Yount!" came a cry in unison, and suddenly the Brewers center fielder disappeared in a crush of outstretched arms and bobbing heads and pleading voices. *Please! Mine! Sign mine! I'm next.* The secret for the players was to keep moving as they signed, to advance steadily toward their secured parking area. From what I could gather, the athletes most in demand were home-run hitters, followed by starting pitchers and relievers. The lesser-known Brewers seemed slightly more accommodating, though I was surprised how patient even the stars were, often staying until the last little boy in line had his autograph and had become part of the bonding between player and fan that is one of baseball's most curious and wonderful gifts.

"Oh, thank you, sir. Thank you," said one of those boys, wide-eyed and reverent. He held the program bearing the autograph of Gus Polidor, a .200 hitter, to his chest with his right hand, raised his left arm in triumph and danced across the parking lot to his father. He held out the scorecard and said, "Who was it, Dad?"

Our heroes had changed, not disappeared, I decided. Though mine may have slipped away, to the boys who are what I once was, to those whose summer days are full of trust and faith, a new generation of giants now walked the earth, and of that I was glad.

Chapter Nineteen

I used to think, as others may think, that the Middle West is supremely ignorant. I was wrong. The Middle West is supremely wise. It goes its own way, hating no man and fearing no man.

—from *A Visit to America*, 1935, by
A. G. MACDONELL

The Class-A Midwest League stretches through four states named for long-vanquished Indian tribes (Wisconsin, Iowa, Indiana and Illinois) and links a cluster of towns that ring with the echo of the American heartland, among them Peoria, Cedar Rapids, Rockford, Kenosha, Appleton. I was back in the minors. The free meals and large crowds and million-dollar salaries of Milwaukee's County Stadium were quickly forgotten and I returned, not unhappily, to a hot-dog diet and little ballparks where I could park free and wander into the clubhouse without a pass and order fast-food lunches with players who always insisted on paying their share of a five-dollar tab.

Each league and each team I had seen had taken on its own identity, but the players themselves were cut from a universal mold. They talked about the same things in Stockton as they did in Elmira, they dressed in El Paso as they did in Harrisburg. No one wore earrings or long hair or outrageous clothes, and I never heard any white-powder jokes or had any hint that cocaine was in vogue. I often felt as though I were back in the fifties and everyone around me had grown up in the Midwest.

The Middle West—which I suppose would have been known as the Near East had we settled the Pacific coast first—was the perfect setting for baseball. Amid fields of corn and long summer nights and steepled white churches that filled to capacity every Sunday was the bedrock of a nation, broad-shouldered, sweaty-browed, fingernails lined with dirt. No one in New York or California paid much heed to the voices that came from this land, yet I knew with certainty that long after crack barons had taken over our cities, long after zealots had shot all the smokers and flag-burners and gays, and the urban family had become a relic studied in high school sociology classes, the Midwest would still stand out here on the plains, as square as it was sensible, feeding us and reminding us of who we were.

At a distance the Midwest had always seemed bland, but with my feet planted on its deep, black glacial soil—soil that "looks good enough to eat without putting it through vegetables," Robert Frost said—I thought it to be the most distinctive region I had found in the United States. The Midwest had a beauty that was unstartling, a way of going about its daily chores that was unspectacular. Yet everything about the place was reassuring: the sense of community, the closing of deals on a handshake, the unabashed expressions of hats-off patriotism (people glared at you in the Midwest League if you talked during the singing of the national anthem), the belief that a day's labor was an honorable pursuit. I even saw whites washing dishes, scrubbing floors and performing other menial jobs in the Midwest, a sight that would strike Californians as peculiar.

Being "average" is seldom a complimentary label, but that, in the kindest sense, is what the Midwest is. Des Moines, for instance, is the most frequently surveyed per capita market in the country by telephone researchers who want to know what the "average" American does and thinks. Milwaukee is second, Indianapolis third. In Peoria I ran across a statistic that reflected what the Midwest had kept and many of us were losing: 75 percent of the city's households were occupied by families, 41 percent had chil-

dren and 65 percent of the parents were married. Back home in
Los Angeles, 47 percent of the households were occupied by families, 22 percent had children and 34 percent were married. Take
away the family as a cohesive unit, and the spread of drugs, crime,
teenage pregnancy and truancy seemed easier to explain.

There is a feeling in the Midwest, as on Huck Finn's raft, that
"nothing ever happened to us at all," and Peoria itself has come
to epitomize all that is ordinary about this unordinary region. "If
it plays in Peoria, it'll play in America," they still say, referring to
the tough vaudeville audiences before which Jack Benny, Fibber
McGee and Molly, Fanny (Baby Snooks) Brice and others performed before taking their acts on the road. When veterans of the
battleship USS *Iowa* wanted to have a reunion, Peoria is where
they came to hold it. Among the choice of dining spots they found
downtown was the Chat and Chew Restaurant.

Peoria's minor league team was the Chiefs, an affiliate of the
Chicago Cubs, and it drew nearly twice as many fans each season
as the city had residents. I drove out to Meinen Field and parked
Forty-niner, as I always did, with its nose facing away from the
diamond to protect my windshield from foul balls, and went looking for the umpire's room. It was huddled in a dark corner under
the grandstand and had a green door bearing the warning, UNAU-
THORIZED VISITORS NOT ALLOWED. I knocked.

The room was about the size of a pantry, with a shower and toilet
in the back, and two folding metal chairs set up by a pair of wooden
lockers. Brian York and Bryan Wilber—who pursued their major
league dream through the Midwest League in a battered '77 station
wagon with two hubcaps and four colors—were stripped to their
shorts, rubbing beautiful white shiny baseballs with mud and tobacco juice. They were happy to have a visitor, authorized or not,
because umpires are so ignored in the low minors that their names
often aren't even included in box scores. The reason: the official
scorer didn't bother to ask them who they were.

I had once prized a new, unmarked baseball more than anything,
and the mud ritual that all professional umpiring crews performed
before every game mystified me. Good "working mud," York and
Wilber said, takes the gloss out of a ball so it doesn't slip from a
pitcher's grip. The mud must have just a touch a grit, though not

enough to scar or discolor, and should be sufficiently slimy to spread easily. Sometimes it is mixed with tobacco juice, spit, shoe polish or other concoctions that umpires fuss over like chefs, each believing he has created the finest recipe for delicate morsels of earth, lightly moistened with Copenhagen or Bull Durham.

The mud used in the majors was discovered in 1938 by a coach for the Philadelphia Athletics, and comes from a New Jersey tributary of the Delaware River. Once a year the family-owned Lena Blackburne Rubbing Mud Company packs the mud into coffee-can-sized containers and ships it off (at twenty-four dollars a can) to big-league stadiums. But minor league umpires must find their own mud, unless they have a friend in The Show who can scrounge them some, and they spend a surprising amount of time checking out riverbanks and rain-soaked golf courses and roadside ditches. Brian York had packed his great find in peanut butter jars and he told me how he got it:

"My grandfather had come over from Ohio to see me umpire. He came into the locker room after the game and I said, 'Come on. We got to go out and find some mud.' My grandfather said, 'Who would want to rub mud on a white ball and make it brown?' He's so laid-back you wouldn't believe it. He's from Kentucky, the smartest man in the world, but he doesn't know anything about baseball. He never had the luxury of playing because he worked in the coal mines and got married when he was sixteen. His wife was fifteen. I just love telling stories about him because he's my best friend, and one of the toughest things that's happened to me in my brief career is that I had to umpire the night of his fiftieth anniversary and couldn't be there.

"So anyway, I wanted him to be part of my experience umpiring and we went down to the stream by Rockford Park. There's a bridge there and the river's right nearby. We pulled up in the car and walked down the hillside to the edge of the water. I stick my hands in up to my elbows, and my grandfather, he's just kind of watching. The first stuff I came up with was sewage. Really gross. But I figured if I found some rocks, there might be good mud there.

"Pretty soon my grandfather's taking all this very seriously. He's found an old headlight cover and he's scooping away, trying to dig down to good mud. I tell him we need grit and mushiness, and he yells out, 'Come here! Come here!' I run over and he's found the greatest dirt in the world. We mixed it up and put it in four containers and brought it back to the motel. I spread the mud out in the parking lot to mix in some other stuff I had. The visiting team's manager comes out of the motel and sees me there, like a kid playing in mud and says, 'How old are you anyway?' My grandfather really laughed. I just thought it was great he got to be part of all this."

York and Wilber were in the only profession I knew where a man was expected to be perfect his first day at work and get better as time went by. They, along with two hundred other umpires in the minors, were competing for sixty major league jobs—a journey that could take ten years to make, and few completed—and their lives reminded me of those of desert nomads. They traveled at night to elude the prairie heat, avoided bars and motels frequented by players whose performance they had to judge, and lived a spartan existence, spending virtually every moment together from a season's first pitch to the last. Each earned nineteen hundred dollars a month, from which he had to pay all his road expenses.

Sometimes fans would see managers giving them a terrible lashing. Their arms would wave and point in exasperation, their heads would bob and their feet would tap-dance in the pattern of a little boy who had to go to the bathroom. It was good theater, but as often as not the manager was speaking in a calm voice, saying something like "You called that play right, I'm just protecting my player. Give me fifteen seconds out here." Then he would wheel, kick some dirt in disgust and stomp off to the dugout.

The mud having been applied, York and Wilber changed into their blue uniforms with padded shoulders and creased pants. They suddenly looked older and sterner. York stuffed the game balls into his pockets and Wilber flicked some lint off his jacket. "It's seven of," Wilber said, looking at his watch. "Time to go." Shoulders straight and heads back, they moved together down the concourse and with deliberate strides walked onto the field to a chorus of boos.

Meinen Field, filling quickly, had the feel of a shopping mall where people came to socialize and wander. Chuck Lewis, back home in Peoria on vacation, was standing with his kids down the left-field foul line, pounding his baseball mitt. "Isn't this what the world's really all about?" said Lewis, the Washington bureau chief for the Hearst newspaper chain. Dick Dutton, a business executive and president of the Booster Club, which provided players with towels, pillows, sheets, silverware and small appliances when they first arrived in Peoria, was recruiting fans for the trip to the Chiefs' upcoming series in Burlington, Iowa: box seat and bus transportation, ten dollars. The mayor's secretary was at her customary place in the concession stand, dishing out hot dogs even faster than she typed.

"Striiiike!" yelled Brian York as the first pitch of the game went by the Beloit Brewers batter waist-high, and the crowd roared.

Peoria had been a wounded town in the early eighties, when minor league baseball returned after a twenty-five-year absence. President Reagan, who grew up eighty-five miles away, had ended U.S. support for the Soviet Union's gas pipeline and Moscow had shifted its purchases of earth-moving equipment to Komatsu of Japan, costing Peoria's biggest employer, the Caterpillar Corporation, $90 million in lost contracts. Caterpillar laid off eight thousand workers. The Pabst brewery and the Hiram Walker distillery closed. Huge farms went belly-up. Merchants fled downtown, and even the Elks and the square dance clubs no longer considered Peoria a good place to hold their conventions.

It may have been only coincidence, but not long after the Chiefs came home, then were bought by Pete Vonachen, a crusty local with an owlish face and a quick tongue, life took a turn for the better in Peoria. The farm-belt recovery started, the restoration of downtown got under way with the building of a convention center and a new hotel, and everyone seemed to get caught up at once with civic enthusiasm. When seventy-six-year-old retired truck driver Charles Harshbarger found himself with more volunteer work than he could handle—he tended flower and vegetable gardens at fire stations and nursing homes around town—the Bellevue Senior Citizen Center came through with a crew of helpers.

"You wouldn't expect women in their seventies and eighties, with hip transplants, backaches and knee problems, anticipating heat, sweat and bugs, to come out at seven A.M. and pick beans," he said, "but they do."

Peoria started believing in itself again, and the symbol of that rekindled confidence was the Chiefs. They became winners and set league attendance records two years in a row. Harry Caray, the Chicago Cubs' announcer and Vonachen's best friend, talked about Peoria often on his national broadcasts, turning the Chiefs into something of a cult. Vonachen installed an exploding score-board, baby-sat for his players' children when asked and let any fan wander into the PA announcer's booth to sing "Take Me Out to the Ball Game" in the seventh inning. Vonachen was a Peoria nationalist. He had spent the winter eating ham and potato salad off paper plates and promoting the Chiefs anywhere he could get a dozen people together, from the Methodist Church to the Elks Lodge and Boy Scout meeting halls. He understood exactly what played well in Peoria and he ran his baseball business the way he would have a neighborhood tavern. He was, I thought, testimony to the strength of what the minor leagues have less and less of—local ownership.

His arm was wrapped in a sling the afternoon I met him in Sullivan's saloon. Vonachen had locked himself out of his home and, trying to crawl through a second-floor bathroom window, had fallen fifteen feet off a ladder. He was full of painkillers and not very happy to have to order some damn yuppie soda drink instead of his regular V.O. whiskey. "I can't drink because I've got all kinds of shitty medicine in me," he said. "I guarantee this seltzer is going to make me puke."

Vonachen was sixty-four, his round face anchored by a sharp chin and creased with smile wrinkles. His great-grandparents had emigrated from Germany, and his grandfather had run an Illinois saloon, the Big Foot, that served free lunches but not women. Saloons, he thought, were where all the most interesting people still met. Vonachen had what he called "that old Midwest gut feeling" about when to get in and out of a business and he had gone from owning the best restaurant in Peoria to running a $23 million-a-year blacktop construction company to operating a cou-ple of motels. "You sit down to talk about a deal in the Midwest, and no one throws each other curves," he said. "You start from a position of trust." The sports editor of the local paper had talked him into buying the recently returned Chiefs in 1984 from a Florida group that was running the team into the ground.

"I like to say I'm streetsmart, but you know what?" he said. "I'm obsessed. I get into something and I'm obsessed with making it the best. I didn't know a damn thing about running a baseball team, but I got obsessed with making the Chiefs the best franchise in minor league baseball. I just can't stand to lose."

One night at Meinen Field, when Peoria was losing, umpire Mark Widlowski made several questionable calls. The rattled Chiefs started arguing. By the ninth inning manager Jim Tracy and four of his players had been ejected, and Pete Vonachen couldn't take it anymore. "Play 'Howdy Doody Time,' " he told the PA announcer and, appropriately inspired, the owner bolted the fence and raced onto the field, screaming every obscenity he knew at Widlowski. The fans cheered wildly.

"Get out of here, or there's going to be a riot," the umpire said.

"You're going to have to throw me out," Vonachen snapped, falling to his knees in a position of prayer. "Go ahead. Do it. I'm praying for you to throw me out."

"You're gone!" ordered Widlowski, a stiff right arm pointed toward the yonder. The owner stomped off the field, pondered the dugout for a moment, and was struck by a TV image of how Billy Martin would have reacted to banishment. In a flash he was raging through the dugout like a tornado, uprooting helmets, gloves, bats and balls. The projectiles flew onto the field and Widlowski deftly danced and hopped his way clear of amputation and castration.

"Here, Pete, you forgot one," said a Chiefs pitcher, running over with the last helmet.

"Thank you, son," Vonachen said, flinging that one, too.

Vonachen knew immediately he had made a bad mistake, and started plotting how best to capitalize on it. "It was a dumb, dumb thing I did," he said. "A guy in my position shouldn't be running on the field. It showed no class." He apologized to the umpires and sent them flowers and a box of Hershey chocolate Kisses. But the damage had been done. George Spelius, a Beloit florist and the Midwest League president, suspended Vonachen, banning him from the park for nine games, and assessed the largest fine in league history, one thousand dollars.

The next night a large crowd showed up to see if Vonachen would defy the ban, but he was abiding by the order to stay out of Meinen Field. Just beyond the left-field fence, 335 feet from home plate, was a little equipment shed and on its roof he had built a platform and there he sat, in a lawn chair, next to his hibachi grill. "And now from the new owner's rooftop box . . . here's Peoria Pete!" boomed the PA man. Vonachen, holding a portable microphone, led the crowd in singing "Take Me Out to the Ball Game" and used a portable phone to call the Cubs' Harry Caray, who told the world of the happenings in Peoria.

Radio station WMBD got caught up in the spirit of rebellion and offered dinner in the "owner's box" to the person who called each morning with the best poem or song about Peoria Pete's dilemma. The nightly winner was escorted across the field by the Chiefs' marketing director, then climbed up onto the platform for dinner with the boss. One woman said she didn't like hot dogs, and Vonachen sent out for lobster tails. The crowds grew larger each night. Five thousand. Six thousand. Then standing room only. The only troublesome moment came when a spark from the grill set the roof afire, but Vonachen extinguished the flames with beer.

The ban ended on the tenth night and Vonachen returned to Meinen Field, wearing an orange jumpsuit and riding in a police van that was led by a motorcycle escort as it circled the field to cheers and applause. "Pete," league president Spelius said, "I knew I shouldn't have let you sit on that roof." The Chiefs estimated Vonachen's suspension had been worth ten thousand dollars in increased revenue.

Vonachen and the Chiefs were as Midwestern as a John Deere tractor, and I was sorry to leave them. My last night in Peoria the Chiefs beat Beloit 10–6, and Vonachen brought a load of hamburgers and potato chips into the clubhouse for the players. "Pete, can you spare twenty till payday?" one of them asked. He rolled his eyes and reached into his wallet. I mentioned that his relationship with the team seemed unusual, especially since I had met some club executives who didn't even let players into their office without an appointment. "Nah," Vonachen said, "I don't do anything special. I just try to be decent."

I left Peoria at dawn the next morning, sipping coffee from my plastic mug and listening to the radio: "November beans are down a dime at five-ninety a bushel. Midwest cash hogs today are any-where from a dollar lower to fifty cents higher. In Peoria they're getting forty-eight even. August hogs are down two, October hogs up twenty-five cents." The murderous heat and humidity came up early and would, I knew, hang about all day. My cab was a sauna. The land flew by unnoticed, hypnotizing in its flatness and same-ness. I yearned for a bend in the road, the sight of hills, a cooling breeze. Only two states—Iowa and Nebraska—separated me from Colorado's snowcapped Rockies and the West. My foot pressed harder on the accelerator.

After a night at Sec Taylor Stadium in Des Moines, at the confluence of the Raccoon and Des Moines rivers, and a day at Rosenblatt Stadium in Omaha, where umpire John Deluca stood behind home plate wearing shin guards over his trousers, having forgotten to pack his uniform pants, I found Highway 81, the route of the Pony Express and the Overland Stage. Trappers and traders and settlers from Independence and Westport (Kansas City, Mis-souri) had taken this road in the 1860s. Not far from Lebanon, Nebraska, a stone's throw past the geographical center of the United States, they had turned west, as I now did, onto Route 36.

The minor league season had only a month to run. I slipped into my cowboy boots and put on my Stetson and poured forty gallons of gasoline into Forty-niner. Then I drove through the night and did not stop until off in the distance, at the edge of the Great Plains, I saw the skyline of Denver and could smell the mountain air.

The West:
Homeward Bound
July 30–August 31

Chapter Twenty

If I could get back in baseball, I'd climb onto that minor
league bus and I'd ride and ride and ride through the
night, and I'd thank God for every mile.

—GARLAND SHIFFLETT,
Denver minor league pitcher, retired

I've never seen a happy-looking
jogger, but those in Colorado appeared particularly anguished.
They were everywhere, like an infestation, pounding over mountain passes, through parks and along city streets, eyes bulging and
tongues protruding from twisted faces, all impeccably dressed, all
gasping in the thin mile-high air. Although my own health regimen
had been disrupted by the trip, I, too, had been a jogger in Los
Angeles, a routine I undertook mainly to offset my intake of whiskey and cigarettes, and I feared I would have little in common with
these Gucci cowboys who got their Rocky Mountain Highs on
Perrier and raw fish.

I had first seen Denver in 1970, when I arrived on a Greyhound
from New York, fresh out of Vietnam, my journalistic blood still
pumping with the adrenaline of Hamburger Hill and Dong Ha and
the besieged Special Forces camp at Ben Het. My new assignment
was on UPI's night shift, rewriting regional news, weather reports

and farm prices for the radio wire, and, soon growing restless, I was gone within the year. Denver, though, was an appealing place in those days, a Western cow town plopped in the middle of nowhere, more quaint than fashionable, having been created on the whim of an army general turned speculator.

Named for a now-forgotten Kansas governor, Denver was founded in 1858 by General William Larimer, who staked out the settlement by crossing four cottonwood sticks in an empty expanse where the Sante Fe and New Mexico roads met on the routes to Fort Laramie and Fort Bridger. This, he wrote, "is the center of all the great leading thoroughfares and is bound to be a great city." In 1869, the federal census taker counted 4,749 Denverites; a decade later, there were ten more.

The men who followed Larimer were the ultimate gamblers, men who would give up their homes and lives in the Midwest and East in pursuit of sudden wealth in an untamed territory. Many made fortunes in gold and silver, and what Mark Twain called the "get-rich disease" struck so many victims that, in the 1880s, Governor John L. Routt walked out of the state capitol in Denver one day and rode to Leadville to take up a new profession as a miner. In short order he became fabulously wealthy.

The great city that Larimer had envisioned emerged in the 1970s, after I had left, when Colorado rode the crest of an energy bonanza to Texas-style prosperity. Scores of high-tech companies and ninety thousand new residents a year poured into the state, and Denver became the center of the Rocky Mountain High, the home of a new breed of transplanted Westerner: smug, yuppified, antigrowth, environmentally fervent. In little more than a decade the city had moved from the cow chip to the computer chip. The pickup truck with a gun rack mounted by the rear window gave way as a symbol of manhood to a BMW with a ski rack. Denver got a new skyline of shimmering office buildings, a Super Bowl–bound big-league football team, a big-league basketball team, a symphony orchestra, sprawling suburbs—and the highest peak carbon monoxide pollution levels of any U.S. city. But Denver never quite got what its power brokers wanted so passionately— Eastern recognition as a big-league city. How, after all, could you accord big-league status to a town that had a minor league baseball team, and one to boot that was the affiliate not of a club in New York or California but, for God's sake, *Milwaukee*?

Denver was a member of the Triple-A American Association that had gone out of business in 1962 for seven years after losing four of its best territories to major league expansion teams: Milwaukee, Minneapolis–St. Paul, Kansas City and Houston. "We just ran out of cities," said Jim Burris, the former league president and Denver general manager. The Denver club, once known as the Bears and now the Zephyrs, played in Mile High Stadium, the biggest baseball arena in the country (with 75,052 seats, about eight hundred more than Cleveland's Municipal Stadium), and had attracted the five largest crowds in minor league history, the biggest of which was announced as 65,666 for a fireworks promotion in 1982. It was a record that probably will never be broken. (More than seventy thousand fans had actually attended the game; Burris fudged the figure downward so as not to be in violation of city fire-code regulations.) Burris overcame the stigma of promoting a minor league club in a major league city by producing championship teams year after year, six of them between 1971 and 1981.

For thirty years Denver had been courting the big leagues, looking for a team, and had come close to convincing a couple of existing clubs to relocate and to winning an expansion franchise. But the Queen City of the Plains was always left standing at the altar. Now the National League was talking expansion again and thirteen cities from Phoenix to Buffalo were lined up for a franchise, which would pump at least $60 million a season into the local economy in direct and indirect spending and provide countless millions' worth of free national exposure.

Baseball's planned expansion had nothing to do with altruism; in fact, big-league owners hated the idea. Why slice up a billion-dollar pie of television revenue when you have a monopoly? Why let an upstart stick his fingers into the $50 billion sports industry, an industry that is the nation's twenty-third largest, bigger even than the automobile and security and commodity brokerage sectors of the U.S. economy? Why expand and end up playing fewer sold-out games between historical rivals, such as the Red Sox and Yankees, the Cards and Cubs, in favor of, say, a Phoenix-Montreal series that no one gave a hoot about? The answer was that baseball was nervous about protecting its antitrust exemption and about the threatened establishment of an unauthorized third major league, and the best way to reduce the heat was to enlarge the fraternity. To join, a new owner awarded an expansion franchise was going to have to bleed a bit first, giving existing team bosses upwards of $100 million to divide among themselves and agreeing not to share in the big-money TV pie for several years.

Denver seemed a natural for the big leagues. It would have the Rocky Mountain region all to itself—of the four time zones on the U.S. mainland, only the Mountain Zone has no major league baseball—and 8 million people passed through the Denver airport each summer, many hurrying straight off to the national parks. The closest major league team would be in Kansas City, six hundred miles away. But Denver had never quite gotten itself organized, and its sports dollar was thinly sliced between the two existing big-league teams, the Zephyrs, a dog track and outdoor recreation. Denver needed a stadium designed for baseball, not football (the Broncos controlled the dates at Mile High and the city didn't give the Zephyrs a penny from concessions and parking revenue); it needed a partnership of local high-profile investors (the Zephyrs' reclusive owners, the Dikeou brothers, had never been part of the city's civic-booster network); and it needed to allay suspicions that a baseball team would have trouble competing with the movie theaters (Denver had the highest per capita movie attendance of any U.S. city) and the mountains and the Broncos.

"Dammit," a fan ahead of me said one night, waiting in line to buy a Zephyr ticket as the last notes of the national anthem sounded from inside Mile High Stadium, "I'm going to miss the kickoff."

The announcement of Colonel William Higgins's execution by Shiite fanatics in Lebanon was accompanied by a grainy black-and-white photograph of the victim, a rope around his neck. The TV channel I was watching in a Chinese restaurant carried the news of his death, my first night in Denver, after an ad that said, "Help stop AIDS. Use a condom." Higgins, serving with U.N. forces in southern Lebanon, had been kidnaped more than a year earlier,

and apparently been killed in retaliation for Israel's snatching of
a Muslim cleric, Sheik Abdul Karim Obeid. Higgins was forty-four
years old, a combat veteran of the Vietnam war, and had written
in his high school yearbook that his ambition was "for my family
to always be proud of me."

I had not known him in Lebanon, but I had spent time with the
UN troops in that nightmarish country and I knew the Associated
Press reporter Terry Anderson, who was among the Western hos-
tages still held captive there, Terry having been chained, I had
heard, to a radiator for four years. My summer suddenly seemed
as inconsequential as baseball itself. I had lost myself in a toy store,
isolated from too many of the things that really mattered, and I
pushed aside my plate and paid the bill. I did not go the ballpark
the next day and instead wrote some postcards to friends I had not
been in touch with for a while.

In the Pioneer League, the Helena Brewers requested that the
flag at Kindrick Legion Field be flown at half-staff in Higgins's
honor, which it was. The *Rocky Mountain News* in Denver set up
a hot line, asking callers how President Bush should respond to the
murder. One caller recommended an "all-out nuclear attack," saying the United States should "hit all the hospitals, then work our
way down." Another said, "Let's not play games like we did in
Vietnam." Several respondents addressed their advice to President
Reagan, one to President Ford. In the end, the United States did
nothing.

It was early August, the dog days of summer for weary minor
leaguers. Hitters started shifting to lighter bats, pitchers had trouble keeping their fastballs down and away, thus giving sluggers an
advantage in Denver, where balls traveled a country mile in the
thin air, and everyone was grousing, about their careers, their
managers, the major league organizations that owned their services. This was the time when, if a team wasn't in a pennant race,
thoughts turned to next year's contract and next spring's assignment; a fast finish in the few weeks of the season that remained
could enhance both. For some injured players, the goal now was
to collect workmen's compensation over the winter, instead of

laboring at menial jobs, and they had already asked their team doctors for written statements that they would not recover for several months.

Fan interest was shifting, too, toward football. The two Denver newspapers all but ignored the city's baseball team, filling their sports pages with story upon adoring story about the Broncos, who had opened their preseason camp in nearby Greeley.

The Zephyrs had edged out the Iowa Cubs for the 1986 league championship by winning their last three games of the season. In 1987 they had won their last eleven to pass the Louisville Redbirds at the wire. But this summer they were fading in the stretch. They had taken a two-game lead onto the road and come home in second place, having lost seven of nine. One night they played fourteen innings, got back to their motel at 2:00 A.M. and had to rise at 5:00 A.M. to catch a 6:00 A.M. flight to Indianapolis for a doubleheader. They lost both games, 2–1. In anger, manager Dave Machemer tipped a bowl of gravy over the clubhouse cold-cut table.

Machemer had slugged a home run in his first major league at bat in 1978. He never hit another one in The Show, and except for twenty-nine games, his seventeen-year baseball career had been spent in the minors, but Machemer was highly regarded and if he did well in Denver he had a good shot at landing a coaching job with the Milwaukee Brewers. Sent back to the bushes after his fine debut fizzled, he had written a ballad called "Compensation" with Dave Egan, a minor league pal now working as a postman in Rochester. As mournful as a coal miner's lament, it is still heard from time to time in minor league clubhouses:

> *The baseball strike of '81 is over and the issue of compensation's been settled for now.*
>
> *Well, have you heard about the minor league veteran? Listen up and you're going to hear it now.*
>
> *You know, it was about ten years ago today I got on that bus and I was going to be a big star with a bat and a glove.*
>
> *I told all my friends, "You're going to be hearing big things about me and real soon."*
>
> *When I joined my first pro team, the manager said, "Dave, we're glad*

*you're here. But we don't have enough uniforms to go around. See if you
can salvage some remains and piece one together over there."*

*And after the first game, I asked the trainer, Hey, what time should we
check in at the airport for that midnight flight?*

*He kinda laughed and said, "Rookie, by the time we board the bus for
Waterloo, the plane'll be plain outta sight."*

*And I said, well, this can't be all bad. You're paying me five hundred
a month to do this.*

*Well, it's years later now, but for me and a lot of other minor leaguers,
conditions seem to be pretty much the same.*

*They talk about compensation. They talk about compensation. Well, I
don't even know what the word means. . . .*

Back in the Milwaukee Brewers' home office, farm director Bruce
Manno watched with alarm as the Zephyrs struggled and slipped.
There was a growing belief that the team had an attitude problem—an assessment that often reflected as unfavorably on the
coaching staff as on the players themselves—and Sam Suplizio was
summoned to Mile High Stadium from Grand Junction, Colorado.

Suplizio was a tall, graceful man of fifty-six, whom the Yankees
had trained as a late-inning defensive caddy for weak-kneed Mickey
Mantle. A week before reporting to New York in 1956, he had
shattered his right hand breaking up a double play against Nashville. Seven operations did not restore the feel of releasing the ball,
and trying to rifle a throw from the outfield, the ball would roll out
of his hand and fall at his feet or fly straight up over his head. He
attempted a comeback, laboring with pick and shovel on a construction gang to strengthen his wrist. The wrist couldn't stand the
strain and snapped again. Suplizio took a job selling insurance in
Grand Junction.

I had met Suplizio at Milwaukee's spring training camp in Arizona the previous March and asked him why most of the coaches
and instructors I saw in the minor leagues were people who, like
himself, had not quite made it. He thought for a moment and said,
"Because we were never fulfilled. We're living our lives through the
kids we teach."

Suplizio now owned the bank and insurance company that had

taken him in as a wounded minor leaguer thirty years earlier. He was the Republican party's former Colorado finance chairman and a millionaire a couple of times over. But whenever the Milwaukee Brewers called, as they did often, needing someone to hit fungoes in spring training or fill in as a coach with the Big Club or work with hitters and outfielders in Denver or El Paso, Suplizio just walked out the door of his financial empire and didn't come back until the assignment was over. He had, he said, the best baseball job in banking.

In Denver, the banker with No. 52 on his uniform checked with Machemer, some of the veteran players and pitching coach Jackson Todd, whose own baseball career had been interrupted by lymphatic cancer fifteen years earlier. The Zephyrs' problem, Suplizio decided, was not attitude; it was fatigue. He tore up the chew-ass speech he had outlined on a pad of legal-sized yellow paper and jotted down some new notes that had the motivational ring of Dale Carnegie. In the Zephyrs' spacious carpeted clubhouse, the players pulled their folding chairs into a semicircle around Suplizio.

"You remember what Vince Lombardi used to say, that fatigue makes cowards of us all?" he told them. "Well, you're young and you may not understand what's happening to your bodies, why you're griping about everything, and everything seems to be going wrong. When you're tired, it's absolutely normal for your attitude and perspective to change. But we've all come too far from spring training, worked too hard, not to give 150 percent in the twenty-eight days that are left. You can't let it get away. You're the person who will suffer if you do.

"Just last Saturday I sat at lunch with Robin Yount [the Brewers' $3 million-a-year center fielder] and I asked him what he'd tell people like yourself if he had my job. He didn't blink an eye. He said, 'Tell them to stop worrying about money. Stop worrying about the organization. Stop worrying about where they're going to play next year. Stop worrying about all these things you can't control, and just go out on the field and beat the hell out of whoever they're playing. The rest will take of itself. The money will come. The fame will come.' "

One of the largest minor league crowds I had seen all summer—fifty-three hundred—showed up that day, but Mile High Stadium was so cavernous that the place felt empty. The names of the Broncos' past stars stared down at the fans in big blue letters painted beneath one of the tiers, and in the clubhouse a sign reminded the baseball players to clean out their lockers by Friday and leave nothing of value behind; the Broncos were taking over the stadium for a weekend exhibition game. The Zephyrs fell behind, 10–7, and it looked as if Suplizio's speech hadn't helped at all.

Then in the ninth Denver scratched out a run with two outs, and loaded the bases on a single and two walks. Louisville brought in a reliever, and Tack Wilson, the Zephyrs' thirty-three-year-old journeyman, reached for an outside pitch and sent the ball fluttering like a badminton shuttlecock into right field, to score two runs and tie the game. Greg Vaughn, Denver's clean-up hitter, battled Cris Carpenter one on one, fouling off half a dozen pitches, then struck out. In the press box, Frank Haraway, the official scorer who had covered the team for nearly sixty years, put his left hand over his ear and with his right slowly clanged an old bell three times, once for each run. From below, the crowd roared back in acknowledgment of each clap: "One! . . . Two! . . . Three!"

Vaughn was the top power hitter in the American Association, laboring in the minors only because Milwaukee already was laden with outfielders, and when he came to bat in the bottom of the twelfth with two out, the score still tied, 10–10, the Redbirds held a conference on the mound to discuss how to pitch him. After letting a fastball go by, Vaughn drilled a slider toward the left-field fence. He took three steps, stopped dead to watch, then circled the bases with long strides as the ball flew out of sight. *Clang* went Haraway's bell, and a chorus of fans yelled back, "One!" Within five minutes, Bruce Manno was on the line from Milwaukee, asking Machemer, "How'd you guys do today?"

Everywhere Vaughn had played—at the University of Miami (where he earned a degree in business), in Helena, Beloit, El Paso and Denver—he had been a star, pursued, applauded, listened to. He was a wonderful athlete, a man, I was told, who played for the team, not just himself. But players in the pubescent stages of fame often were not easy to approach. The day after his home run, I asked Vaughn if we could get together for lunch or a drink. "I'd prefer the clubhouse if you want to do an interview," he said. I explained that I didn't want to interview him per se and really just wanted a chance to sit and talk. But I acquiesced and met him in front of his locker after batting practice.

This, I discovered, was a demeaning setting for a journalist, rather like staking out a politician's house hoping he would grace you with a quotable remark as he hurried out the door to his car. The player maintains control when stationed at his locker, because those few feet are his turf and all visitors are intruders. By seeing people on that stage he agrees not to sharing a conversation but only to holding court. Vaughn's eyes wandered constantly as we talked, and sometimes he got distracted by something a teammate was saying several lockers away. "I'm sorry," he would say, "would you repeat that question?" He was bored, and I realized I hadn't asked him anything he hadn't been asked before and wouldn't be asked again. I thanked him for his time after a few minutes and left, remembering a remark the wife of Dodger outfielder Von Joshua had once made to the wife of Ross Newhan, the *Los Angeles Times'* premier baseball writer. "You know," she had said, "if it wasn't for *my* husband, *your* husband wouldn't have a job."

Standing at the batting cage my last day with the Zephyrs, talking to Lamar Johnson, the Brewers' roving batting instructor, my thoughts drifted off and I understood that a secret mission had brought me to Denver: I was the forty-nine-year-old journalist who had come to save the pennant for the Zephyrs. My feet remained planted in dirt but my mind raced across the grass, and from the empty stands behind me the crowd's roar grew.

The catches I made were miraculous. Every ball—a liner to left, a towering drive into the alleyway between center and right— found its way into my glove after a long run, and pretty soon the Zephyrs put down their bats and stepped away from the cage to watch. My arm was a cannon, not at all like the chicken wing that had strained in grammar school to get the ball from short to first, and the strikes I fired from right field struck the catcher's mitt with a loud pop, arriving on the fly, a foot off the ground.

Johnson waved me in and I took my place in the cage. I felt loose and strong and invincible. The bat was light as a broom handle and

the first pitch I drove high over the outfield fence. I set my feet
again. Bugles sounded "Charge!" The pitches came in machine-
gun-fire succession, faster than even Steve Dalkowsky could have
thrown them, and each one thundered off my bat and hurtled
toward the clouds. The Zephyrs had found their Hurricane Bob
Hazle and together we would rope the stars and conquer the
heavens.

I carried the fantasy with me on the way out of Denver, plotting
the story of the mysterious stranger whose astonishing skills had
been hidden for half his life. The summer journey had broken the
chains of journalism and freed my imagination. I no longer felt
bound, as I had in Lebanon and Uganda and Vietnam and so many
other places, merely to gather facts, present them in an orderly
fashion and interpret without emotion or subjectivity. Now, bound
for Salt Lake on Route 40, slipping through the Eisenhower Tunnel and climbing the Continental Divide, I knew I had been af-
flicted with the dream disease of the minor leaguer. It was a voice
that asked, "If someone is to be chosen, am I the one?"

And the answer always came back: "Why not?"

Chapter Twenty-one

This ain't football. We do this every day.

—EARL WEAVER, *former Baltimore Orioles manager*

A gale came up crossing the Rockies and an air-vent flap that I had forgotten to close on Forty-niner's roof broke loose from its hinges and blew away with a clatter. The rain poured in, and I pulled off the road near Steamboat Springs to save the cushions at my dinette table from drowning. Back home, I was useless around the house and would summon a plumber for a leaky faucet before I'd think of picking up a wrench. But now, I thought, I'd grown rather clever. I knew how to prime generators and fix busted latches on cabinet doors and find the flattest spot to park so the gas flame that fired my refrigerator would not tilt toward an unprotected surface.

My safety matches were wrapped in an airtight Ziploc bag to prevent them from igniting by friction when the road was rough. My plastic plates and glasses were mounted with rubber skidders and held steady even when I braked suddenly. Clothespins kept my pants from falling off swaying hangers, and two cardboard cartons, fastened to the wall by bungee cords, provided a secure repository for my notes and team programs and stack of computer paper.

I climbed the ladder attached to Forty-niner's hinder. From a metal clothes hanger I fashioned a spoke to hold in place a temporary vent cover, which I concocted out of my plastic rain coat, a pad of legal-sized notepaper, two pieces of string and several paper clips. The soiled shirts in my laundry bag proved an adequate substitute for mops and towels, and by the time I found a saloon in Steamboat Springs, Forty-niner and I were dry again. The bar was crowded, its patrons mesmerized by the live TV broadcast of two football teams we had exported to Tokyo for a game, the Los Angeles Rams and the San Francisco 49ers. I decided we had sent them there as revenge for Japan's bombing of Pearl Harbor.

I enjoy football, but after a summer immersed in the passive beauty of baseball, I resented the sight of crashing bodies and wounded gladiators hobbling off the field and tangled legs and arms protruding from human piles. What we had exported was a Kojak show that had elements of all the worst aspects of our society; it was violent, aggressive in a bullying sort of way and strangely impersonal with faceless combatants wrapped in athletic armor, responding to commands relayed by walkie-talkie. Clearly, though, I was the only one in the bar who felt that way, and the man next to me shrugged when I offered my observations. "My team, the Yankees, are finished, so I'm ready for this," he said.

The return of football reminded me that my season was ending, and perhaps that's really why I felt resentful. It was the top of the ninth and I still had things to do. I wanted to spend some time with the Salt Lake Trappers, dawdle in Montana and get back to Stockton to see how the Ports had done. For the first time since I had left California more than four months ago, I roughed out a tentative itinerary so as not to waste a day.

The Salt Lake Trappers were the Rocky of Baseball, unwanted, undrafted and gutsy as hell, an independent team with no major league affiliation and enough bruised egos to fill a hospital ward. "Everyone," said manager Barry Moss, "comes here pissed off, with something to prove—that they're good enough to play."

Tony St. John was one of the rejects. He had pitched for a small liberal arts college in Oregon, and a week before the June draft—a lottery in which major league teams divvy up the country's best fourteen hundred or so high school and college players—the Montreal scout who had been bird-dogging him said, "The Expos like your stuff, Tony. We're going to draft you. I'll give you a call next week as soon as the draft's over." The scout drove off and St. John never heard from him again.

That would have been the end of his baseball dream were it not for the Team of Second Chances, an outfit comprising ballplayers no one else wanted. The funny thing was that when this gang of miscasts put on the uniform of the Salt Lake Trappers, year after year they produced some of the best teams in minor league ball. St. John paid his way to a tryout camp in California, secured himself a job at $550 a month and last night had rewarded the Trappers with the best performance of his brief professional life, striking out nine over six innings and showing nearly perfect control. Tonight, though, the Hawaiian-born right-hander faced a tougher challenge than the one the Billings Mustangs had offered. Ten thousand fans had filled Salt Lake's Derks Field to capacity and St. John's knees shook like jelly. "I'll bet he doesn't have the guts to go through with it," his roommate, Ray Karczewski, said.

St. John had brought his college sweetheart, Elizabeth Tindle, into Salt Lake and, much to her dismay, had arranged for her to throw out the honorary first pitch. She took her position on the mound, with St. John crouching behind the plate, and aimed a pitch for home that was a mile wide. "I knew she'd choke," St. John mumbled out loud. Elizabeth heaved a sigh, relieved that her ordeal was over, and walked toward the plate to scattered applause. St. John stood there, holding the ball to present her.

"Wait a minute, Elizabeth," came the voice of PA announcer Mike Runge. "Don't leave the field yet. Turn around. There's a message for you on the scoreboard."

She turned. The message said in big, bright letters, "ELIZABETH, I LOVE YOU. WILL YOU MARRY ME?"

A murmur went up from the crowd. It started softly in the seats around the field, then rippled back into the grandstands, growing louder and stronger row by row until finally the whole park rocked with cheers and laughter. "Oh my God . . . yes!" she shouted. St.

John raised his hands to the fans, thumbs extended skyward. The crowd, on its feet now, roared, and St. John's teammates—every one a reject—rushed from the dugout to pound and hug him as though he had thrown a no-hitter.

Then Salt Lake got down to business and thumped Billings. Watching this bunch of mavericks was like rooting for Gary Cooper over that gang of gunslingers who got off the train in *High Noon.* The team was, I thought, the perfect metaphor for Utah itself.

Fleeing religious persecution and in search of Zion, the Latter-Day Saints, or Mormons, arrived in what they called Eastern California one July day in 1847. Their ailing leader, a Vermonter named Brigham Young, propped himself up on an elbow in his bed in Wilford Woodruff's carriage and looked out at the Great Salt Lake Valley below. The snowcapped mountains of the Wasatch and Oquirrh ranges surrounded an empty oblong plain big enough to build an empire in. "This is the place," Young said, a comment St. John and scores of other young ballplayers would echo for different reasons more than a century later.

The Mormons, forever the underdogs, forever scorned by the establishment because they marched to their own drummer, built a society that was self-sufficient, industrious, prosperous and family-oriented. Although the first organized baseball game in Utah Territory was played just twenty-two years after the pioneers' arrival—a game between Eurekas and a group of soldiers from Camp Douglas—the Mormons were a serious and devout people with little tolerance for frivolity or dalliance. "Joking, nonsense, profane language, trifling conversation and loud laughter do not belong to us," Young told his flock on the way West. Salt Lake still lives in the image of those principles, and from a twenty-eight-story office building, the tallest in the state, next to City Hall, the Mormon bureaucracy and its elderly leadership look down on a city where everything feels extraordinarily logical and wholesome.

Salt Lake is a Perry Como kind of place, an America of the fifties holding out against the beat of heavy metal. It's a place where trends and fads go to die. The city leads the nation in per capita consumption of bubble gum and Cracker Jack. It harbors no

X-rated movie theaters, no jolts of wickedness, no raised voices or raucous debate. The streets are laid out in numbered grids, eight blocks to a mile, each boulevard 132 feet wide—big enough for an oxen-pulled wagon to make a U-turn. Traffic signals chirp like electronic canaries to aid the blind in crossing, and no one jaywalks.

It was difficult not to feel a little bit holy walking the streets, for Utah is the only state that still lives by the teachings of a church. In schools the words "condom" and "sexual intercourse" had been banned, even in after-class voluntary lectures on AIDS prevention, and anyone ordering a drink at the hotel bar was dispatched by the bartender to a pantry-sized state liquor store down the corridor to first buy one of those miniature bottles that airlines serve, as though the extra effort would somehow tinge his cocktail with guilt. (Sinful though drinking may be, liquor taxes raise more than $8 million annually in Utah, and the money is used to support the school-lunch program.)

At Derks Field—named for the former sports editor of the *Salt Lake Tribune,* a throwback to an era when baseball counted writers among the good guys—the Trappers sold more snow cones than cups of beer; kids under five were admitted to games free, in keeping with Salt Lake's family traditions. The Trappers had the best attendance in the Pioneer League, outdrawing the Medicine Hat Blue Jays twenty to one, though on Sundays, a day locals saved for church and family, you could rattle around an empty ballpark and hang your feet over two rows of seats without getting in anyone's way.

The Pioneer League was a rookie circuit that ran for seventy games, mid-June to late-August. It reached from Salt Lake, up through Idaho and Montana, to just across the Canadian border at Medicine Hat, a team Toronto staffed mostly with homesick Latino players who had a dickens of a time adjusting to the bone-chilling climate and the first games they had ever played under lights. (The Blue Jays' record in 1988 was 12–58, the worst in league history.)

The league was not a favorite of farm directors: the bus trips were too long and draining, the weather too cold, the towns (except for Salt Lake) too small and out of the way. But for the fans, the Pioneer was nothing short of a glorious obsession, a tapestry of little ballparks set in the shadows of grain silos and perched on the doorsteps of mountains, the setting for hungry young players, away from home the first time, struggling with the demons of loneliness and distant dreams, trying to unlearn all the bad habits that had become part of their amateur repertoires. "You really have to deprogram a lot of kids at this level," said the Helena Brewers' pitching coach, Ray Burris, a fifteen-year major league veteran. "You have to take away the old way of thinking and install new microchips." If Norman Rockwell had wanted to paint minor league baseball, I'm sure he would have landed in the Pioneer League, and probably with the star attraction, the Salt Lake Trappers.

To find the roots of the Trappers' success, you have to go back to the seventies, to the Southern California beach colony at Malibu, where an artist and documentary film producer named Van Schley (rhymes with sly) had a crazy notion: that a minor league team could be successful and prosperous as an independent entity, scouting and signing its own players, free from all major league subsidies, directives and on-field instruction. His inspiration was the now-defunct Portland Mavericks, whose manager was once suspended for throwing a chair at an umpire and whose players used to cruise the streets of the towns where they were playing, insulting citizens from the windows of their bus and making disparaging remarks about the home team. Their terror tactics did wonders, and the Mavericks filled the stands night after night and won the Northwest League championship every year they were in the league, from 1973 to 1978.

About that time, Schley read that an all-independent circuit in Texas, the Lone Star League, was dying. He put away his easel and traveled to San Antonio to attend a league meeting, feeling as misplaced as, well, an artist at a baseball assembly. At some point during the discussions he raised his hand, and the next thing he knew, he was the owner of the Texas City Stars. The cost was five hundred dollars. The following August the Gulf States owners canceled the play-offs. The announced reason was the danger posed by an approaching hurricane. The real reason was that

Corpus Christi didn't have enough money to pay its players. The league soon folded.

Schley found his way to Salt Lake after stops in five other bush-league towns, and, with little more than an American Express card, a telephone and the savvy to judge talent, began competing against major league teams with dozens of scouts and multimillion-dollar development budgets. His modus operandi is this: he and Trapper manager Barry Moss, a California realtor and former minor league outfielder, run off-season tryout camps, scour colleges and tournaments and ballparks off the beaten path, track down young athletes bypassed in the June draft, sort through the five hundred unsolicited applications the Trappers receive every year, and maintain an informal network of college coaches, baseball writers and ex-players to tip them on likely prospects, most of whom had some athletic flaw that scouts considered professionally fatal. The reward for finding a player the Trappers sign is a free trip to Salt Lake City.

I asked Schley how he would characterize the way he ran his operation. He thought for a moment, rubbed his trimmed beard and said, "Loosey-goosey."

Without a major league affiliation, of course, a player's career begins and ends in Salt Lake. So the prayer of every Trapper is that he will be sold at season's end—a top performer fetches about five thousand dollars—to a club in The Show, thus giving him the chance to work his way up through an organization. Schley has answered more than forty prayers in the past few years, including those of Tom Candiotti, who now throws knuckleballs for the Cleveland Indians.

But August had settled over the Pioneer League, and although scouts gathered in the seats behind home plate at every Trapper game with their radar guns and notepads, there was no word of any pending sale, and players were growing antsy, pondering a future that perhaps didn't exist. Then one morning the Montreal Expos phoned. That afternoon Schley and Moss summoned the team's two best players, infielders Mike Grace and J. D. Ramirez, out of the clubhouse and into the manager's office, twenty minutes before the game with Helena. Ramirez was hitting almost .400 and Grace was playing so well at third that he was a strong candidate for the

Trappers' MVP award, an honor that earned the winner two roast
beef sandwiches at Arby's, with French fries and a soft drink. (The
team's stolen base leader got a free Jiffy Lube.)

The office was small and dark. Schley was sitting on an old,
tattered sofa, Moss behind his desk. The two young men stood off
to the side, fingers softly drumming the side of their legs, forcing
smiles that asked, What's this about? What made them most uncertain, I think, was to see me, a stranger, sitting next to Schley, with
a camera, and they waited for someone to speak.

"Well, I've got some good news for you," Schley said, and you
could sense the tension lift like passing storm clouds. "I talked to
the Expos this morning and they're buying your contracts. Congratulations!"

Grace looked startled. His eyes grew wide but his brow furrowed.
"You're playing some kind of joke on us, right?"

Ramirez let out a whoop. "You're not messing with us?" His eyes
darted from Schley to Moss and back to Schley, begging confirmation.

"No, it's on the level," Schley said. "You'll finish the season
here, though there's a chance one of you might get moved up to
Jamestown, in the New York–Penn League, the last week of the
season. We haven't finished the paperwork yet, but the Expos are
good on their word. It's definite."

Ramirez, no longer able to contain himself, was swaying back
and forth on the balls of his feet. Grace still looked numb. "Is this
like a late April Fool joke?" he asked. "Is this really straight up,
skipper?"

"You're here with the boss," Moss said, nodding toward Schley.
"Don't look at me."

"Straight up," Schley said. "One thing. The Expos don't want
to release it to the press yet. But you can tell your teammates."

Grace and Ramirez rushed through the door, and hardly got ten
steps into the clubhouse before being swept up in the clutch of the
other Trappers, who slapped high-fives and hollered in celebration, and from somewhere in the sea of bodies, I could hear one
of the new members of the Montreal organization yell out, "We're
married!"

· · ·

Though some of the Pioneer League's teams were among the worst in baseball a few years back, Schley worked magic with the Trappers. They won the first year he came to town, 1985. They won the second year, too. And the third. Major league clubs with teams in the Pioneer League started getting defensive about Salt Lake's success and began stocking their clubs with better talent. "How'd you like a job with a *real* organization?" a Los Angeles Dodgers official asked assistant general manager Holly Andretta. "Not on your life," she shot back.

Salt Lake started the 1987 season with the usual cast of odd characters: a pitcher recruited from a Chicago pizza parlor, a part-time model, a designated hitter born in Pago Pago who made earthen pottery, a pitcher from Kobe, Japan, who said he played "baseba-ru." The Trappers split their first six games that year, then beat Pocatello, 12–6, in the home opener, and kept right on rolling. They reeled off ten straight victories—fifteen straight—twenty—twenty-five—twenty-six. On a Friday night in late July they hit twenty-seven, tying the record for the longest winning streak in professional baseball's 117-year history, a mark shared by the 1902 Corsicana Oilers of the Texas League and the 1921 Baltimore Orioles of the International League. "This team," said Koichi Ikeue, "play strong baseba-ru."

The next night ten thousand fans jammed Derks Field. Scores more climbed trees beyond the outfield fence. Scalped tickets—unheard of in the minors—went for ten dollars each. "I prayed a lot before I came out tonight," one fan said. Salt Lake's opponents were again the Pocatello Giants, and they surrendered quietly, 13–3, for the Trappers' twenty-eighth in a row. The crowd stood and cheered for five minutes. ABC's Wide World of Sports named the Trappers the Athlete of the Week. In the home-team clubhouse, awash with champagne and clogged with cigar smoke, the once-ignored overachievers formed a circle, arms over one another's shoulders, and unleashed a mighty war cry:

"Re-jects! . . . Re-jects! . . . Re-jects! . . ."

The Streak—and the pennant that followed—ended the Trappers' domination of the Pioneer League. Chagrined, the Los Angeles Dodgers began loading their Great Falls team with high-round draft choices; Milwaukee jacked up the talent in Helena; other clubs brought in former college players and before long the quality of competition in the Pioneer was as good as some Class-A circuits. The Trappers were struggling along in third place the night I left Derks Field but were still what America loves best—the underdog. They were the only team in the minors who were independent by choice, the only one whose players took on every day as if it were their last.

The Trappers appealed because they were us. They were a team dedicated to everyone who has ever closed up a bar alone at two in the morning or lost the daily double in a photo finish. They were proof there would be another day and another race. If you didn't embrace them, you were probably one of the people who rooted for Goliath over David and never believed reindeer could fly.

Chapter Twenty-two

Support Your Local Tavern.
—Sign on outfield fence of Butte Copper Kings

To get from Derks Field to the Montana towns of the Pioneer League—Helena, Billings, Great Falls and Butte (which Jack Kerouac passed through in the sixties and later wrote that everyone he saw on the streets was drunk)—you turn right out of the Trappers' parking lot, take a left by the Quality Inn, and head straight north for ten hours. For a couple of hours I followed the Helena Brewers' bus. The driver, Jim Hankinson, had turned his garage back home into a butcher shop and a few times each season bestowed his highest honor on favorite members of the team—an invitation home for an elk dinner. Hankinson was too well rested for Forty-niner and me to keep up with him. To prepare for his all-night drive, he had forced himself to stay up the previous night, then had slept all day, and somewhere near the Continental Divide, my eyelids weighted with weariness, I pulled into the dying cattle town of Lima and parked until dawn next to an abandoned two-story brick building that had once been the Merrel Hotel.

Montana's beauty was a lonely beauty that gnawed at you. This was the frontier of the nation's Empty Quarter, a vast, unpeopled place of high plains and mountains and endless sky and million-acre ranches. Wealth and professional achievement didn't count for much on their own in Montana, and the state had no social strata to speak of, except that descendants of the first settlers had a leg up on "honyockers," the transplants from elsewhere. Montana was a meat-and-potatoes, drink-your-beer-from-the-bottle place, as unpretentious as Colorado was trendy, and when people around the state disparaged the tiny capital, Helena (population 24,000), as snotty and aloof, what they meant was that occasionally you saw folks there wearing a coat and tie and speaking with Eastern accents. Of all the states I had been in since leaving California, I liked Montana the best.

Back in my Randolph Scott days, when I was twelve or thirteen and wore a buckskin jacket my mother had given me as a birthday present, I had been taken with the romance of the most Western of the Western states. I fired off letters from Boston to the governor in Helena, to county sheriffs, to dude ranches that advertised in *Field and Stream*, to historians who could tell me about Chief Joseph ("From where the sun now stands, I will fight no more forever"), the regal leader of the Nez Percé Indians. Almost all wrote back, and before long my cardboard box marked "Montana" overflowed with information. I signed my test papers at school with my new nickname, "Montana Dave," and ignored my parents unless they addressed me properly. A Montana State University banner hung in my bedroom. The affair with Montana eventually ebbed and the cardboard container was replaced by shoe boxes of baseball cards, but driving into the Prickly Pear Valley now and looking for temporary quarters on the streets of Helena, I felt, in a strange way, as if I had come home.

Montana, the nation's fourth largest state, was once the private domain of the Anaconda Copper Mining Company. The Company, as it was called, ran Montana like a colony, owned all the major daily newspapers but one in the state until 1959 and was so defensive about opposition voices that letters to the editor were barred. No one contested an Anaconda official's boast in the forties that The Company had lost only one governorship since statehood. The relationship with Anaconda was important, I thought, because it helped explain why so many Montanans today were antibusiness, protectionist and firmly on the side of the greenies (environmentalists) instead of the boomers (developers).

In a little town called Wisdom on the shoulder of the Rockies, I happened upon the Antlers Saloon one day and fell into conversation with the owner, Daryll Jacobson and his friend Jerry Rutledge. They were drinking Coors Lights and discussing Montana's fortunes. Sooner or later, I was told, every conversation at the Antlers got around to the two hottest local topics—the state's sagging economy and whether to restore the old weathered schoolhouse up the road or tear it down and build a new one.

"All you need is some more tourism to get things moving," said Rutledge, a rancher whose ancestors had settled in Wisdom a century earlier. "Spend some money and advertise our natural resources. That's better than bringing in industry and all that stuff from the East."

"Goddamn right it is, Jerry. You get industry in and we start losing our life. I mean, where else can you be this free?"

"As I see it, industry'd just turn us into another Wisconsin or Minnesota, and who wants that? If you want to keep the better things for generations to come, you gotta preserve them now. Course, everyone wants to make a livin' and it's hard to talk rationally about these things when you see some quick money."

"Yeah, there's no simple solution to this development thing. It's just like that schoolhouse," Jacobson said. His retriever, Charlie, got up from in front of the wood-burning stove, stretched and went back to sleep.

"Personally, I'd rather see them pick some amount of money and fix it up," Rutledge said. "Christ, Harvard University's got buildings two hundred years old and they're still standing. It just pisses me off, you get someone who hasn't been in this valley but maybe fifty years, and he comes in and wants to take the school down. That school was good enough for me and my father. It oughta be good enough for the kids today. I mean, those bricks were made right here in Wisdom. That place is our heritage. You don't tear down your own heritage."

"Damn, why didn't you get up at the meeting and say it just like that? That makes a lot of sense to me. I love that old school, too, just like I love these mountains, but I never heard anyone express it just like you did."

"Oh, hell, Daryll, you know me at those meetings. I don't say nothing. Nobody'd listen to me anyway."

Just off Helena's main street, Last Chance Gulch, was the ball-park, Kindrick Legion Field. It had been built in 1946, when all the games were played during the day, and faced the wrong direction, south-southwest, for a night game, with the setting sun shining directly into the eyes of a right-hand hitter until about 9:00 P.M. For the fans, though, this was a blessing. Rather than looking at the aluminum sheds of a recycling plant and the Burlington Northern train tracks behind home plate, what we faced was Mt. Helena rising out of a low chain of pine-clad mountains and, just beyond the outfield fence, a white church, its steeple topped by a gold cross, that stood amid a row of tidy wooden homes. On one of them, the owner had painted a target—a huge yellow mitt—as a reminder of Gary Sheffield's home run that had hit the side of his house on the fly a couple of years back.

If I had gotten to Helena and the Pioneer League at the beginning of the season, instead of the end, I might not have left all summer. Kindrick was small—its seats extended only thirteen rows back from the field—and felt as cozy as a village green. Game time was three hours away and I plopped into a seat behind the first-base dugout. The mountain backdrop, the rural residential setting, the sight of a solitary teenage Brewer running wind sprints across the outfield of the empty park made me catch my breath, the way I did at a parade when the drum and bugle corps marched by. My promise to Jim Pringle, made during the tank attack in Beirut seven years earlier, had, I realized, been fulfilled. I had found the Montana ballpark and the summer sunshine I had dreamed of that day my life was in danger. I wondered what had become of Pringle. Was he still catching midnight flights to cover wars and coup d'états in forgotten countries of the Third World? And I wondered if I could ever return to that high-adventure life of the wandering foreign correspondent. It seemed so far away.

The Helena Brewers trickled onto the field in threes and fours as I sat there. I liked the way a ballpark came slowly to life each afternoon, precisely at four o'clock, as though a silent alarm had rung from California to the Carolinas. Over by first base, Ron Romaneski, the owner, was raking away at the mud, mixing in kitty litter, in hopes the rain-drenched earth would be dry by game time. He was forty-six and, after his second heart attack, had gotten out of the title insurance business in Yakima, Washington, as a wealthy man and had bought the Brewers, thinking minor league baseball would be a fun and stressless way to slip into early retirement. But Romaneski had a character flaw: he pursued perfection, not just excellence. He poured the same high energy into his new business that he had into the old one, spending thirteen and fourteen hours at the ballpark and participating in—or at least overseeing—every detail, then at game time working himself into a state of high tension rooting for the Brewers. By season's end his doctors would warn him that he had to slow down if he expected to complete his allocation of at bats, and Romaneski, reluctantly ending the most joyful experience of his life, would sell the team after having been an owner for just seventy games.

"How you coming on that mound, Randy?" Romaneski yelled out from first, but Randy Bruce, who had given up his job as a machinist to become the Brewers' groundskeeper, didn't hear him. He and five players were sculpting the mound, adding moist clay so the pitchers had something to dig into with their toes and scraping away bumps with a flat board. The pitchers got down on their hands and knees to more closely examine the slope and texture and smoothness. Though Bruce thought the mound was in fine shape, he remained tolerant of the teenagers' own pursuit of perfection.

"You want me to take a little more off?" he asked.

"Yeah, just a bit more over there, in front of the rubber," one pitcher said. "I'm always landing on that hump when my front foot comes down. . . . There you go. Now pound that down. I'm beginning to like this mound more already."

Helena's opponents were the inept Medicine Hat Blue Jays, who always finished last in the Pioneer League and drew fewer than fourteen thousand fans for the entire home season. They stumbled off their bus, run by the Carefree Express Company, at 5:00 P.M., scratching their crotches and looking dazed and numb after the seven-hour trip from home. The Brewers ignored them as they filed onto the field, led by their scrappy manager, Rocket Wheeler, whose face was still scratched and bruised from a bench-clearing brawl in Butte. Wheeler had been coldcocked from behind by a six-foot-one Texan that night, and before he could gather his wits, the monster outfielder was sitting on his chest, fist in the recoil position. Wheeler escaped further damage only because another of the Butte Copper Kings had grabbed the outfielder and screamed, "Jesus, that's the manager! You don't hit the *manager!*"

The skies had turned dark and threatening by the time the Brewers' sole ticket seller opened for business. I felt the bite of autumn in the evening chill and went out to Forty-niner to fetch my sweater. An Eastbound train out of Spokane rumbled past the park, whistle wailing, and from the PA announcer's cubbyhole, the voice of Ray Charles's "America the Beautiful" floated across the emerald-green infield. I watched an Indian, maybe thirty years old, get off his bicycle by the admissions gate. His jet-black shoulder-length hair made his skin appear even redder than it was, and his shoulders were stooped beneath the faded plaid shirt. He ambled toward the ticket booth, then retreated and took up his position with the children who had staked out the parking lot where foul balls might fall.

The crowd was small, only a few hundred, and Joe Roberts, a former state legislator and deputy attorney general, flipped a dozen hamburgers onto his Weber grill, figuring he'd be lucky to meet expenses tonight. He had been a defeated candidate for lieutenant governor of Montana and had recently left the legal profession in favor of a mid-career change, though he didn't know how long he could survive financially as the Brewers concession's manager. "I've loved being around baseball, but I may have to go back to the real world soon," he said. When the governor had come to Kindrick Field on opening day to throw out the first ball and had seen

Roberts engulfed by smoke, sticking burgers in buns, he winked at a friend and said, "See, that's what happens to politicians who lose."

Many of the fans coming into Kindrick Field for the game with Medicine Hat seemed to know each other, and I found the park an easy place not to be a stranger. Mary Gunstone, who bought a sixty-dollar season ticket every year, was one of the first to arrive. She wore a blue Brewers warm-up jacket and held a 35-mm Canon with zoom lens. She carried twenty-five photo albums—each a photographic chronicle of the season—that she had put together over the past three months. The albums were carefully wrapped in plastic, and each bore the name of one of the Brewers.

"Mary, why don't you just give them doughnuts?" the owner of the bakery where she worked had asked. "You could get them for free."

"No," she replied, "you can't take home doughnuts. I want them to have something they can keep, something to remember their season in Montana by."

She waited at the railing beyond the dugout, calling the Brewers aside one by one to make her presentation. The young men blushed, mumbled thanks and seemed very pleased. "Come here, Emmett," she called. Emmett Reese, a retired California fire captain who worked the summers as Helena's clubhouse custodian, walked over and quickly scanned the album she gave him. "Oh, Mary," he said, giving her a hearty hug, "this is beautiful. Really beautiful."

A light rain had started to fall. The PA announcer put on a tape of the national anthem. The two young umpires, Keith Denebeim and Steve Beaver, stood at home plate, the Helena catcher fidgeting between them, the tips of their shoes perfectly aligned with the chalk line at the rear of the batter's box, and they did not move a muscle until the final words "and the home of the brave" had sounded. The Brewers pounded out of the dugout like a herd of horses and I could hear their manager, Dusty Rhodes, clap his hands and yell, "OK, let's get the job done!"

By the fourth inning the Brewers rookie starter, Bob Vancho, had given up nine hits and made two wild pitches, and, with

Helena trailing 4–0, pitching coach Ray Burris walked to the mound with long, deliberate strides and stood there in the classic American pose of exasperation, feet wide apart and hands on hips. Vancho listened, his head bowed. "Oh, Jesus, what's going on here?" came the gravelly voice of a fan wearing cowboy boots. "Next inning let's get a real pitcher in there."

Overhead thunder boomed. The black skies opened and torrents of rain swept across the field. Fans dashed for cover.

Romaneski, the owner, jumped out of his seat and headed for the field. His twenty-four-year-old general manager, Duane Morris, a couple of fans and a former forest-fire fighter nicknamed Cochise followed. Emmett Reese ran in from his clubhouse in right field, Randy Bruce sprinted across the concourse. The players poured out of the dugout. From the stands they appeared as formless shadows, nearly obscured by the swirling storm. In a moment they all were pulling and tugging at the tarp, hauling the huge green canvas across the infield. As much as anything I had seen all summer, the sight of that group, soaked and splashing through the rain, captured the shared awareness in the low minors that everyone was in this thing together.

The irony was that these same players, if they had a future and continued to advance, would become part of the most militant body of athletes in professional sports, the innocence I had witnessed this rainy night replaced by attitudes hardened during the long, tough minor league journey ahead. In a year or two the thought of leaving their dugout to save the field from rain would not even occur to them. A few years beyond that they would complain if they had to carry their bags up to their $150-a-night Hilton Hotel rooms. But for now all that mattered was that the game get played.

Helena never did recover, and the final score, after a two-hour rain delay, showed Medicine Hat 5, the Brewers 2. Only forty shivering fans were in the stands for the midnight finish, including eight-year-old Heidi Goettel, who used her allowance each week to buy a bagful of snacks and groceries that she presented her favorite player, Bo Dodson, before every road trip. In the clubhouse, Emmett Reese knocked on the door of the manager's office, where

Dusty Rhodes and Ray Burris were filling in game reports to be phoned to Milwaukee, and asked, "Would you fellows drink a pot of coffee if I made one?"

Reese had been a good college player who knew his limits—he could hit but not run—and had opted for a life as a fireman. Now at fifty-eight, the oldest traveling clubbie in the minors, he would be in the clubhouse till after 3:00 A.M., washing fourteen loads of laundry and hanging each player's uniform to dry in front of his locker. "I just heard that on the Billings club, the kids have to wash their own uniforms and personals," he said. "To me, that just isn't hygiene because you know they're not going to do it every day." Reese came up to Helena from his retirement home in Arizona every June and had made only one request when Romaneski bought the team and became his new boss.

"I'd like to be able to use the office phone twice a week to call my wife," he said. "We've been married thirty-nine years."

"You use it to call her every day if you want," Romaneski replied.

Reese scurried from locker to locker, scooping up jerseys, socks, jockstraps. I asked him where he stayed when he was in Helena. "I had an apartment the first year," he said, "but it was a nuisance, so now I just live here." He nodded toward a rollaway bed that was folded up next to the washing machine and said that not having to commute was a real plus. He spent his own money for the team's supplies—soap, insect repellent, sunflower seeds, chewing tobacco, fungus powder, rags to rub pine tar on the handle of bats—and received from each Brewer twelve dollars per paycheck, which came every two weeks. Of the twenty-four players on the club last year, twenty-one had sent him a Christmas card.

Kindrick Field emptied in minutes, leaving groundskeeper Randy Bruce alone under the lights. He pounded and raked and poked at the infield, a performer on an abandoned stage. The two umpires ate a hurried dinner—pizza and a beer—then stuffed their blue duffel bags into Keith Denebeim's Bronco and took off for Pocatello, which they would reach by dawn. General manager Morris retired to his office to count the night's receipts, and the official scorer, Gordie Higgins, a college student majoring in philosophy, who earned twenty dollars a game, came down from the press box to join him. It would take Higgins an hour to put together his box score proof—Helena's runs plus men left on base plus Blue Jay putouts had to equal Helena's at bats, base on balls, sacrifice flies and hits, bases awarded because of interference and hit-batsmen— and fax it to the league statistician.

After a while the field had been manicured to Bruce's satisfaction, and he parked his cub tractor by the bull pen in right field. Morris and Higgins walked out of the office together and locked the door. One of them hit the main electric switch and the field darkened as though a candle had been blown out. "Night, Emmett," Morris called through the open clubhouse door. Reese was stuffing uniforms into a washing machine and did not hear him.

I found a motel at the edge of town. In the first weeks of my journey, I had usually asked permission of the motel manager before staking claim to a free "room" in his parking lot. When I didn't, I was always careful to park near the motel and not to use my interior lights, so security officers would think I was just another traveler who had checked in for the night. When I slept in Forty-niner on a city street—which was illegal—I never drew my curtains or scattered clothes on the bench by the dinette table; any policemen who bothered to look through my windows would have thought Forty-niner was empty.

The more a state catered to tourism, the more likely its lawmen were to be lenient with the indiscretions of RVers. But as the trip proceeded without a hitch, I got careless, usually spending the night wherever I grew tired. At the motel in Helena, to avoid the mounted security lights that sometimes kept me awake, I parked at the farthest end of the lot, fifty yards from the building and almost as far from the nearest vehicle. I was awakened several hours later by men's voices and a banging on my door. My heart raced and I lay very still. They banged again and a voice called out: "Police! Open up in there."

I jumped out of my bunk over the driver's compartment, and for some reason or other fumbled to put on my Stetson before opening the door. I was relieved that the two uniformed men outside really were policemen.

"This is private property you can't park on," one of them said. "You'll have to move on."

"I'm leaving for California in the morning," I said, "but I'm really too beat to start driving now. Isn't there someplace I can grab a few more hours' sleep?"

"Sure. Go up the hill past the motel, about half a mile. You can park on the right-hand side of the street. Nobody'll bother you there."

Wearing just my underpants and Stetson, and feeling as foolish as I must have looked, I drove off in search of my new home. But I never did get back to sleep and I headed out before dawn, bound for Stockton. Forty-niner's transmission slipped out of gear twice, making me uneasy, and I eased off the accelerator as I climbed into the high country, where cattle grazed and Montana, in the final days of summer, seemed as remote as anyplace on earth.

Chapter Twenty-three

When you get right down to it, I guess it's just a game.

—DUSTY RHODES, *manager, Helena Brewers*

Six hundred miles east of Montana, in San Mateo, California, the workday of statistician Bill Weiss was just beginning about the time I left Kindrick Field my last night in Helena. From Stockton, Tucson, Butte, Reno, Spokane and more than a dozen other Western cities, the faxed box scores of minor league games were chattering into the den of his home. It was past midnight. Weiss and his wife, Faye, took each player's nightly numbers and transcribed them onto that athlete's personal ledger. "Oh, oh," Weiss muttered, eyeing the pounding Helena's Bob Vancho had taken, "this young fellow better not have too many more nights like this if he wants a job." The Weisses adjusted batting averages, figured E.R.A.s, made lists of the top batters in the five leagues they handled, and searched for errors— perhaps a forgotten base on balls or a misplaced strikeout—when a proof sheet didn't balance.

"Although there are some obvious flaws—like the game-winning

RBI, which has no meaning—I think more than any other sport, baseball stats reflect a player's ability," said Weiss, the minor league's premier statistician for more than forty years. "The game has maintained a uniformity which is conducive to stats having a continuous meaning. Rip Van Winkle could wake up today and still pretty much recognize baseball as the same game he had seen before he went to sleep."

Weiss, a balding, bespectacled man who could pass for a college professor, worked with pencil and typewriter, accepting grudgingly that he soon would have to give up his trusty tools in favor of a computer. "It's difficult to justify the additional expense in terms of income," he said. Around him were cabinets and file cases stacked high and boxes full of three-by-five cards, each the statistical narrative of a life. Rows of baseball books lined the wall, and in one corner was a brown armchair with recliner footrest where, for a few minutes in the middle of each night, Weiss would stretch out to catnap.

Seven nights a week during the season Weiss worked at what was both his passion and his livelihood, stopping about 7:00 A.M. to read the newspapers and breakfast on fruit and orange juice. He played out eighteen or twenty games over the night, compiling the lists of statistics that he would fax to the teams and newspapers and leagues that retained his services. By midmorning, when he finally climbed into bed for two or three hours' sleep, in scores of minor league towns and cities across the country, another baseball day was beginning.

With a week left in the season, I made the ten-hour drive from Spokane to Bend, Oregon, in a single leap. It was the wrong way to travel, moving so fast. I took no notes and cheated myself by letting everything slip by in a blur of miles. I don't remember much about the Bend-Boise game in the Northwest League, except that the night was cold and the Boise manager, Mal Fichman (known as Malfunction when he had managed Rocky Mount to a 20–114 record in 1980), had put a fifty-dollar bounty on Bend's annoying Elk-man mascot who wiggled its fanny in front of his players during batting practice. The money would go to any pitcher who bopped the creature with an errant warm-up pitch.

I looked forward to my return to Stockton. For the first time all summer, the next stop would take me back to a familiar place and people I knew. The thought of not having to introduce myself or explain what I was doing seemed a great luxury. I spent the night outside Bend's Vince Genna Field and went to sleep reading an edition of *The New York Times*, several days old, that may have explained why all the joggers I had seen in Colorado looked so punished. They had heartburn. The paper cited a new medical study and quoted one of the doctors involved saying: "The pool of acid down in your stomach sloshes around and you're more likely to get that coming back up when you run."

The article reminded me of all the self-denial fanatics I would soon encounter in Los Angeles. How dull life must be for them, never enjoying an occasional excess. The funny thing was that the people I had met in the heartland towns weren't obsessed with low-cholesterol diets and secondhand smoke and abstinence, and they looked fine. I now knew what had happened to those obnoxious kids we all had gone to high school with and no one liked. They had become the health Nazis.

Five months and sixteen thousand miles after I had left Stockton, I returned. Just inside the city limits Forty-niner wheezed and shuddered, its engine racing in third gear when it should have shifted into second. My transmission was dying. It was as though Forty-niner had said, "I got you over the Rockies and I've brought you home, now I need to rest." I thought of the barren stretches of road where a crippled vehicle would have left me stranded for days, and felt grateful.

There was an RV repair shop not far from Billy Hebert Field, and I stayed in Forty-niner and made coffee and turned on my portable computer while the two men wrestling with my transmission tugged and pounded and made expensive sounds. The insurance policy I had taken out to protect myself against major engine problems like this had expired five hundred miles ago, somewhere around Yakima. I typed in several pages of notes and was surprised that, after so long on the road, the journey had not bleared. Every time a town's name came up on my screen, the image of a specific ballpark slipped into sharp focus. What I remembered most clearly was not home runs or dazzling plays or even who was a prospect and who was not; it was the faces of people who happened to play baseball for a living, each fighting his own private war, each wanting not much more than what we all aim for—to look back at the end of a day or a season and be able to say, "I gave it my best shot."

I picked up a copy of *Baseball America* from the stack of magazines in my sink: Dan Fitzpatrick, the Stockton Ports' sore-armed reliever, had retired at the age of twenty-six, taking with him a lifetime mark of fifteen wins and eleven defeats over five minor league seasons. He had quit, with his arm finally mending, just before his first scheduled mound appearance of the season, and just before the Ports' road trip to Reno, his favorite Cal League city. It was as though he didn't want even to be tempted anymore by the dream.

Outside the garage I found a pay phone and called Fitzpatrick in Maryland. He was driving a furniture delivery truck now and had applied for a post office job. He planned to get married in February and had no regrets about leaving Stockton. He had found, he said, that there were ways to compete in life without being a ballplayer.

"The thing was, I wanted to get on with building a future," he said. "I tried to enjoy myself those last couple of months in Stockton, but that's tough when you don't feel you're going anywhere. I just sat down with myself, I talked with Mo [pitcher Steve Monson] and my girlfriend, and I guess I realized maybe I was kidding myself a little at the end, thinking I was a prospect."

The America where Fitzpatrick had played—and I had passed through, however briefly—was not the America we read about in the big-city dailies. It was a place that seemed largely at peace with itself, a place I could wander for countless miles and months and never feel threatened or get hassled or be part of a crime statistic. Maybe I was just lucky. Or maybe this was the America I had sought in the first place, the rural America of my youth, where there was plenty of open land on which to build a baseball diamond and sufficient time to play a game that theoretically could go on indefinitely.

If this was indeed what I sought, I was lucky to have found it before it slipped away. Baseball is a rural game and we were becoming an urban nation, still regionally distinct, yet homogenized by television and commercial franchises. So many of the community ball fields I had passed in towns across the country were unused that I had to wonder if perhaps baseball didn't mean less to today's youths than it did to people of my generation. Believing in our teams and institutions and favored people must be tougher for teenagers now than it had been for me, and I hoped they would have the chance, as had I, to meet tomorrow's stars before they got 900 numbers or peddled their memorabilia on TV. I hoped they would understand the truth in Faulkner's words "The past is never dead. It's not even past."

It was hard to know how long the minor leagues' Second Golden Age with its inflated franchise values would last—certainly not forever. One day, it seemed, the major leagues would discover they could save money by putting their development dollars into college baseball and into low-classification leagues that shared a single modern complex in Arizona or Florida, playing games at 8:00 A.M. to avoid the heat (and drawing no spectators). When that happened, the pint-sized parks in Helena and Bluefield and Elmira and scores of minor league towns in between would become memorials to a bygone time, just as Birmingham's Rickwood Field had. The minors were, I thought, a last holdout from a vanishing America.

The majors had already become a money-driven institution, operated in partnership with television (which provided 47 percent of baseball's revenues, compared with 37 percent for ticket sales). I don't begrudge the players and owners for taking their millions; I'd take them, too, if my editors were kind enough to offer. But all the money-driven institutions to which we once gave trust—from the savings and loan associations to collegiate recruitment programs—have fallen victim to the greed for money or success, and in the process violated our faith. Though we may call baseball our national pastime instead of a mere sport, I know of no reason why it alone should be able to withstand the temptations that have brought others down. Granted, we would still go to the games and we would still cheer, but would we still believe?

On the day I arrived back in the California League, Pete Rose's season-long ordeal ended and Commissioner Bart Giamatti banished him from baseball for life. Rose, an addicted gambler, went defiantly, admitting no wrongdoing. Like many circuits, the Cal

League season is split in half to sustain fan interest; come mid-June, the slate is wiped clean and a new race begins, with the winner of each half battling for the championship in a play-off at season's end. The Ports had finished second in the first half. But by July manager Dave Huppert was at the helm of a marvelous team, a team that turned double plays and got clutch hits and had strong pitching and won without superstars or prima donnas, and now the Ports were just one victory from clinching the second half's Northern Division pennant.

There had been many changes while I had been gone. The Ports had picked up a solid reliever to replace Fitzpatrick, Tim Fortugno, who earlier had learned that the Phillies organization had dismissed him when he showed up for work one day and found that his uniform had been removed from his locker. Carl Dunn, the Ports bus driver, stopped by a California highway patrolman on Highway 99, had been unable to talk his way out his first speeding ticket in thirty years of professional driving. "Don't worry, busie," yelled Brian Drahman from a rear seat, "I gave him the finger so he had a good look." "Did you do it *before* or after I got the ticket?" Dunn asked. "Both," Drahman said. And Katie Derksen, the nineteen-month-old daughter of the Ports pitching coach, had learned "Take Me Out to the Ball Game" from start to finish and, now knee-high, could strut among the naked men in the clubhouse, serenading them without missing a word.

Forty-niner's transmission overhaul kept me hanging around the garage until nearly 7:00 P.M. and depleted the last of my traveler's checks. When I finally got to Billy Hebert Field, the park I had left in April to climb the snow-covered Sierra on my way East, the Ports' game was in the second inning. From the parking lot I could hear the buzz of the crowd and the amplified refrain of the Diamonds' "Little Darlin' ": "Wella, that's my lova. My darlin', I neeeeed you, to call my own and never do wrong. To hold in mine, your little hand. . . . Pleeeese, hold my hand." The record faded and Buddy Meacham's voice rose from the press box: "Fans, here's another lucky bingo number from the card in your program . . . I-27 . . . I-29 . . . N-35 . . . Now, leading off for the Stockton Ports, Bobbeeeee Jones! . . ."

I felt as though I had never been away.

The Ports scored early in pursuit of their division title and led
the San Jose Giants, 6–3, going into the ninth. Chris George, one
of Milwaukee's top prospects, took the mound for Stockton. He
gave up a long single, then whizzed a ninety-mile-an-hour fastball
by Steve Hecht for the first out. Jamie Cooper followed with a fly
to right that Jones caught easily. Designated hitter Juan Guerrero
was the Giants' last hope. He slapped a grounder to second. Pat
Listach hurried to his left, scooped it up and fired to first to put
the Ports in the Cal League play-offs for the fifth straight year.
"Ladies and gentlemen," announced Meacham, "your 1989 Stockton Ports!" I had expected elation to erupt in the stands and on
the field, but it didn't. The crowd, numbering fewer than a thousand, drifted off quietly into the night, and the players hurried
across the diamond and disappeared through the gate in left field
that led to their clubhouse. For several minutes Hebert Field was
quiet. Then from the direction of the clubhouse a chorus of shrieks
and whoops erupted.

In the majors, pennants are celebrated with champagne. In the
minors they use beer. Putting my wallet and camera in a plastic
Ziploc bag, I walked toward the clubhouse and entered, at my own
peril, a tribal ritual of spontaneous joy. "Reporter! Reporter! Reporter!" came the chant, and the spray from twenty beer cans hit
me at once, just as a five-gallon bucket of water cascaded over my
head. Drenched in beer, dressed only in their underwear, the
barefoot players danced and cavorted and hollered and shouted
toasts to one another on the long benches in front of the plastic
sheets trainer Jim Poulin had tacked over their lockers. The secondhand rug that had once covered the floor of a bank squished
under foot and the waves of laughter grew more raucous as the pile
of cans deepened.

"I just want say," someone shouted, "that you guys are the best
bunch of . . . of *pricks* I ever played with!"

"Here's to Chris Cassels. He doesn't have much range at third,
but what he gets to, he drops."

"Here's to the only team in the whole fucking organization who
as of right now, right this minute, is going to the play-offs!"

"Let's not forget the departed Ports. Here's to Dan Fitzpatrick."

This was a party to match the ones I had known at the Beta

House back on the University of Maine campus. It was an affair
of the heart played out privately, beyond the reach of TV cameras
and, except for me, outsiders. It was a celebration of team triumph,
not individual achievement. The pressure of a long season had
lifted and, for these few moments, tomorrow no longer mattered.
Steve Sparks, the night's winning pitcher, tilted back his head to
chugalug a can of Miller. "Sparky's going to make himself puke,"
cried a delighted teammate. Sparks wiped the foam from his mouth
with his arm, yanked the notice off the bulletin board that listed
the times of the morning workouts and ate it. Rob Derksen, the
pitching coach, tore up the poster announcing the prohibition
against gambling—"No more of that Pete Rose stuff!" he bellowed—and ran wide-eyed for the shower to refill his water bucket.
"Derk goes crazy at these things," observed manager Huppert, the
elder statesman of the crew.

The party had the momentum to go on all night. A delivery man
showed up with nine pizzas, and Huppert fished seventy dollars out
of his jeans and sent out for more beer. In the parking lot out back,
the wives and girlfriends waited patiently in their cars. It was nearly
midnight when I slipped out the door, coated with beer and needing a shower. I walked toward the parking lot, and from the clubhouse behind me the voices rose through the stillness of Billy
Hebert Field: *"Pros-pect! Pros-pect! Pros-pect!"*

That night back in Milwaukee, Bruce Manno, the Brewers farm
director, addressed a telegram to Huppert and the Ports, and called
Western Union. The cable said: "Congratulations on clinching the
second half championship. In spite of the injuries and various
player moves that have taken place, you have played hard and
shown a great desire to win, which is a credit not only to your
ability but to your character as well. You are accountable for your
own performance, but you are also accountable for the performance of your team. You have all done a great job. We are proud
to have you represent the Milwaukee Brewers in the play-offs and
good luck the rest of the way."

The Ports' season ended three games later in San Jose, on Ted
Williams's seventy-first birthday, a night the Giants dedicated to
a local boy, six-year-old Alex Vlahos, who had leukemia and

needed a bone-marrow transplant. They set aside one dollar from every ticket sold for his medical bills, and Stockton's trainer passed an envelope marked "For That Kid" among the Ports, who contributed an additional $136.55. Alex had been scheduled to throw out the first ball, but was too sick to attend the game.

I had grown alarmingly comfortable with my nomadic life and was in no hurry for it to end. My days had no structure: I dressed as I chose, ate when I was hungry, moved on when I was restless. Yet I did not feel idle because I had a mission, and my notebooks filled with jottings of a summer's game played on real grass and memories of a time when Eddie Mathews and Warren Spahn ruled the world. I had planned to return with the Ports to Stockton for the play-offs. But in the seventh inning of the final game, with the Ports losing, I understood that my journey was complete. It had ended with the Ports' victory celebration. That was the memory I would carry with me, the moment that captured the exhilaration of being young and being winners and, as Roger Kahn said, being good enough to dream.

While the Ports showered I took a piece of white cardboard from one of my shirts that had come back from the laundry and, with a Magic Marker, wrote in large, bold letters, FOR SALE. I taped the sign in Forty-niner's rear window. Carl Dunn's old Greyhound waited nearby, its engine running. After twenty minutes Sparky and Jonesie and Hup and the other descendants of the Mudville Nine got on board, lugging duffel bags and munching hot dogs. "I'll see you in Stockton," I said to one of them, but I knew that I wouldn't. Dunn turned left on Eleventh Street and headed out onto the interstate, taking the northbound ramp toward San Francisco. His bus gathered speed. I was of a mind to follow, but when the exit for 101 South approached in the night, I took it, as though some reflex had overpowered my thoughts. Los Angeles lay a night's drive ahead.

The season I had stolen from adulthood was, I knew, not mine to keep. Summer was over and it was time to go home.

Epilogue

Over the winter the Milwaukee Brewers received the Topps award as the Minor League Organization of the Year. The National Association announced that minor league attendance had hit a thirty-seven-year high (surpassing 23 million). *Baseball News* chose the Salt Lake Trappers' twenty-nine-game winning streak as the top minor league story of the decade. Johnny Neun fell critically ill in Baltimore, and for the first time in seventy years spring training would go on without him.

The Stockton Ports had not fared well in the California League championship series the previous September—losing all three games to the Bakersfield Dodgers, the last two by shutouts—but they won more games in the decade (824) than any team in minor league baseball, and manager Dave Huppert got his promotion to the El Paso Diablos. The Diablos' bright and talented second baseman, Frank Mattox, got *his* to the Denver Zephyrs, and the Zephyrs' slugger, Greg Vaughn (the American Association's Most Valuable Player in '89), his to Milwaukee, where major league pitching didn't seem to mystify him a bit.

The two young Salt Lake Trappers whose contracts had been bought by Montreal moved up a notch, to Jamestown in the New York–Penn League, in the final days of the season and became overnight folk heroes. J. D. Ramirez knocked in eleven runs in his fourteen games with the Expos, and Mike Grace's double in the final game enabled Jamestown to defeat Pittsfield, 1–0, for its first championship in thirty-six years.

In Tucson, former major leaguer Ron Washington put together one of his finest seasons, hitting .320, but never got the call to join the Houston Astros. He shopped around in the off-season and, at age thirty-eight, signed on with the Texas Rangers, which sent him to their Triple-A club in Oklahoma City. Dave Butts overcame his nightmarish slump with the Durham Bulls, got his average up to .253 and retired. He was twenty-six. "I told my wife that if I wasn't going to make the big leagues—and it was pretty clear Atlanta didn't have any plans for me—it was stupid to keep playing," he said. Stockton's graceful outfielder Bobby Jones, in his fifth year of professional ball, a Cal League All-Star the past two seasons, was released by the Brewers in March 1990, during spring training. "He didn't really develop," said a Milwaukee instructor. Said Jones: "I know there's another team out there that wants me. It's just a matter of making some calls." And in the Pennsylvania town of King of Prussia, Max Patkin—the Clown Prince of Baseball— packed his overnight bag on opening day, as he had done every opening day for forty-five straight years, and rode another bus to another minor league town, hoping his gags would still make people laugh.

The Atlanta Braves hired Frank Howard to replace Eddie Mathews as their minor league hitting instructor, ending Mathews's twenty-seven-year association with the Braves as player, manager, scout and instructor. No one from the organization called Mathews to tell him he was about to be fired; he read about it in the morning newspapers. "I treated people good," Mathews told *Baseball America.* "I've got no regrets. I don't know why I should even think about living life any differently. Because somebody in Atlanta thinks I drink too much? Screw 'em."

And me?

Well, it took six months to sell Forty-niner. I was sorry to see him go and sorrier still the new owner had no appreciation of the roads he had traveled or the ballparks he had seen. Then I moved back East, to the *Los Angeles Times'* Washington bureau. I still think of the West often, of its mountains and byways and restless people. And every once in a while I dig out my old calendar to see where I was on this day a year ago.

The Minor Leagues of North America

TOWN	TEAM	LEAGUE	AFFILIATION	PARK CAPACITY
ALABAMA				
Birmingham	Barons	Southern	Chicago (AL)	10,000
Huntsville	Stars	Southern	Oakland	10,250
ARIZONA				
Phoenix	Firebirds	Pacific Coast	San Francisco	7,983
Tucson	Toros	Pacific Coast	Houston	9,500
ARKANSAS				
Little Rock	Travelers	Texas	St. Louis	5,975
CALIFORNIA				
Adelanto	Mavericks	California	San Diego	3,500
Bakersfield	Dodgers	California	Los Angeles	3,000
Modesto	A's	California	Oakland	2,500
Palm Springs	Angels	California	California	5,185
Salinas	Spurs	California	Independent	3,540
San Bernardino	Spirit	California	Seattle	3,000
San Jose	Giants	California	San Francisco	5,200
Stockton	Ports	California	Milwaukee	3,500
Visalia	Oaks	California	Minnesota	2,000
CANADA				
Calgary	Cannons	Pacific Coast	Seattle	7,500
Edmonton	Trappers	Pacific Coast	California	5,000

TOWN	TEAM	LEAGUE	AFFILIATION	PARK CAPACITY
Hamilton	Redbirds	N.Y.–Penn	St. Louis	3,200
London	Tigers	Eastern	Detroit	5,400
Medicine Hat	Blue Jays	Pioneer	Toronto	2,800
St. Catharines	Blue Jays	N.Y.–Penn	Toronto	2,000
Vancouver	Canadians	Pacific Coast	Chicago (AL)	6,500
Welland	Pirates	N.Y.–Penn	Pittsburgh	2,500
COLORADO				
Colo. Springs	Sky Sox	Pacific Coast	Cleveland	6,130
Denver	Zephyrs	American	Milwaukee	75,052
CONNECTICUT				
New Britain	Red Sox	Eastern	Boston	4,000
FLORIDA				
Baseball City	Royals	Florida State	Kansas City	7,000
Charlotte	Rangers	Florida State	Texas	6,026
Clearwater	Phillies	Florida State	Philadelphia	7,385
Dunedin	Blue Jays	Florida State	Toronto	6,218
Ft. Lauderdale	Yankees	Florida State	New York (AL)	7,211
Jacksonville	Suns	Southern	Seattle	8,200
Lakeland	Tigers	Florida State	Detroit	7,500
Miami	Miracle	Florida State	Independent	5,000
Orlando	Sunrays	Southern	Minnesota	6,000
Osceola	Astros	Florida State	Houston	5,100
Sarasota	White Sox	Florida State	Chicago (AL)	7,500
St. Lucie	Mets	Florida State	New York (NL)	7,347
St. Petersburg	Cardinals	Florida State	St. Louis	7,004
Vero Beach	Dodgers	Florida State	Los Angeles	6,500
W. Palm Bch.	Expos	Florida State	Montreal	4,392
Winter Haven	Red Sox	Florida State	Boston	5,000
GEORGIA				
Augusta	Pirates	South Atlantic	Pittsburgh	4,000
Savannah	Cardinals	South Atlantic	St. Louis	7,500
IDAHO				
Boise	Hawks	Northwest	California	4,500
Idaho Falls	Braves	Pioneer	Atlanta	3,800
Pocatello	Pioneers	Pioneer	Co-op*	2,580

TOWN	TEAM	LEAGUE	AFFILIATION	PARK CAPACITY
ILLINOIS				
Kane County	Cougars	Midwest	Baltimore	3,200
Peoria	Chiefs	Midwest	Chicago (NL)	5,000
Rockford	Expos	Midwest	Montreal	4,200
Springfield	Cardinals	Midwest	St. Louis	5,000
INDIANA				
Indianapolis	Indians	American	Montreal	12,500
South Bend	White Sox	Midwest	Chicago (AL)	5,000
IOWA				
Burlington	Astros	Midwest	Houston	3,500
Cedar Rapids	Reds	Midwest	Cincinnati	6,000
Clinton	Giants	Midwest	San Francisco	3,600
Davenport	Angels	Midwest	California	5,000
Des Moines	Cubs	American	Chicago (NL)	7,600
Waterloo	Diamonds	Midwest	San Diego	5,500
KANSAS				
Wichita	Wranglers	Texas	San Diego	7,488
KENTUCKY				
Louisville	Redbirds	American	St. Louis	33,500
LOUISIANA				
Shreveport	Captains	Texas	San Francisco	6,200
MARYLAND				
Frederick	Keys	Carolina	Baltimore	4,500
Hagerstown	Suns	Eastern	Baltimore	6,000
MASSACHUSETTS				
Pittsfield	Mets	N.Y.–Penn	New York (NL)	5,200
MISSISSIPPI				
Jackson	Generals	Texas	Houston	5,200
MONTANA				
Billings	Mustangs	Pioneer	Cincinnati	4,500
Butte	Copper Kings	Pioneer	Texas	5,000
Great Falls	Dodgers	Pioneer	Los Angeles	4,000
Helena	Brewers	Pioneer	Milwaukee	2,700

TOWN	TEAM	LEAGUE	AFFILIATION	PARK CAPACITY
NEBRASKA				
Omaha	Royals	American	Kansas City	15,000
NEVADA				
Las Vegas	Stars	Pacific Coast	San Diego	9,370
Reno	Silver Sox	California	Independent	4,500
NEW MEXICO				
Albuquerque	Dukes	Pacific Coast	Los Angeles	10,510
NEW YORK				
Albany	Yankees	Eastern	New York (AL)	5,700
Auburn	Astros	N.Y.–Penn	Houston	3,575
Batavia	Clippers	N.Y.–Penn	Philadelphia	3,000
Binghamton	Mets	Eastern	New York (NL)	6,200
Buffalo	Bisons	International	Pittsburgh	19,500
Elmira	Pioneers	N.Y.–Penn	Boston	5,100
Erie	Sailors	N.Y.–Penn	Independent	3,200
Geneva	Cubs	N.Y.–Penn	Chicago (NL)	2,200
Jamestown	Expos	N.Y.–Penn	Montreal	3,328
Niagara Falls	Rapids	N.Y.–Penn	Detroit	2,800
Oneonta	Yankees	N.Y.–Penn	New York (AL)	3,200
Rochester	Red Wings	International	Baltimore	12,503
Syracuse	Chiefs	International	Toronto	10,500
Utica	Blue Sox	N.Y.–Penn	Chicago (AL)	5,000
Watertown	Indians	N.Y.–Penn	Cleveland	3,500
NORTH CAROLINA				
Asheville	Tourists	South Atlantic	Houston	3,500
Burlington	Indians	Appalachian	Cleveland	3,500
Charlotte	Knights	Southern	Chicago (NL)	10,917
Durham	Bulls	Carolina	Atlanta	5,000
Fayetteville	Generals	South Atlantic	Detroit	3,000
Gastonia	Rangers	South Atlantic	Texas	3,200
Greensboro	Hornets	South Atlantic	New York (AL)	7,500
Kinston	Indians	Carolina	Cleveland	4,100
Winston-Salem	Spirits	Carolina	Chicago (NL)	4,280
Zebulon	Mudcats	Southern	Pittsburgh	5,000

TOWN	TEAM	LEAGUE	AFFILIATION	PARK CAPACITY
OHIO				
Canton	Indians	Eastern	Cleveland	5,600
Columbus	Clippers	International	New York (AL)	15,000
Toledo	Mud Hens	International	Detroit	10,025
OKLAHOMA				
Oklahoma City	89ers	American	Texas	12,000
Tulsa	Drillers	Texas	Texas	8,234
OREGON				
Bend	Bucks	Northwest	Co-op*	3,000
Eugene	Emeralds	Northwest	Kansas City	7,200
Medford	Athletics	Northwest	Oakland	2,900
Portland	Beavers	Pacific Coast	Minnesota	26,500
PENNSYLVANIA				
Harrisburg	Senators	Eastern	Montreal	5,600
Reading	Phillies	Eastern	Philadelphia	6,500
Scranton	Red Barons	International	Philadelphia	10,004
RHODE ISLAND				
Pawtucket	Red Sox	International	Boston	6,010
SOUTH CAROLINA				
Charleston	Rainbows	South Atlantic	San Diego	4,300
Columbia	Mets	South Atlantic	New York (NL)	4,000
Greenville	Braves	Southern	Atlanta	7,023
Myrtle Beach	Blue Jays	South Atlantic	St. Louis	3,500
Spartanburg	Phillies	South Atlantic	Philadelphia	3,900
Sumter	Undetermined	South Atlantic	Montreal	4,000
TENNESSEE				
Chattanooga	Lookouts	Southern	Cincinnati	8,000
Elizabethton	Twins	Appalachian	Minnesota	1,500
Johnson City	Cardinals	Appalachian	St. Louis	3,500
Kingsport	Mets	Appalachian	New York (NL)	8,000
Knoxville	Blue Jays	Southern	Toronto	6,412
Memphis	Chicks	Southern	Kansas City	10,000
Nashville	Sounds	American	Cincinnati	18,000

TOWN	TEAM	LEAGUE	AFFILIATION	PARK CAPACITY
TEXAS				
El Paso	Diablos	Texas	Milwaukee	10,000
Midland	Angels	Texas	California	3,800
San Antonio	Missions	Texas	Los Angeles	3,500
UTAH				
Salt Lake City	Trappers	Pioneer	Independent	10,200
VIRGINIA				
Bristol	Tigers	Appalachian	Detroit	1,200
Hampton	Pilots	Carolina	Seattle	4,330
Lynchburg	Red Sox	Carolina	Boston	4,200
Martinsville	Phillies	Appalachian	Philadelphia	3,200
Norfolk	Tides	International	New York (NL)	6,162
Pulaski	Braves	Appalachian	Atlanta	2,000
Richmond	Braves	International	Atlanta	12,000
Salem	Buccaneers	Carolina	Pittsburgh	5,000
Woodbridge	Cannons	Carolina	New York (AL)	6,000
WASHINGTON				
Bellingham	Mariners	Northwest	Seattle	2,200
Everett	Giants	Northwest	San Francisco	2,400
Spokane	Indians	Northwest	San Diego	10,000
Tacoma	Tigers	Pacific Coast	Oakland	8,002
Yakima	Bears	Northwest	Los Angeles	3,148
WEST VIRGINIA				
Bluefield	Orioles	Appalachian	Baltimore	3,000
Charleston	Wheelers	South Atlantic	Cincinnati	6,500
Huntington	Cubs	Appalachian	Chicago (NL)	2,500
Princeton	Reds	Appalachian	Cincinnati	1,500
WISCONSIN				
Appleton	Foxes	Midwest	Kansas City	4,300
Beloit	Brewers	Midwest	Milwaukee	3,800
Kenosha	Twins	Midwest	Minnesota	3,500
Madison	Muskies	Midwest	Oakland	3,923

*Co-ops are quasi-independent teams that have limited working agreements with a major league affiliate.

TRIPLE-A LEAGUES: American Association, International, Pacific Coast.

DOUBLE-A LEAGUES: Eastern, Southern, Texas.

SINGLE-A LEAGUES: California, Carolina, Florida State, Midwest, New York–Penn, Northwest, South Atlantic.

ROOKIE LEAGUES: Appalachian, Pioneer.

Source: *Baseball America.*

DAVID LAMB has traveled the world as a correspondent for the *Los Angeles Times* and has lived in Egypt, Kenya, Australia, Vietnam and a dozen American cities. He is the author of two highly acclaimed previous books and is an eight-time Pulitzer Prize nominee. At present he covers the United States from the *Times'* Washington, D.C., bureau.